The American Regime

Christian Alexander Secor

THE

AMERICAN REGIME

WRITTEN BY

CHRISTIAN SECOR

A JANUARY 6TH PRISONER

ANTELOPE HILL PUBLISHING

Cover art by Swifty.
Edited by Tom Edwards and Harlan Wallace.
Layout by Margaret Bauer.

Antelope Hill Publishing | www.antelopehillpublishing.com

Paperback ISBN-13: 979-8-89252-061-4
EPUB ISBN-13: 979-8-89252-062-1

To the two Toms who made this book possible. Without them, this would be an inferior work to that which is presented to the reader. Their knowledge, critique, and wisdom were invaluable. I would also like to thank the family and friends who have remained by my side, through thick and thin.

This book is dedicated to all the patriot dissidents held as political prisoners or otherwise repressed by the satanic regime which has seized power in the United States, but most especially the following:

ASHLEY BABBIT, an Airforce veteran who was shot in the neck, though she was unarmed, and whose murderer remains at large.

JOHN ANDERSON, a Marine Corps veteran murdered in prison by the state while being held indefinitely and illegally on fake charges. His murderers remain at large.

ROSANNE BOYLAND, who was beaten to death by Capitol Police, and whose murderer remains at large.

BENJAMIN PHILLIPS, hit on the head with a flashbang grenade. The police refused to help him while his heart had stopped. His murderer remains at large.

KEVIN GREESON, also killed by a flashbang grenade to the skull. The police refused to resuscitate him. His murderer remains at large.

MATTHEW PERNA, driven to suicide by the media and state because he trespassed in the "people's house."

To the prisoners and exiles of the **RISE ABOVE MOVEMENT**, whose only crime was to defend peaceful MAGA demonstrators from Antifa.

These are only a few. The regime's many illegal acts of state terror are so numerous that they are difficult to count, but not a single one will be forgotten or unaccounted for.

I am proud of what I did. May these enemies of the people suffer many times what they have inflicted.

They will not replace us.

CONTENTS

One morning, like over nine hundred other Americans and counting, I found myself faced with the reality of state power. For the great blasphemy of voicing our nation's feelings in the supposed House of "Representatives," my house was invaded and my family was traumatized by militarized political police. I was not the first. It sadly looks like I was far from the last. I thank God that at the very least the rabid lapdogs of the regime didn't "accidentally" kill anyone when they came for me, as they did at Waco, or when they caused Christopher Kuehne's wife to have a miscarriage after making her stand outside in the snow.[1]

To protect my identity, I can't give more details now. The mere fact that I have exercised my First Amendment rights in writing a book would be used against me—so much for the "land of the free." Free speech, like many of our traditional customs and rights, has come to exist only as a pathetic shade of its former self on moldering scraps of paper.

While I was neither the first nor the last to endure the wrath of state power when the American Regime's shoddy veneer of legitimacy was discarded after January 6th, I do intend to be the first to turn around and reverse the full-scale rout that the right currently is in. Too many conservatives, having failed to conserve anything, as usual, have blubbered and begged for scraps off the table in the

---

[1] Fairbanks, "Wife Suffers Miscarriage."

wake of January 6th. For what? For a few more months until they too turn into pariahs, and in the meantime are made to walk on the eggshells of what is considered to be "problematic" in our supposed democracy? For a few more dollars from their mega-donors? For the ever-elusive vote of senile NPR listeners? For the applause of leftists who openly despise them? So much for the "home of the brave."

I admit that I have thought about slinking off to the woods and letting this dystopian nightmare collapse upon itself while quietly raising chickens. Like all of the political prisoners from January 6th, I have largely been abandoned outside of the dissident right. Even the most strident of mainstream Republicans seem to take the luke-warm stance that we should all be thrown in jail, *but only after we have a fair trial and proper procedure is followed* without being tortured via solitary confinement or other methods.[2] "I know thy works, that thou art neither cold, nor hot. I would thou wert cold, or hot." (Rev. 3:15) Why should I care about a nation that doesn't care about me, or about the veterans, students, workers, family, friends, and neighbors who were and continue to be tortured and held in solitary confinement?

But when it became clear that the regime was going to throw everything at me in an attempt to permanently ruin my life in a hissy fit of spite, I decided to do the opposite: something more ancient and absolute than the desire to take the well-trodden path of least re-sistance awakened in me. This has become my personal *hour of decision.*

No, I was not the first to be targeted. But unless I am pleasantly surprised by someone else taking point between now and the pub-lication of this book, I do intend to be the first to dedicate my life to undoing their evil works. *Was this ordeal supposed to "deradicalize" me?* If so, they have failed. As they would have it with me, let it be so with them. Others have, and will, suffer far worse than I have. But I

---

[2] To put the abuses of the DC Gulag into perspective, Rule 43 of the United Nations Standard Minimum Rules for the Treatment of Prisoners states: 1. In no circum-stances may restrictions or disciplinary sanctions amount to torture or other cruel, inhuman or degrading treatment or punishment. The following practices, in partic-ular, shall be prohibited: (a) Indefinite solitary confinement; (b) Prolonged solitary confinement; (c) Placement of a prisoner in a dark or constantly lit cell; (d) Corporal punishment or the reduction of a prisoner's diet or drinking water; (e) Collective punishment.

intend to impose a hefty opportunity cost for their depraved acts of state oppression. I will not cower before corn-fed traitors and diversity tokens awkwardly roleplaying as Rambo. It is less *what* the regime has personally done to me, per se, and more *who* they and their lapdogs are, and *why* they are doing it, that has galvanized me. I will not debase myself before these lesser creatures, who are anathema to all that is good and natural.

But what is the American Regime, anyway? Is it not a distinct entity from the American nation? They call us traitors, but we are not. We are rebels. There is a great difference, though the misunderstanding between state and nation causes this subsequent misunderstanding. How can the historic American nation be treasonous toward itself? This, on its face, makes little sense. What we are witnessing is a divergence between these two structures, a divergence that must be accounted for if we are to properly address this accusation that patriots are traitors, and subsequently that internationalists are patriots. It is this peculiar entity, distinct from the body politic, which is to be examined in this work.

To explain this nebulous occurrence, I have first attempted to briefly summarize key moments in American history and how they specifically lay the groundwork for the current regime. It is necessary to examine which moment in time we are in, as based on the observations of history, sorting through the propaganda of pop history, to properly understand the regime. A fish can only obtain a basic understanding of reality if it knows more than just the nature of the water that surrounds it.

After this, the institutions that control our lives, as well as different models on how this array of institutions actually fit together into a web, are explored, as this is the meat of this study, since we are attempting to answer what this regime actually is. These separate models are often the source of division among those who essentially have the same goal, which is the critique and weakening of these very institutions. However, what I have found is that these models can be synthesized, and all have a great deal of truth to them. Thus, rather than focusing on the blind-spots of the separate theories of power as applied to the American Regime, I have attempted to streamline and connect them into the same language so that we might not get bogged in the mire of perfection.

Finally, not only have I attempted to synthesize the various models of power, but I have furthermore synthesized these models of power within my own model of meta-historical movement: two of the great foci of the modern, energetic right. I have combined this with some metaphysics, as among many great schisms that are rarely spoken of between the true right and left are not only the nature of history, but also the question of the parallax between ourselves and our ancestors, the ancients.

The left is content to judge the past based on *post facto* notions. I prefer to ask the more interesting question: what would *they* think of us? And where would they see us, and the regime, going?

The writing of *The American Regime* was done during the most stressful time in my life. I was just released from a detention center after over a month in inexplicable solitary confinement (which ended up being much worse than prison) and was held under house arrest until further notice. I had no idea when all this would end. I was suspended from studying political science at UCLA and facing decades in prison for fake crimes, trumped up by a regime that I hope our posterity will hardly be able to believe. Under the guidance of my friend David Zsutty, now the director of the Homeland Institute, I began using my newly freed schedule to write for *Counter-Currents* under the pseudonym Aquilonius. At the time, I had no idea that these would become a part of my prison notes corpus.

Doing little more than studying and writing, I figured that I should put my now more cemented worldview into a book as something that could not only explain myself, but also the grievances that led to the uprising at the Capitol. Furthermore, I found that few had tried to synthesize such complicated matters into a single place. Samuel T. Francis attempted this but died before he could finish *Leviathan and Its Enemies*. Since the release of the First Edition, Auron MacIntyre's *The Total State* has attempted this, though it relied perhaps more on anecdote than a general narrative of historical and cultural trends, and avoids certain subjects that I could not omit if I wished to do what I have always tried to do: tell the unadulterated truth, warts and all. I would not be surprised if he read the First Edition and tried to tamp it down for a more general audience.

The last edits were made over the course of November 2022, at the end of which I knew I would be interred in prison for the foreseeable future, and the book was released in time for the second anniversary of January 6th. In prison, I continued writing for *Counter-Currents* from behind the fence, as well as studying—indeed harder than I ever had—multiple hours a day. The free time is the only thing I miss about that place.

The American Regime is a product of its time, and while editing the new edition I found that this is why it shines. It is not merely a textbook of facts and trends, but a view into one of the most admittedly radical voices in America speaking out during the most oppressive period that America has seen in decades—perhaps since Reconstruction. If I were to tone down the language in some aspects, it would only take away from the context in which it was written. For that reason, my edits consist only of updates, corrections of grammatical errors that slipped through the cracks, and clarifications where further explanation was needed.

The book took over a year to write, as not only was I starting from scratch but also learning to write and research at a level higher than would be expected of an undergraduate. At the time, it felt like my own personal graduate thesis. Because of the length of time the book took to complete, I was able to take a more macro-level perspective on trends, rather than producing essays or articles shaped by the story of the day and the author's momentary state of mind. There were many instances in which news events appeared to contradict arguments I had advanced in the book, prompting momentary doubt, only for those events to reveal themselves months later as aberrations, with the broader macro-level trends once again vindicated.

I expect some readers will conclude that, with Trump's reelection, these trends have been reversed. Reality could not be further from the truth. What we find with Trump is a vindication of the Spenglerian dichotomy of Caesar versus collapse. Trump represents a sort of centrist Caesar attempting to make as many people happy as possible—especially elites. By contrast, a Left that no longer appears ascendant increasingly embodies social disintegration rather than historical momentum. With Trump enjoying the backing of Big Tech, we see what this Caesarism could look like—a future dominated by artificial intelligence, automation, transhumanism, and so on. If we are not careful, the warnings which I once directed at the entrenched Left may become no less relevant to the entrenched Right. Only time will tell.

This represents a markedly different landscape from the one in which the First Edition was written. It was a time when woke corporations and Big Tech exclusively sided with the Left. Again, I have left the book basically as it was written to stand up for itself.

It is often said that a thinker should wait some time before writing their first book, as their thoughts are likely to change drastically over the course of their formative years. Eighteen months in prison afforded me ample time to develop my ideas, and while my positions have surely shifted back and forth in various respects over that period, the book's central theses remain my steadfast position. I continue to regard them as largely unassailable for readers willing to approach the work with an open mind and a readiness to learn, rather than with preconceived notions or modern sensibilities.

PART ONE

OUR PLACE IN HISTORY

1

FOUNDATION MYTHS

"It is in general more profitable to reckon up our defects than to boast of our attainments."

—*Thomas Carlyle*

As with all societies, in the United States our view of ourselves and our history creates a unique worldview that influences us in all aspects. It is important to understand that this worldview is not necessarily objective, but rather a subjective one specific to a group of people within a certain geographic zone at a particular time. For example, an Englishman likely has a far different view of the American Revolution than an American, and indeed, we would likely find that an American in 1920 or 1820 would have a much different view than an American in 2020. Our perception of history and its effects on our worldview are formed by foundation myths. These foundation myths form "truths," and the people who are subjected to those "truths" have their opinions, historical as well as philosophical, constrained by them. Thus it is pertinent to explore these foundation myths, which are so formative to the American mind, in order to understand what has gone wrong in America.

I

Before beginning to understand modern America, we must start at the beginning. Every culture has a foundation myth. The Romans had Romulus and Remus, who, as the story goes, were raised by a she-wolf and went on to found what would become the Roman Republic. As for Americans, we have the Revolution for our independence, a story that has often been simplified down to one word: "liberty." A foundation myth need not be wholly fantasy. Many, if not most, are based in truth. However, a foundational story necessitates an element of myth which characterizes a people. According to the American myth, after decades of subjugation by the British, we had enough of their repressive taxes and domination, and declared our independence from Great Britain, defeating them in battle by virtue of our superior spirit, and created the first free nation of the era, modeled after high classical civilization. Some oppressors were tarred and feathered, and the rest is history.

This, unfortunately, is largely quite imaginative with respect to the actual events. For decades, the American colonies lived in relative independence from the British Empire. However, during the French and Indian War, Britain was pressed with insurmountable debt as a result of protecting the colonies from French invasion. Due to this, some taxes were levied on the Thirteen Colonies in an attempt to make up for a small part of the debt which had been incurred by protecting the colonists.[3] Rather than the colonists being grateful for the protection, this resulted in a boycott of the British Empire's goods by Patriot Party-aligned colonists, the purpose of the establishment of which was mercantilism, which itself was to monetarily benefit the Empire and demographically benefit the Anglo-Saxon people by providing for, and defending, a place for the posterity of Albion to live at a time when a population boom meant a highly crowded British Isle. The colonists even colluded with enemies of the British—illegally buying tea from the Dutch rather than paying more for it to support the Empire, for instance. Eventually England removed the taxes except for those on tea, but nevertheless, the colonists refused to pay for this tea and

---

[3] See Fisher, *True History of the American Revolution* for this discussion.

continued colluding with the enemy for the purchase thereof. The British leniently began subsidizing East India Company tea to prevent the state-sponsored corporation from being bankrupted by the practices of the defiant colonies. As an aside, at that time British tea was actually cheaper than Dutch tea. This attempt at incentivizing cooperation between the Crown and subjects was not taken well and resulted in the act of protest known as the Boston Tea Party. No one was hurt, although the modern equivalent of around a million dollars in property damage was suffered by the traders. In modern times, the apparent parallels between protests like these and modern-day leftist protests should not be simply ignored. The colonies refused to pay back these damages, and other tea shipments were boycotted, causing more surplus tea to rot in storage.

During this era, the Patriot-leaning colonists vandalized the property of Loyalists, and tarred and feathered those who expressed the wrong opinion. Furthermore, they began seizing weapons from Loyalists and stockpiling these arms in places such as Concord, Massachusetts. As the British went to confiscate the often-stolen weapons which were being stored in preparation for revolt against the British, they were attacked at Lexington, thus beginning the War of Independence. The fact that the Patriots seized the weapons is a testament to the organizational abilities of the future rebels years before the war began.

During the first years of the war under General Howe and his brother Admiral Howe, the British did everything in their power not to destroy the rebel army, while still fighting to keep the colonies under Imperial rule. Throughout the early years of the war, there are numerous recorded occasions in which the Continental Army could have been completely destroyed and yet was not, due to the liberal Whiggery of the Howe brothers.[4] By the time the British were ready to crush the rebellion in proper anti-partisan fashion (as was seen in Ireland), France, Spain, and the Netherlands declared war on the British Empire. The result was that it became immensely more difficult for the British, with their military now spread across the

---

[4] See Fleming, "The Enigma of General Howe."

globe, to sufficiently close off its American theater. The rest is history.

What is the point of this seeming defamation of the Founding Fathers, whom those of the conservative movement revere as saints? Before answering this question, some nuance should be introduced. The Founding Fathers were hardly radical left-wing extremists. If we are to be honest, they were everything the modern left hates, and if they saw what it meant to be a "radical left-wing revolutionary" today, it should go without saying that they would be absolutely disgusted. The Patriots also had perfectly valid reasons for wishing to split off from the motherland of England. Religiously they were much different, for example, a fact that is reflected in the First Amendment to the Constitution. This is but one of the easier examples which can be used to demonstrate that, by 1776, the colonists had become its own, albeit similar, people separate from the English of England proper.

This is far from an ignoble story. It is one of self-determination and, of course, liberty and freedom. However, it is still necessary for the right to come to terms with the fact that the story of the Thirteen Colonies is not a right-wing story, but rather, a progressive one with some parallels to the modern left in terms of the historical cycle. Both groups behaved unreasonably and were never satisfied with concessions from a somewhat empathizing government, resulting in a shift in the Overton window (or in other words, the spectrum of acceptable political opinion shifted from the right to the left). Both were highly organized and willing to use violence against groups with rival opinions who supported the status quo of an earlier era. Both had a government which was all but aligned with them and, therefore, were able to act with less resistance than was to be expected, in contrast to the Irish of the eighteenth century and the American right today. And, regrettably, both these modern groups and the Founding Fathers propounded a situationally left-wing ideology. The founders claimed to be liberal, the Enlightenment philosophers they studied claimed to be liberal, and the proponents of their ideology today often claim to be "classically" liberal. Therefore, it seems silly and counterproductive for conservatives to concede this liberalism as the catalyst of their ideology. Entire books could be written on the subject of the other side of the Revolution, as indeed they have.

This is not to say that the Founding Fathers were evil men at all. Rather, they were expressing a legitimate reaction to what they saw as a foreign occupying force which no longer represented them. Over the course of the seventeenth and eighteenth centuries, the colonists became a wholly new nation which saw England as alien to them, as has often been the case in the ancient world when colonies rebelled against their founding city, such as in the case of the war between Corinth and Corcyra in the fifth century BC. A true tragedy is that the foundation myth of America has been transformed from one of nationalism and self-determination into one of classical liberal ideals, partly due to the theme of "liberty" having somewhat changed in meaning over the centuries.[5]

The Founders were great men, among the greatest of the time, with legitimate grievances. However, if Americans are to reclaim themselves, it will be necessary to transcend a foundation myth with such subversive themes. That the central piece of the original foundation myth of the American nation is a radical revolutionary movement of agitators with arguably left-wing ideals, utilizing a Jouvenelian middle-low versus high revolutionary strategy, paints a picture of the true potential in this nation for a reactionary traditional ethos.[6] Generally, there is nothing more traditional, by definition, than a foundation. Therefore, it is impossible for any spiritual or political awakening to occur which can be characterized as being further to the right of the origin story of the nation. Furthermore, even harkening back to the true ideals of the Revolution, which despite their flaws are still far superior to any political development in the US over the past 150 years, has been impossible for many decades. As America continually undergoes new foundations through new myths, the quality of the successive founders becomes more apparently lacking.

---

[5] See Robertson, "What Did the Founders," and Rushdoony, "The Changed Meaning."
[6] See de Jouvenel, *On Power.*

II

The second founding myth is that of the American Civil War. Founding myths act in a similar fashion to the Old and New Testaments of the Bible. While the New Testament reigns supreme in instances of contradiction, the Old is also often valid when no such contradiction is present. Such is the case with the second founding myth. The story of the Civil War is that the evil White Southerners wanted to keep Blacks as slaves and, when Lincoln attempted to force their hand, they seceded, attacked the North, and were defeated by the gallant, biracial army of the North. This depiction is, like the story of Independence, partly embellished. There are some obvious contradictions, like within the New and Old Testaments, which are apparent between the first and second foundation myths. First, we must touch on the inaccuracies.

To be sure, slavery was and still is an unfortunate fact of life in preindustrial society, one that will not meet its demise any time soon. It should be emphasized, though, that slavery was a *necessary* evil for much of human history, including long before the Atlantic triangular trade. It is also relevant that slavery, hardly an efficient system in modern times, would have likely been abolished soon after 1860 in the Southern states, simply because of its untenability as an economic system. The rise of abolitionist sentiment coincided with the rise of coal energy, which replaced slave energy.[7] It is also worth mentioning that our modern comprehension of the history of slavery in America is mostly based off of abolitionist propaganda tracts such as *Uncle Tom's Cabin* and other works fed to us at a young age in school. The "villains" of the story, of course, had no reasonable opinions, and their stories need not be told, according to a government and an information network that *surely* has the masses' best interest at heart.

Furthermore, there is a fallacy invoked on the subject of slavery. While surely the modern person would not want to be an African slave in the antebellum South, this hypothetical modern man would also not want to be a serf during the same era in Russia, or an Irish manual laborer in the Northern US, or any manual laborer in the

---

[7] Bier, "Matt Ridley: How Fossil Fuels Helped End Slavery."

mid-nineteenth century, for that matter. Calling slavery inhumane by modern standards is unfair if it is not acknowledged that *all* lower-class labor up until, and even arguably during, recent times, even in the developed world, is inhumane. This produces a problem as to why slavery is considered an inhumane practice. Is it due to the labor, which was a normal way of living up until recently? Is it the bondage that slaves owe to their masters? If it is the labor factor, then should civilization be abolished to avoid any injustice lest anyone is forced to work for his daily bread? If it is bondage that supposedly causes the inhumanity, can this viewpoint really be defended within the context of a time when most people never traveled more than a few miles from their home, a phenomenon that produced a more cohesive society and closer personal relations than the atomized and "free" world of today?[8] This is not to defend the ownership of other humans, which is wrong, but to put into perspective the period in which slavery was abolished.

There is a debate which continues to this day as to whether the Civil War was truly even over slavery in the first place. The correct answer is that it was over both slavery *and* states' rights.[9] However, the reason is clear why the left and the mainstream focus on slavery, as do conservatives, who at least used to focus on states' rights. The liberal supports social justice while the conservative supports freedom and self-determination. After all, the conservatives intuitively see the contradiction between our first two foundation myths. Freedom and self-determination were two of the main values of the War of Independence. By consequence of the victory of the Union, these older values became subservient to the new and degenerated values of social justice and equality. Of course, Lincoln didn't even want to free the slaves, nor did he ever believe in racial equality, preferring repatriation to Africa for the former slaves.[10] However, a foundation myth is exactly that: a myth. And for practical purposes, modern interpretation is more relevant than what actually happened.

---

[8] Press, "Myths About Slavery and Lynching."
[9] See Pierce, "The Reasons for Secession," and Davis, *Rise and Fall.*
[10] Lincoln spoke of "restoring a captive people (American Blacks) to their long-lost father-land" in an 1850 speech commemorating the recently deceased Henry Clay.

The fear of losing the freedom of home rule due to the heavy urbanization and population amassment in Northern states was a valid reason for Southern angst. After all, very few Southerners voted for Lincoln. Lincoln won with less than 40 percent of the *nationwide* vote while carrying virtually no Southern districts, most of which were easily carried by Breckinridge. Therefore, why was it right that Lincoln would be the president and have dominion over not only his supporters in the North, but also his enemies in the South? Especially relevant is the fact that states were much more autonomous at that time, the US often being referred to as "*these* United States," emphasizing this pluralism. The Civil War historian Shelby Foote notes that "[b]efore the war, it was said 'the United States are'—grammatically it was spoken that way and thought of as a collection of independent states. After the war it was always 'the United States is.'"[11] If the will of Southerners could be swept aside in this election, in what other political issues would the rural South become irrelevant in the decision-making process due to the economic and demographic behemoth of the industrial, urban North? Thus, while Lincoln was not yet threatening to end slavery, the South could see the writing on the wall, and seceded from the North to maintain their freedom from electoral subjugation. Here again, the parallels between the past and the present are easy to see, and, here again, the conservative movement takes a position that is obviously counterintuitive. Just as Southerners feared in the 1800s, today, conservative America is dominated by the industrialized liberal centers. The difference today is little more than geographical. In 1860, the Northern states were generally industrialized, urbanized, bourgeois, and liberal, while the South was agrarian, rural, aristocratic/paternalistic, and conservative. This has evolved into an urban/rural distinction within states as the cities in all states have grown exponentially. However, the problem remains nearly identical. And yet, the position that the conservative movement has taken is that somehow "Democrats are the real racists," as the South was Democrat-dominated many years ago, ignoring the more important and ideologically relevant characteristics of the Civil War.

---

[11] Burt, "'These United States.'"

American conservatives in the twenty-first century now idealize Abraham Lincoln simply due to the fact that he started the Republican Party. However, a modern Lincoln would likely be someone who would deny Republican states and localities their rights through federal decree. The Lincoln Club, a far-left organization masquerading as a Republican organization, is ironically an example of the true spirit of Lincolnism in our time. How can a conservative movement which now idealizes Abraham Lincoln, the destroyer of home rule and independence, some of traditional America's most important and existential values, survive intellectually or practically? It obviously cannot and, as a result of these terrible philosophical positions that are adopted without much further thought, conservatives are easily outgunned by the radical deconstructionist left. Blunders like these are what allow the far left to manipulate contradictions of the system.

III

The next foundation myth of America is the Second World War in combination with the Holocaust. Once again, what truly matters in our study is the modern cultural interpretation of history rather than the true history itself. Pop history reigns supreme in popular culture—"pop" signifying mass consumption. The tale of America supplying the Allies before entering the war and boycotting Japanese raw material shipments before being attacked by Japan and then Germany, which now had a proper excuse to attack American shipping, is a much less propagandistic story than America fighting "fascism" and "racism" to save the Jews and other minorities from the clutches of the far right. However, the latter narrative is what is understood by the public and what is taught in the education system. From here, there are some archetypes which the story portrays. The Jews and minorities in general are the utmost good, while the Nazis and Fascists are the utmost evil. It takes little imagination to stretch the concept until "minorities" becomes anyone who is not, like a Nazi, a straight White male. Therefore, the utmost good becomes all minorities, women, sexual deviants, and even simply abnormal people. "Nazi" is translated into straight White male, and anyone else who lies on the political right, while the Allies generally were on the left, such as the resistance groups, the USSR, the FDR administration, etc., and are used as mascots of a new and unrecognizable left wing.

In this case, the American right does not have a contradictory view in opposing the Nazis, who were an enemy of their nation at the time. However, where they stumble is in how they always allow the left to control the narrative completely. Rather than frame the war as perhaps a "Great Patriotic War," as even the Bolshevik Russians—of all people—did, the war today is touted as war of a multicultural, multiracial conglomeration of democracies acting united against a block of White, traditionalist authoritarians (apparently ignoring the race war against Japan in the Pacific)—in defense of the Jews.

The right is once again playing by the left's rules. While the communists under Stalin were "bad" (and many leftists may even contest this), the Nazis were far worse due to the *racism*, and especially anti-Semitism, of their policy of death and destruction— "racism" being another loaded word the left loves to use to undermine their opponents, who already agree on their historical framework and are thus already defeated in the debate room or strung along to their insane motte-bailey conclusions. The communists were, of course, much worse than the Nazis. Death is death, and motivation hardly matters. To say that racism is a terrible motive could be countered by the blatant racism of the Soviet regime in exterminating and deporting minorities who sought autonomy, such as the Kurds, Crimean Tatars, Chechens, Balkars, and others.[12] If racism is evil, why is the institutional classism and racism of the USSR not also evil?

For our purposes, a simple look at the death toll under Nazism, even combined with the other fascist regimes of the era, comes nowhere near that of the USSR alone. And yet today Nazi imagery, rather than that of communism, has become synonymous with evil, despite the Cold War and even the anti-USSR consensus between the right and Western far left during the Cold War years. The colors red,

---

[12] See Human Rights Watch, *"Punished Peoples" of the Soviet Union*, and Aurélie, "The Soviet Massive Deportations."

white, and black, as well as the *totenkopf*, both of which have their origins long before the Nazi era in Germany, are universal symbols of evil in American media.[13] However, today it is perfectly admissible to be a communist or socialist in polite society, especially in the country's most influential positions of power where, in many cases, those of the far left sympathetic to Marxism may actually be in the *majority*.[14] Minus a small amount of flak, it may even be socially acceptable to excuse the atrocities of socialist regimes or perhaps deny they ever happened.[15] The opposite is obviously not the case with Nazism or fascism. A modern "fascist" could disavow every fascist regime, perhaps calling himself a "moderate fascist" or "fascist with a face," who is against any wonton violence, and the results would be that this person would be banished from polite society, which makes little sense, as the whole point of "anti-fascism" apparently was to counter the perceived negative and destructive effects of Fascism during the 1920s through the 1940s.

Thus, we finally see the conclusion to the left-wing version of the Second World War: fascism, and therefore anything distinctly to the right, is evil, not because of the destruction and death that it causes, but in and of itself. At the same time, communism and socialism are admissible always and in spite of the death and destruction that they inevitably and *admittedly* cause. And the kicker is that conservatives actually tend to agree with this blatantly subversive leftist message. It has become controversial even in conservative circles to have the opinion that the USSR was more evil than NSDAP rule in Germany.[16]

---

[13] Skull or literally "death head" in German, traditionally used by Prussian cavalry but largely made known in modern times by its use by the SS.

[14] This is often the case in social science departments in modern American academia, with Marxist concentrations typically in fields such as sociology, anthropology, and gender/ethnic studies.

[15] Perhaps the most famous case of this was French academic and existentialist philosopher Jean-Paul Sartre. From the 1950s through 1970s, as the Gulag Archipelago and other accounts of Soviet atrocities behind the Iron Curtain became widespread, Sartre the Stalinophile denied the possibility of the USSR's immense cruelty, now acknowledged by the Russian government. Today, Sartre, along with his fellow French colleagues who have other heinous views (specifically on pedophilia), is an icon and hero in mainstream academia and even the "moderate" left. See Cheah, "Michel Foucault."

[16] As of the publishing of the Second Edition, this has apparently begun to change due to the tireless work of activists and commentators who have risked and sacrificed their livelihoods to spread the truth.

The most culturally relevant part of the Second World War and the subsequent foundation myth is the Holocaust, which continues to hover around the American mind today. There is a Holocaust memorial in just about every American city, despite the fact that it occurred on another continent. Many Hollywood movies have been made on the subject, but virtually none on the Armenian Genocide or the Ukrainian Holodomor. This constant stream of reaffirming media creates an environment in which Jews are seen as carrying a generic protagonist archetype by default due to their victim status. Due to the migrant waves of Jews before, during, and after the war, along with their can-do-no-wrong status, leftists, largely of Jewish immigrant or first-generation immigrant origin, were able to form their own foundation myth out of the Second World War over the next three decades.

IV

Our last stop on the time machine is appropriately the most recent past foundation myth that America has added to its stack up to the modern day, which is the civil rights era of the 1950s and 1960s. The theory of civil rights is today official American doctrine and arguably a state religion, even more so than the previous American legends, likely owing to its relatively recent occurrence. The watershed moments of this foundation myth were *Brown v. Board of Education*, the Civil Rights Act of 1964, the Hart-Celler Act, and the anti-war movement in reaction to the Vietnam War.

Today, civil rights has become part of the American national canon. There is no debate in mainstream politics on the validity or merits of these new rules as, after decades of enforcement, the very seams which America has been sewn with have become intertwined with civil rights law. In the case of most of these laws, the removal of them from the equation would mean a major disturbance in how modern Americans on both the mainstream right and the left understand their country.

To tackle this, we must start from the beginning with the first major legal action of the era: *Brown v. Board of Education*, which, although today taught *a priori* as a feat and step forward in legalism, was in fact a feat in the bastardization of the law. The Constitution has always been interpreted as saying that, as education is not an enumerated right of the government, the states will have control of education. And yet, with the ruling in this court case, the federal government has banned the states, in the case of school segregation, from legislating education in their own state. Today, as the left has taken control of all aspects of life, it is impossible to say this without becoming a pariah. This view on Supreme Court jurisprudence is not held by anyone in Washington, at least not publicly, and yet not long ago it was a mainstream opinion. In his famous book *Conscience of a Conservative*, 1964 Republican presidential candidate Barry Goldwater writes:

> *The federal Constitution does not require the States to maintain racially mixed schools. Despite the recent holding of the Supreme Court, I am firmly convinced—not only that integrated schools are not required—but that the Constitution does not permit any interference whatsoever by the federal government in the field of education.* [17]

Goldwater was, of course, hardly a radical George Lincoln Rockwellite, but an ardent constitutionalist and libertarian, who in fact naively founded the NAACP of his home state of Arizona, desegregated the state's National Guard before the national military, and was against segregation. However, as Jonathan Haidt has pointed out, conservatives value more than just equality. [18] Goldwater's gripe, one that should still be valid but sadly is not in the modern conservative movement, was the problem of the federal government encroaching on the issue of desegregation. By the right

---

[17] Goldwater, *Conscience of a Conservative*, 27.
[18] In Haidt's *The Righteous Mind*, he postulated that there are six major values. While conservatives have a moderate preference toward all values (care, justice, loyalty, authority, sanctity, and liberty), liberals place an emphasis on care, justice, and liberty, while mostly ignoring the other three. Libertarians tend to place almost all emphasis on liberty. Thus, while the libertarian-conservative Goldwater was against segregation on principle, he also valued the liberty of states and especially private businesses. Liberals emphasize care and justice more than conservatives and libertarians, and therefore usually cannot understand Goldwater's admirable distinction and adherence to principles, preferring to simply label him as an evil racist and every other *ad hominem* attack in their book of labels which stifle debate.

conceding such an existential issue as the very right to freedom of association, the left has taken an arrow out of the quiver of conservative thought, apparently never to be seen or used again, as the Overton window slides to the left, *and only to the left.*

The next and perhaps most important event in this era was the signing of the Civil Rights Act of 1964 by President Johnson, which banned discrimination in most aspects of life based on race and sex, though today it has been construed to ban discrimination against any type of sexual deviant or pervert, a caveat which was not expressed by those passing the CRA originally and certainly not intended by the electorate who voted for the politicians who passed the CRA. Once again, this has been held as a step forward for society, that the sacred right to freedom of association had been removed from the American people. A most conspicuous part of the law which was clearly aimed at creating public consent for the revocation of rights in favor of the wholly artificial "civil rights," was the purely abstract legal notion of "public accommodations" created out of thin air, which is a blatantly misrepresentative term used to shield its true definition, which includes public *as well as private* facilities. Essentially everything public or private was banned from practicing freedom of association, at least for Whites. The only real exceptions to this today are clubs but, as culture is downstream from the law, it has become untenable today for these clubs to continue to operate. To ban discrimination by private individuals in their private business is quite literally "none of your business," a notion which was only recently made a taboo talking point. People, liberal or conservative, discriminate every day in who we allow in our homes. With the sneaky use of the term "public" to mean "public and private," America was tricked into revoking this right outside the home.

Today, like in the other foundation myths, American people across the political spectrum take this epochal change of culture and opinion for granted. "The Democrats are the real racists," says the average conservative, not realizing that by saying such a thing, he has conceded that racial tribalism and favoring your own people (a human phenomenon present in any successful society, and often absent in dying ones) is an evil that the left is correct in wanting to be vanquished. How, then, does the conservative counter the liberal who believes the Founding Fathers, and just about every figure in the history of mankind, has been racist? Usually, he or she will say they were "flawed but good," which is not a satisfactory answer. The real answer should be "Who cares if the founders were racist?" If the standard for having respect for a historical figure is that said figure must abide perfectly by modern sensibilities, there will be little respect for any figure who lived before our time. The left establishment that wishes to wholly destroy the past of Western civilization and demoralize its inhabitants unsurprisingly finds this to be quite an attractive option.

This cult of the "anti-racist" is hardly a legitimate inquisitive endeavor at finding the truth, but rather a cynical political weapon against Whites everywhere. This is further demonstrated by the fact that just about any "racial prejudice" by one group against another, even when neither are White, can, through sophistry, be used against Whites. The fact that lighter skin and pigmented eyes are sexually selected for and, as a result, the higher castes in most societies have lighter skin and eyes than the lower classes, even in societies which practiced this long before they ever met a White person,[19] is clearly an example of supposed "White supremacy," always sure to ignore the infinitesimally more brutal subjugation under other non-European warrior bands such as the Mongols, Manchu, Bantus, Comanche, Turks, etc.[20] Blacks attacking Hasidic Jews in New York and Mexican and Black gang members murdering each other in Los Angeles can be chalked up to "internalized White supremacy," I'm sure. There are an untold number of pseudo-esoteric word games invented by academics and used by their protégés in an attempt to seem intelligent by redefining words every other year and acting baffled when their adversary has not "read the literature" of some obscure, mediocre intellectual who was assigned reading in their sociology 101 course at XYZ State University.[21]

---

[19] See McCool, "China's White Skin Obsession."
[20] See Coulter, "Ann Coulter: Have a Historically Accurate," and Chakra, "The Brutal Military Tactics."
[21] James Lindsey has written extensively on the "woke" dialect jargon. There is also evidence that this phenomenon is not unprecedented in history and that the elite class of the late Ottoman Empire embraced a diverging vocabulary to a point where the laymen could barely understand the language of the elites. Andrzej Łobaczewski

Again, the conservative has bought into a game created by the left, hook, line, and sinker. If you say, even in conservative circles, that you do not support St. Martin Luther King Jr., you will be amazed to find yourself a *persona non grata* outside of a few fringe groups.[22] It amazes me that today, if you ask an elder if they were one of the tens of millions of White Americans who did not support the civil rights era legislation and action by the government such as the use of the National Guard, the 101st Airborne and their bayonets, and "busing" (which was seen as so extreme in that era that it was actually banned by name in the Civil Rights Act), you will seldom hear the affirmative answer. It seems clear that the oldest living generations have been shamed into pretending that they did not counterprotest against civil rights. It is naive to believe that, on the current trajectory, this pattern will not continue with subsequent generations.

The next stop in the era of civil rights is the Hart-Celler Act, which introduced the era of near-unlimited immigration, irrespective of the demographic consequences, to America. Once again, this was passed by Congress due to deception. Famously, Ted Kennedy testified that the passage of this new act would have no effect on the demographic makeup of the country.[23] Less than sixty years later, White children are in the minority among their peers in America. In the cities, where just about everything important in America happens, Whites are a small minority, composing only 36 percent of the population as of 2020.[24] The few that do live in the cities are usually those who, in fact, often have an *outgroup* preference,

---

also wrote on language evolution in *Political Ponerology: A Science on the Nature of Evil Adjusted for Political Purposes*. As a psychologist in Warsaw Pact Poland, he too noticed a trend toward jargon and complicated dialect utilized by nefarious and often psychopathic elites in the Polish and Soviet governments.

[22] Again, this has greatly changed since 2021 due to tireless efforts at shifting public consciousness.

[23] See Kennedy, "How the Immigration Act.": "'The bill will not flood our cities with immigrants,' lead supporter Sen. Edward 'Ted' Kennedy (D-Mass.) told the Senate during debate. 'It will not upset the ethnic mix of our society. It will not relax the standards of admission. It will not cause American workers to lose their jobs.'"

[24] Frey, "US White Population Declines.": "For the first time there are more children who are minorities than who are white, at every age from zero to nine."

meaning that they dislike fellow Whites and prefer nonwhites, a wholly unique and unprecedented phenomenon.[25]

Today, Americans are taught that America is a "nation of immigrants," equating the modern immigrants, many of whom come to America illegally, to the men and women of the seventeenth through nineteenth centuries who largely *settled*, not immigrated to, America, fought the "poor defenseless" Native Americans tooth and nail, and suffered from starvation and crop failure. Many died drowning in the Atlantic before ever stepping foot in the New World. Even after the settling of America, the European immigrants to the cities, such as the Irish and Italians, were a step above what we are used to today. They received no benefits, worked in harsh conditions, and some even starved to death as late as the Gilded Age. Many simply returned to their home countries as the harsh "dog eat dog world" of America wasn't to their liking. They all, of course, had to go through an immigration inspection, and many were sent back after long voyages due to various illnesses and worry of potential illegal activity. There was a long period in which only Whites were allowed to enter America as prospective future citizens and, until 1965, there were quotas to keep the demographics of America stable. Despite this, America's history has been rewritten, as happens after the assertion of all foundation myths, into something wholly alien.

The Hart-Celler Act ended America as it was pre-1965, and modern conservatives have once again bought into the progressive lie. America is not a nation of immigrants but a nation of settlers and, at best, a nation of White immigrants living beside an internal nation of Black descendants of slaves. While the US underwent a large migrant wave in the nineteenth century, immigration hardly defined the US then as it has since 1965. Even then, the introduction of White immigrants was protested, and it was not for decades that these immigrants were able to assimilate into White American society.

And yet, the conservative will seldom advocate for the pre-1965 system or even entertain the idea of a complete stop on immigration. That they don't understand that it is in large part *legal*

---

[25] Uhlmann et al., "The Motivated Use."

immigration that is causing every city in America to be ethnically cleansed of its White population, and many traditionally Republican states, to become swing states, or even deep blue states (such as the case in Colorado of the conservative Mountain West, and Virginia of the conservative South), is a testament to the incompetence and often the controlled opposition of the so-called representatives of conservative thought and vote in America. To see the droves of these critters fawn over the uncharismatic Jeb, the plastic Mitt Romney, the two-faced careerist Lyin' Ted Cruz, or the weakling Little Marco paints an accurate picture of the corporate conservative America that has long abandoned the mass migration issue in any real capacity.

Today, conservatives are accused of being anti-immigration. Lamentably, this is not the case. Conservatives tend to reply, "I'm not against immigration as long as they come here legally." The main immigration issue in the Republican Party is illegal immigration, which would be basically irrelevant compared to legal immigration were it not for the fact that Democrats have used an incredibly sly tactic of getting these illegal aliens status as legal residents for the end purpose of providing a "pathway to citizenship" for illegals and formerly-illegals. This they do by using some sob story to somehow claim that being able to bubble in some voting papers every other year is *that* much of an improvement over simply living here in peace, working, and paying taxes. It should be painfully obvious that the "pathway to citizenship" is a backchannel for the Democratic Party to pump out votes for themselves. They admit as much, though from the smarmy weasel look they make when one brings this up, it's clear that they are not used to *even this* coming up in a discussion on immigration.

Finally, this era culminated in a true foundation myth, which continues to enamor the minds of generations of young Americans to this day, through the combination of civil rights with the counterculture and anti-war movement. As will be discussed in greater depth later on, it was here that the new academic and information elite, largely consisting of Jewish immigrants and second-generation immigrants, newly empowered by the Holocaust foundation myth, were able to truly form America into something new. The civil rights era legislation provided what essentially became a new constitution, providing legal backing, while the community organizing of the 1950s and 1960s provided infinitesimal opportunities to network with fellow left-wing dissidents on the streets and at elite American universities. Once the legal avenue was stable, culture was simply downstream from politics. And once subsequent movements popularized in this era such as second wave feminism, post structuralism, postmodernism, Black liberation, anticolonialism, etc., were solidified within elite circles, the seeds of the next foundation myth were already sewn.

V

But what is the next foundation myth of America? At the time of writing, the reader is indeed living in it. After countless race riots over the last few years, it should be clear that, once again, America is changing drastically and, already, the America of today is something completely different from what it was only a few years ago. The legalization of gay marriage (another issue the right has conceded) is but a microcosm of the new American experience. Some point to the beginning of this phase being the Obama campaign in 2012 blatantly switching its targeting from the White working class, as the Democratic Party usually did, to minority issues.[26] Others point to the Gamer Gate controversy, a relatively obscure affair over leftist coverage of video games on gaming news websites. Whatever it was, clearly something transformed and divided the culture into two distinct camps in the early 2010s.

On the activist left was a coalition of oddities and professionally offended activists made up of students, "alternative lifestyle" advocates, and the self-righteous mass of professional and amateur agitators, often highly active on social media, especially Tumblr and

---

[26] The logic of this switch in campaign strategy was not by accident, but quite well thought-out, as the demographic change in America, and especially the Democratic Party base and demographics which could be courted by the Democrats, had shifted dramatically over the decades since Hart-Celler. At the same time, Whites were a decreasing percentage of the population (and as of the 2020 census *numerically* shrinking in actual numbers), and the working-class White demographic has especially seen a near-disappearance relative to only a few decades ago. Nicholas Jones et al., "2020 Census Illuminates Racial." See also "The Great Replacement."

later, Twitter. The term "social justice warrior" or "SJW" was created to label these people as a single category. On the grassroots right were the ruralites, the religious, and many in the White suburban working and middle class: generally those who led traditional lifestyles on the activist side. These two camps together are a minority of Americans today, but they are the epicenter of the culture war which only now the rest of the American people are being swept up in. Rather than calling the far left "SJWs" as many young people do, a common term used by all age groups on the right is "the loud minority" while the right is "the silent majority." As time has carried on, the right has become less silent and more numerous (though never *actually* constituting a majority).[27]

This culture war seemed to hit a tipping point with the 2016 presidential campaign of Donald Trump. As a whole, politics has become deeply influenced by this culture war. For this reason, Donald Trump was able to win the White working class, much of which was either apolitical or Democratic-voting for decades. On the flip side, people like Elizabeth Warren and Hillary Clinton had to change their position from a working-class message, to more of an elitist message targeting the upper middle class. The Democratic Party quickly changed gears from a mainly pro-worker and middle-class party to a party of the untouchable dregs of the lumpenproletariat on the bottom, and a coastal elite of upper middle class and wealthy people on the top, comfortable enough to adopt the luxury positions espoused by the new Democratic platform, but wealthy enough not to be negatively affected by them. There is a tacit agreement between the top and bottom to squeeze the middle—seemingly a common occurrence during the consolidation of power—described famously in Bertrand de Jouvenel's *On Power: The Natural History of its Growth.* Predictably, an upside-down caste system is forming, similar to the Soviet Union, where the lunatics come to run the asylum, in what can be called no less than a *satanic* inversion. And when referring to something as satanic, we are not necessarily saying that it is literally of a demonic origin in the

---

[27]As of the Second Edition, the labels "SJW" and "loud minority" have fallen out of fashion in favor of "Woke," and the time from the mid-2010s–mid-2020s has become known as the "Great Awakening."

spiritual or metaphysical sense (though religious people are free to subscribe to this view), but rather in the traditional meaning: that of an inside-out, upside-down, topsy-turvy morality which contradicts a perennial and natural understanding of the world which is universal to all civilized cultures from ancient Egypt to the West up to only a few years ago.

The 2016 election was a backlash (or as the Black Van Jones of CNN not inaccurately coined it: "Whitelash") to the open insanity of the left. In 2008, the year that Obama was elected, only a fringe of the American population supported gay marriage. By 2016, it had been made legal in every state by federal decree through the Supreme Court. In 2016, supporting the self-castration of the transgender community was also only something found on the fringe. Today, child castration is in vogue in the Democratic Party's base. Pedophilia is now only accepted by the fringe. This, of course, has been coming since at least the 1960s (and if the reader wonders where this garbage comes from, he should really pay more attention to what they are teaching in the universities).[28] "Existential philosophy" and "queer theory" are codes for trains of thought which lead to the acceptance of pedophilia.[29] Within the Democratic Party, will there be a majority in support of "pedosexuals" or "minor attracted persons" (MAPs) in 2024? Or how about 2028?[30] And if

---

[28] S.G. Cheah, "Michel Foucault." "It was a time when social taboos were broken on principle, for the main slogan of the 1968 student uprising was 'It Is Forbidden To Forbid.' Nothing is out of the question. No behaviors should be deemed too repulsive. No human desire should be deemed taboo. Not even pedophilia."

[29] See the previous footnote on Sartre. Of course, this is an oversimplification, and Heidegger was hardly a supporter of pedophilia. However, it is hard to unsee the shoddy character of many of the fathers of these "disciplines" after short research. For example, the founding document of queer theory and gender theory, *Thinking Sex* by Gayle Rubin, supports pedophilia. These disciplines are highly influential in academia and on the left at large to this day. It would be naive to assume that there is no intent to promote these practices, especially considering the proven prevalence of creepers within the government and wealthy private elite. See Dreher, "Can You Normalize Queerness without Pedophilia?"

[30] As of 2025 and the publishing of the Second Edition, the progressive movement has not adopted pedophilia *per se* but continues to support the spiritual and psychological rape of children's minds, leading to self-castration or suicide. Rather, they have gone in a different direction in terms of stigmatizing age gaps. Instead of promoting pedophilia, shaming normal heterosexual couples for any age gap has become in vogue, with college student vigilantes physically assaulting college seniors for the crime of dating freshmen. Orwell's prediction of an anti-sexual leftism, a

Republicans only barely defeat the pedophile party in these elections, while the culture nevertheless slides ever more to the left, will this be a victory or a defeat? By now, it should be obvious that this shift in the Overton window does not originate in the era of left-wing domination that we live in today but is part and parcel of the nature of history that has just been described. Theodore Roosevelt, a progressive of the turn of the century, would put any modern "conservative" politician to shame today. The left has won in the field of sexual deviancy in every aspect outside the legalization and acceptance of pedophilia which, credit given to the American people, is not yet tenable. Thus, for the time being, they have largely moved on to "racial injustice."

The most prolific movement of this era is the Black Lives Matter movement, a completely astroturfed movement which venerates criminals of all races, though predominantly Black, who have the support of every institution in the United States, and whose main purpose is to act as the Brownshirts or Red Guard of the regime against what I have referred to as "traditional America" but what Łobaczewski simply called "normal people." These protests were labeled "mostly peaceful" by the left and the media.[31] It should be known that, in my experience in the right-wing protest movement of 2020, if there are counter-demonstrators who lack police protection, "mostly peaceful" becomes *exclusively* violent. They carry knives, pistols, clubs, razor blades, pepper spray, tasers, and who knows what else to "protect themselves" from the five sixty-year-old Trump supporters who counter them and attempt to protect the once majority-White and conservative city which they lived in for their entire lives. The reader can guess which side gets beaten half to death and which side is excused as "mostly peaceful."

It is a mistake to believe that Black Lives Matter is simply a moral organization whose protesters sometimes get carried away and begin to destroy private property or harm private citizens. The first evidence of this is the fact that if BLM was a moral organization, they would have found a way to "organize" that wouldn't cause mayhem

prediction that has earned him no awards over the years, just may bear some insight here.
[31] See the infamous "fiery but mostly peaceful protest" ticker tape from CNN; Daily Wire News, "Watch: CNN Claims"; see also Houck, "Anarcho-Tyranny 2020."

and death in its wake. The leaders of this group are aware of this and yet continue to lead riots which are tacitly supported by the government, an inference that can be made due to their failure to stop or prevent them. Dozens have been killed by BLM's riots and countless others have been injured and harassed.[32] Rather than take responsibility for the actions of the "protesters" under their wing, they excuse themselves by saying that these rioters were not actual members of the organization (very few people are *literally* members of the nonprofit "Black Lives Matter").

Even more damning is that while BLM does not take credit for their destruction, they also don't seem to really condemn it, either. There is a reason for this. The destruction is part of their tactic. Not only do their members get to *de facto* legally loot businesses, but by using this tacit threat, they are able to extort support from the local populace. One look at any downtown city, full of pro-BLM propaganda on the windows of restaurants, will demonstrate this. It is a mistake to interpret this as BLM having the undying support of the people. The parallels between today and the famous Nazi flags "voluntarily" being hung outside windows when the German army entered Austria, or Soviet propaganda strewn about on the streets of a Soviet city, are eerie to say the least. It is in this way that the phenomena should be viewed. Businesses and especially restaurants, being the heart and soul of a city, are used to lull people into believing that supporting BLM is the normative, default state. Eventually, this perception becomes reality memetically. It becomes "cool" to support Black rioters destroying the city. "Everyone else is doing it." In reality, the only difference between the modern American "deep state" regime extorting support out of a city's downtown and the Nazis or Russians extorting support from Viennese and Muscovite flag wavers is that, in the America regime, violence is exported to groups like BLM and adjacent organizations. There is a tacit *quid pro quo*, meaning that the government doesn't enforce the rule of law on rioters, while the rioters unwittingly carry out the bidding of the government and big business.[33] Mega-

---

[32] Beckett, "At Least 25 Americans."

[33] For example, in a democracy, it is highly important that the state maintain a semblance of law, order, and fairness. Thus, siccing state-paid enforcers on protesters would attract ire from all angles. In contrast, using private individuals and groups

corporations undoubtedly look at a few smashed windows as just another operating cost, and one worth paying if it means the small business competition goes out of business from accrued costs.

It is unsurprising that BLM does not condemn its own rioters. Why condemn them when the US government and every business that matters in America support them? The media surely do not condemn BLM, unless your news is a right-wing source. It is here that we see why we are truly living in a foundation myth today. While the right believes that these issues are still on the table to be debated, the government and private sector has side-stepped normal America altogether, making support for causes like BLM and the aforementioned gay rights movement the official stance of the US government. While Trump was in office, a massive "BLACK LIVES MATTER" logo was painted on a street in DC.[34] In California, to do burnouts on a BLM street mural was prosecutable.[35] "Liberty Plaza" in DC has been renamed "BLM Plaza." BLM and Antifa paramilitaries were allotted a space right in front of the White House balcony to protest every day and every night with personal bodyguards paid for by the taxpayer (that is, the DC Metro Police).[36] Embassies such as the one in Seoul, South Korea, have massive BLM murals, and US embassies now raise the pride flag, a symbol of occupation and global homogenization (also known as "globohomo"). The same can be said for various other buildings owned by the US government all over the world. Even the Trump administration was extorted for pro-Black legislation which no Trump-voter asked for, as a result of rioting in DC.

The FBI also works hand in hand with BLM, Antifa, and sympathetic journalists, using them as their eyes and ears where the government possesses no agents or cameras to do their work.[37] Tyrannical governments in the Soviet bloc and elsewhere also used

---

and punishing them with a light hand is more reasonable tactic. Furthermore, similar to minimum wage laws, big business can take the brunt of a detrimental policy if it means eliminating competition which can't. See Sibarium, "Insurance Companies," and Vance, "Fighting Woke Capital."

[34] Austermuhle, "Bowser Had 'Black Lives Matter' Painted."

[35] Farberov, "Two California Men."

[36] Dwyer, "'Black Lives Matter Plaza.'"

[37] See "U.S. Capitol Violence."; Taylor, "The Proud Boys and Antifa."; Hood, "FBI Arrests White 'Serial Rioters.'"

their own citizens against one another. However, what is most disturbing is the fact that these governments had to *threaten* their populace to comply with acting as informants. In America, we have been subjected to such a spiritual, mental, and even physical deconstruction, that among the people there are many who simply enjoy using power to destroy others.

These are only some of the few ways in which we can see the government has embraced the new mythos. The new cringe-worthy advertising campaign for the military and CIA, glorifying homosexuality, minorities, and even mental illness and the antinomian riot movements of the new era, demonstrate this well.[38]

The ideology of BLM is also unsurprisingly evil. The left has mastered title propaganda. If BLM was called the "Black Nationalists for the Extermination of Whiteness" or "BNEW" (pronounced Be New) for short, they would get less support from the public. To say "I don't support Black Lives Matter" sounds to the average person like "I don't think any Black lives matter." This is, of course, by design. However, the ideology of BLM is not "believing that Black lives matter and therefore they should not be murdered by police." It's not even about being proud to be Black, which there is nothing inherently wrong with, as long as Whites and other races are allowed to as well (Whites are most certainly not permitted to be proud of their race under this regime). What it really suggests contextually, however, is destroying Whites and promoting radical left-wing politics. The founders of BLM have claimed to be "trained Marxists" and famously, in a now-deleted page on the BLM website, said that the organization supports the destruction of the nuclear family, something that has ironically already happened in the Black community and is a major cause of the problems that afflict African Americans today.[39] The current non-deleted demands of BLM on their website are no better, and basically amount to "give us power so that we can make sure White interests are never represented in government again,"[40] something that unfortunately has already

---

[38] For the woke CIA: CIA, "Humans of CIA."
[39] John, "Black Lives Matter."
[40] Some of BLM's demands: Convict and ban Trump from future political office, expel Republican members of Congress who attempted to overturn the election and

been largely granted, though they don't yet realize it, as they are advocates of the "permanent revolution," a mindset highly intoxicating to the pathological "rebel without a cause" who subjects society to perennial torment for reasons which normal people cannot fathom.[41]

The final reason we can be sure that BLM is a malicious organization is the way in which they exploit normal procedure while ignoring real tragedy. Many point to George Soros' historical predilection toward fomenting social upheaval for profit, though he is just a small part of this superstructure and a useful scapegoat.[42] It is no coincidence that cases in which the Black person killed is armed, resisting arrest, being otherwise violent, or dies by outside forces are used by BLM to rouse masses of Blacks and liberal "allies" who are often not versed in the actual circumstances of the death, while actual cases in which an officer kills a Black person in a way that could be easily avoided are ignored.[43] The former cases are divisive and are thereby used to sow division between Blacks and Whites, while the latter everyone can agree are tragic and, at best, caused by stress (of police officers worried that the perpetrator is armed, possibly deranged and/or on drugs, and therefore not thinking about having to endure a life sentence, a fear that is not unreasonable to anyone who has witnessed body camera footage).

Normal run-of-the-mill liberals are similar to some Muslims in that, though they don't participate in terrorist attacks, they also don't necessarily condemn them. Of course, there are many Muslims and liberals who are principled and do condemn the terrorism in the case of Muslims, and rioting, doxing, harassment, etc. in the case of liberals. However, I fear here it is too often a matter of optics rather than genuine belief when the liberal condemns rioting. The most common defense is that the rioting is somehow "mostly

incited a white supremacist attack, permanently ban Trump from all digital media platforms, defund the police., among others.
[41] Neal, *American Extremist.*
[42] Perazzo, "Black Lives Matter." "Through his Open Society Foundations (OSF), Soros in 2014 gave at least $33 million to support already-established pro-BLM groups that, as *The Washington Times* wrote, 'emboldened the grass-roots, on-the-ground activists in Ferguson' after the death of Michael Brown."
[43] It should be noted that the number of unarmed Blacks killed by police is quite small. Taylor, "Police Racism: A Manufactured Crisis."

peaceful," which of course means that the potential victims were able to evacuate the area before the army of the Red Guard descended on them. I'm sure the police who are in striking range of these supposed pacifists would beg to differ when the day turns to night and the rowdiness of the crowd is not subdued by officers kneeling in a pathetic display of "solidarity."

Their lack of genuineness is easily displayed by the fact that, while defending the rioters as "mostly peaceful," they may also quickly change their tune to "show me where it says protests are supposed to be peaceful," as in the case of CNN's Chris Cuomo.[44] The point here is not to simply display the "hypocrisy of the left," a time- and energy-consuming rabbit hole that so many have fallen into. As Solzhenitsyn said, "we know they are lying, they know they are lying, they know we know they are lying, we know they know we know they are lying, but they are still lying." It is a moot point which only has the purpose of preaching to the crowd. Hypocrisy and lying are tools that they use and, as long as this tool produces results, it will continue to be used. Conservatives have no counter to their hypocrisy but to call it out, which the liberal ignores or laughs off. They don't care, and the right is naive to believe that this is any counter worth pursuing. While the right says that the left are not evil but merely misguided, the left happily exclaim from the rooftops the evil of the right. Nevertheless, the left has been effective at using this imagery, as evidenced by their portrayal of contemporary Republican candidates—including their now-beloved John McCain in his 2008 campaign—as some parallel to Nazism.[45]

To the left, conversion to conservatism is to fall under the shadow of evil, of ultimate sin. The mainstream right, clinging to Enlightenment notions, morally accepts apostasy from the right to the left and blames themselves for failing in "the marketplace of ideas." It is too ironic that the main pusher of this ideology, the libertarians and classical liberals, have consistently failed in their "marketplace of ideas," as their ideas have only lost ground in electoral politics to left-wing, big-government encroachment. This one-two punch from the left and the so-called right has crippled true

---

[44] See Neale, "Chris Cuomo." and Kirkpatrick, "FBI Announces War."
[45] 62 Vena, "Madonna Compares John McCain."

conservative thought. This has been done with the idea that truth and righteousness can be commodified and democratized, which is, of course, a side effect of the failed (and oxymoronic) political branch of right-wing democratic thought, such as what the modern right subscribes to today, and which must be abandoned if there is any hope of the survival for the forces of natural order.

The aim of pointing out this failure of modern conservative theory is to demonstrate why the right is incapable of doing the one action that is capable of countering the left's hypocrisy. Many a subscriber to this Enlightenment theory has fallen down the rabbit hole of criticizing liberal hypocrisy rather than calling out liberalism, hypocrisy and all, for what it really is, which is simply the embrace of disorder. It is the wholesale rejection of what Christians call Logos, the Absolute, or God, what Taoists call *Tao* (The Way), or what Hindus call *Brahman* (the Absolute). Twenty-four hundred years ago, Plato remarked similarly, writing that liberal, late-stage democracy results in a rationalization of this antinomian chaos, what we in the modern world in shorthand simply refer to as "evil":

> *It insults those who obey rulers as willing slaves and good-for-nothings and praises and honors, both in public and private, rulers who behave like subjects and subjects who behave like rulers. . . . It makes its way into private households and in the end breeds anarchy even among the animals. . . . I mean that father accustoms himself to behave like a child and fear his sons, while the son behaves like a father, feeling neither shame nor fear in front of his parents, in order to be free. A resident alien or a foreign visitor is made equal to a citizen, and he is their equal. . . . A teacher in such a community is afraid of his students and flatters them, while the students despise their teachers or tutors.*[46]

It is striking that Plato's caricature of a failed city, in taking liberal democracy to its conclusion immediately preceding the transition to a tyranny, is simply describing our own society two millennia into the future.

---

[46] Plato, *Republic*, 562d–563a.

It is not simply inalienable rights that we are endowed with by our Creator, but certain universal truths which are intuitive and natural. Until conservatives are capable of labeling liberals as evil, as liberals do to conservatives, there will be no counter to liberal hypocrisy. With the lackadaisical way in which conservatives oppose liberalism, one would doubt that "thou shalt not bear false witness" was even part of the Ten Commandments.

If things continue down this path, we may see the following narrative mold the future of America as the new foundation myth and truth regime: "In 2015 and 2016, the evils of fascism resurfaced in America as the demonic Whites betrayed *Our Democracy* with the help of the Russian government and elected the dastardly Donald Trump into power, attempting to re-enslave Blacks and exterminate the Jews of America. Luckily, a coalition of minorities, White allies, LGBTQIAP2S++ individuals, and our lovely corporate overlords were able to vanquish this plot by bravely protesting and speaking truth to power against the evil middle- and working- class White 'Middle American Radicals.' However, these MARs struck back by raiding the sacred seat of *Our Democracy* and attempted to overthrow and kill elected politicians, the representatives of the people. Luckily, this was to no avail, and the brave men and women of the Capitol Police were able to round up and imprison these uppity rebels. Peace was restored to the nation." This may seem like hyperbole, but considering how each foundation myth has drifted further and further away from the truth, this version of the modern foundation myth will likely not even be the left-wing version, but rather the "moderate conservative" opinion in the next era.[47]

---

[47] Readers of the Second Edition in the age of Trump and post-Trump may protest that this scenario has been altogether avoided. We can certainly hope that there is truth to this! However, let us recall that all of the foundation myths remained intact during and after the Reagan era, who has long been seen as a champion of the right in America. Indeed, it was he who instituted the federal holiday for St. Martin Luther King, Jr.! Our theses are not based on fluctuations of current events but on centuries-long trends.

VI

The right-minded person should have realized that the actions of the modern-day forces of liberalism which are commanding the most recent foundation myth of this country are evil and indefensible. What I have seen personally I will never forget. How can you forget masked paramilitaries beating the elderly with clubs while the police watch? How can a liberal convince you that BLM is peaceful when you saw the aftermath of a BLM gunman murdering five police officers in Dallas, or have visited their website where they glorify communism? How can you unsee the SUV terrorist attack of Waukesha which ran down dozens of white elderly women and children, killing six, and which was committed by a Black career-criminal who openly embraced anti-White hate and supported BLM? I have personally seen a BLM woman use another "activist's" infant as a human shield as she attacked counter-protesters, and then run to the police claiming that a counter-protester assaulted "her" child. However, if history was hidden or erased, how would one know? How will one's children and grandchildren know the truth? If one has seen this reality unfold but assumes that the tactics, antics, and actions of the "winners" of history were not the same, then one is mistaken that the next generation will recognize the truth. We assume that the Founders did not use dirty tactics, or perhaps explain it away, despite the fact that Patriot rebels sniped at British officers—an unheard-of tactic at the time. We forget the scorched-earth subjugation of the South during the Civil War and Reconstruction. We ignore the bombings of Dresden and the war crimes against German POWs after the Second World War. And most of all, we have been lied to about the race riots and outside agitation of the civil rights movement, and denied the truth about the counter-demonstrator movement of that time. History is written by the victors.

Of course, despite the flaws of our past epochs, the traditional order in those times often justified the actions of revolutionaries and the march of history along with them. It may seem as though I have defamed said movements of the past which conservatives and liberals alike view as sacred cows. The colonists did not declare independence from Britain for no reason, nor did Lincoln invade the

South or Martin Luther King, Jr. march on Washington due to a lapse in judgment. Historically, liberal or leftist movements have arisen due to problems which can reasonably be understood, despite the fact that the actors of progress, seeing themselves as reformers, are unknowing participants in the spread of chaos and corruption. This is no longer the case. The Founding Fathers were not mentally ill villains, despite their flaws, nor was Lincoln. The same cannot be said for the outwardly satanic modern left, which boasts its mental and spiritual illness, wallowing in its decadent and self-indulgent corruption. The past banner-carriers of revolutions were radicals. Today, they are extremists, deranged lunatics who hide under the flag of ideology to tear down society from within. The foot soldiers of leftist activism know what they are against, but not what they are for. Often, they are not even aware of what they are against, and without exception hold multiple contradictory opinions.[48]

It is no surprise that this watershed moment has been thrust upon the normal people of America, the West, and indeed the world. Our institutions were built by fallible men whose principles, in retrospect, were hardly as universal as the Enlightenment philosophy believed itself to be at the time. It is a rational conclusion of history that America's faulty bedrock values, beginning with autonomy, nationalism, and freedom in colonial times; to unity, subjugation, and imperialism during and after the Civil War; all the way to social justice, equality, and the preference for supposed fairness above freedom in the twentieth century, would further degenerate into the value of what is truly evil and the disdain for what is good. This is seen in the anti-philosophy of the current foundation myth, which the powers that be are attempting to institute via a Maoist-style cultural revolution, that will end only once it loses momentum and destroys itself and all under its dominion, or is stopped by heroic action.

---

[48] Malkin, "Beware of the Flu Shot Bullies."

2

ON META-HISTORY

"A civilization or a society is "traditional" when it is ruled by principles that transcend what is merely human and individual, and when all its sectors are formed and ordered from above, and directed to what is above."

– *Julius Evola,*
Ride the Tiger, *2*

In the previous chapter I outlined the foundation myths which dictate how Americans see their country, and the social phenomena that have followed. What has been shown is that, despite legitimate and often noble concerns, the myths which define America are all liberal and in rebellion against order. The parallels even to the most irrational and chaotic elements of the modern era can easily be seen in the Enlightenment revolt that was the founding of America. Furthermore, the historical events become more and more chaotic and indefensible as time drags on.

As has already been discussed, the Revolution is the original founding myth, the Civil War and emancipation, the Second World War, the civil rights movement and the countercultural revolution, and the current social revolution of today are what have followed. Why these revolutions have progressed in the way that they did, and why they are continuing to this day in their modern avatar, is the concern here. To further understand the basic groundwork of the modern era, it is necessary to comprehend the true nature of history: a nature which hardly resembles that which is taught in the lecture halls of modern academia.

I

The modern academic class largely claims to be nominally progressive (if not outright Marxist), and thus views history through a progressive, linear lens.[49] To view history any other way would go against the sacred cow of the modern civic religion. Linearism is also largely in alignment with the themes of popular Christianity and the other Abrahamic religions. There is the beginning of the universe, as detailed in Genesis, and then the end, found in Revelation. Whether this is a correct interpretation of the Bible is unimportant. This is simply the societal theme of the modern West, which relies on Christianity and a progressive lens that originates from the Revolutionary period to the Victorian era as its social bedrock. This is in contrast to the majority of other religions and cultures, traditional Western and pre-Western Indo-European culture included. The Zodiac, astrology, Hindu doctrines, the doctrines of European paganism, and arguably the traditional symbolic view of Christianity all view history as operating in cycles. It is the phoenix which rises out of the ashes or the ouroboros snake of ancient lore, seen from Egypt to the Yucatan, which eats itself in a never-ending struggle. What if the linear view fails to explain the world around us in a sufficient manner? Perhaps the alternative view, seen in these other cultures throughout time, must be considered.

There is also the secular philosophical element. The Hegelian dialectic, a mode of development in ideas, is inherently progressive. Marx viewed the world as constantly progressing, with the end result being the revolution of the proletariat, the abolition of private property, and the end of history resulting in a classless society. It may seem ridiculous to some, but it makes sense if the linear assumption is made. It is progress, but to what destination? An end

---

[49] Bergman, "Ratio of Liberal to Conservative Professors."

implies the inability to progress further. An end implies the lack of a restart. The intellectual class has an interest in suppressing views contrary to linearism, as the modern academics almost exclusively descend intellectually from Marx. Furthermore, there is no disincentive to perpetuating such views, as academics do not feel the consequences of their faulty reasoning. Rather, they are rewarded for keeping their head down and nodding in agreement with other academics. Indeed, "It is the arrogance of the urban intellect, which, detached from its roots and no longer guided by strong instinct, looks down with contempt on the full-blooded thinking of the past and the [ancient] wisdom."[50]

There is some truth to linearism. It is clear that history progresses for certain minimal periods of time, especially in the case, as noted by Joseph A. Tainter, in which a new energy source is founded which can push back decline and collapse for a certain period of time.[51] The Marxist dialectic understood the supplanting of the monarchy by the aristocracy, and then the aristocracy by the bourgeoisie. It was a rational assumption that the bourgeoisie were the last obstacle until the proletariat, the final and lowest class, would supplant them and institute the rule of the workers. Marx views this as a positive, and that it will institute the end of history. However, upon examination of history, this does not appear to be accurate. If this were the case, why did it not occur at any other point in time? Why do we not today live in a time when History (in the sense that Hegel, Marx, or Fukuyama would use the word) and the other classes are a long-forgotten memory? The Industrial Revolution was not the first time that monarchy was supplanted, or even the aristocracy and bourgeoisie. For example, Aristotle is attributed with observing in his time that:

> when the people become prey to lawlessness and wantonness, and the state is managed by worthless men, it tends to change into a democracy of the extreme type.[52]

And:

---

[50] Spengler, *Hour of Decision*, 21.
[51] Tainter, *Collapse of Complex Societies*.
[52] Aristotle, *Politics*, Book IV, 1296a.

> *democracies are generally overthrown by the wantonness of demagogues... who... stir up the people against the upper classes... and thus they are apt to produce a tyranny.*[53]

This is simple common sense, but every society in which the peasantry revolted and overthrew their masters simply degenerated into mob rule and then collapsed. It is clear that this has been "accomplished" in just about every failed society directly preceding its collapse, not out of a glorious class revolution, but due to the de-organization process as a strategy to fight for the very survival of the soon-to-be subsumed culture, as notably seen in the case of third through fourth century Rome or the Maya of the first millennium AD.[54] As early as the fourth century BC, Plato remarked in the *Republic* that it was indeed democracy that was the catalyst toward tyranny.[55] Indeed, tyrannies in classical Greece were often instated by a representative of the pre-Dorian lower class ethnic group, overthrowing the Dorian aristocratic order.[56]

Julius Evola, among the most dedicated philosophers of history of the twentieth century, summed up the alternative, cyclical model of history thusly:

> *Recently, in contrast to the notion of progress and the idea that history has been represented as the more or less continuous upward evolution of collective humanity, the idea of a plurality of the forms of civilization and of a relative incommunicability between them have been confirmed. According to this second and new vision of history, civilization breaks down into epochs and disconnected cycles. At a given moment, and within a given race a specific conception of the world and of life is affirmed from which follows a specific system of truths, principles, understandings, and realizations. A civilization springs up, gradually reaches a culminating point, and then falls into darkness and, more often than not disappears. A cycle has ended. Perhaps another will rise again some day, somewhere*

---

[53] Aristotle, *Politics,* Book V, 1303b-1304a.
[54] Tainter, *Collapse of Complex Societies.*
[55] Plato, *Republic,* VIII.
[56] Sealy, *A History of the Greek City States.*

else. Perhaps it may even take up the concerns of preceding
civilizations, but any connection between them will be strictly
analogical.[57]

It is in this way that history must be viewed if we are to understand
the nature of our world, put the puzzle pieces together, and
determine the patterns which will lead us to creating a roadmap
toward a world which we are proud to pass on to our posterity. Our
environment is but a case study as to what we can expect from an
inaccurate premise that so dictates how we view the world.

There is an inherent problem with the idea of unending progress.
It is curious that those who abide by the Marxist view of history fall
into the same pitfall of the capitalists, their mortal enemy.
Capitalism relies on infinite growth, though this is impossible.
Linearism relies on infinite progress up until the end, which is also
impossible. While Marx viewed the revolution as finally ending once
his view of the world was instituted, all this demonstrates is Marx's
lack of imagination of the destructive capability of man. Marx would
never have been able to predict the depravity and degeneracy that
is becoming mainstreamed in our collapsing culture. In this way, any
witness to the later years of their society, whether they might be
from Rome, Teotihuacan, or Babylon, would have more predictive
power than Marx, simply by relaying their experiences. From the
genital mutilation of children, the admiration for eunuchs, the
sexual deviancy, and potentially much more disturbing
developments, history rhymes indeed. Just like all fallen societies
who came before us, we will find that infinite progress is simply not
possible.

II

The phenomenon of the cyclical nature of history has been studied
by scholars whose insights into what is to be expected and what has
occurred, using the patterns of those great peoples of the past which
fell into almost precisely the same situation we face today, can be of

---

[57] Evola, *Hermetic Tradition*, 13.

use in our decayed age. On the level of empires, Sir John Glubb (a scholar of history and British General of the Arab Legion of Transjordan during the Second World War and 1948 Israeli War of Independence) has done marvelous work, compiling some of the parallels which he saw as constant in declining societies, specifically in his short but succinct masterwork on cyclical history, *The Fate of Empires*.[58] Perhaps his most important insight was that empires tended to last roughly 250 years, give or take a few decades. In other words, a society would only last ten generations past the initial imperial outbreak stage before disintegrating. It should go without saying that this is highly relevant considering that the US is quickly approaching destiny as an empire (in the sense that it began expansion into Indian lands immediately after proper independence) beginning roughly in 1783. According to Glubb's studies, the US is a decade to midnight if we use the precise number of two hundred and fifty years.

To illustrate the rise and fall of great empires, Glubb divided the empire's existence into several stages, the first being "the outburst," in which a formerly backward and irrelevant people begin to conquer often larger, more geopolitically relevant groups, despite the burgeoning people's small size. The second era is that of mercantilism and commerce, in which an emphasis is placed on capitalizing on the newly acquired land and resources gained from the expansion. After this is an era of affluence, which supplies the people with luxury and introduces decadence to the former warrior people. This wealth leads to the ability to fund progress in thought, and therefore, an age of intellect. Intellect is the final age of greatness and, since there is scant more to accomplish, the civilization fights a battle for new records while going into a downward spiral, cushioned by mass wealth, arts, luxury, and further decadence. The choice is simple and, while some last longer than others, the result is always the same. Glubb notes that various political systems have been implemented in an attempt to maintain an empire for longer than his thesis claims is viable, all of which were in vain. This is corroborated by Tainter, who found that, after a certain point of complexity, a society will hit a point of returns on

---

[58] Glubb, *Fate of Empires*.

investment so egregious that the only viable strategy becomes dissolution.

It is not difficult to see the parallels in US history. The US, of course, experienced its outburst period when it conquered Indian lands, defeated the Mexicans, and became one of the largest countries on Earth within a few decades of its founding as an independent nation. We see precisely the same breakout period in Alexander's Macedonian Empire, the Rashidun Caliphate, the Seljuk Turks, and many other great peoples. There is a great outburst by a strong, founding warrior generation. Often times, this warrior band will become the aristocracy which rules over a larger conquered people such as the Dorians of the Peloponnese, the Medes and later ethnic Persians of Achaemenid Persia, the Aryans and later Mughals of India, and the Normans of Medieval England.

The second era (in Glubb's terms) for America began in the mid- to late 1800s. The conquered lands, previously uncultivated, were made useful, largely due to immigrants from Northern and Western Europe, while the industrial centers were manned by Americans of older stock, along with Southern European and Irish immigrants. By the Second World War, the US had become the industrial powerhouse of the world, able to supply itself and the Allies during the war, something which it also did in the First World War.

In the aftermath of this era was an American age of prosperity never before imagined. The US was rich enough to rebuild much of the world after the war and develop an advanced economy in which a working-class family could thrive on a single income and afford to raise a large family, sparking the Baby Boom. The US government was prosperous enough to send men to the moon and simply outspend its chief competitor, the USSR. The American Empire *de facto* controlled most of the developed world and much of the third world through leadership of both NATO and the UN. This era of prosperity was the age in which the Boomers grew up.

Beginning with Reagan, the US government began pushing for the masses to enroll in higher education, giving further fuel to the age of intellect, which arguably had its roots in the tumultuous 1960s, in which the universities and their staff and students became disproportionately influential in all cultural enterprises. And after the Second World War and the G.I. Bill, no longer would university education be only for the old elite. Within a few decades, the number of young people with degrees skyrocketed, beginning in 1960. The 1960s saw the height of high school diploma recipients, in fact. On the surface, it was a golden age of education. However, the motivation that the government inspired rested on an incomplete argument, which assumed that correlation was proof of causation: that college-educated people are more successful and therefore more people should be pushed to attend college.[59] This false premise planted some of the seeds for the later American decline, as seen in the student debt bubble and the decline in homeownership and children in favor of pursuing an increasingly expensive and time-consuming educational path.

Of the various empires which he studied, Glubb found many symptoms that also plagued Britain at the time of his writing, and which today plague the United States. For example, the decline of sexual morality, the popularization of pop music often accompanied by erotic lyrics and guitar-like instruments (think the British Invasion), and the belief that their empire would usher in what is described as "the end of history" in contemporary Western circles. Other symptoms include having outside peoples do their hard work and warfare for them as a result of their belief in cultural superiority, resulting in the natives pursuing bread and circuses. Generosity becomes a curse, the high culture begins to relinquish its resources to help alien peoples who will turn on the empire at the right chance, and welfare is made a state policy.

While Glubb was an Englishman and was not specifically focused on the US, his predictions rang true. His essay *Fate of Empires* was written in 1978 and was largely based on the disintegration of the British Empire (which fell apart soon after WWII), and yet it has perhaps translated even better to the modern American predicament. What lies in wait for us remains to be seen, though the patterns of history are a good roadmap as to what we should expect. Put simply, the progressive theory of linearism is anything but correct over the long term. Their prediction that history will end *this time* is not a sober gamble. Regardless, the academic and

---

[59] Emmons, "Education and Wealth."

bureaucratic classes won't be affected one way or another in the short term, if their predictions and linear views should be ignored.

III

While Glubb's cyclical theory is in large part correct, it is also quite materialistic in its worldview. In the Traditionalist view articulated by René Guénon and Julius Evola, which draws heavily from Hinduism, the cycles of history are regarded as coinciding with the castes—the priests, the warriors/aristocracy, the producers and merchants, and the peasantry/ proletariat. There is much of value in Glubb's study of empires; however, the four-caste model can also be used in the case of the cycle of an empire, as well as greater cycles.

The age of the priests is an age of a phoenix arising from the ashes, or being born for the first time. It is a time when a new way of thinking, a new *weltgeist*, is formed. For Americans, this time is the era before and shortly after the Revolution. It was a time when America was becoming not a simple cluster of British colonies, but its own nation with its own customs, ideology, assumptions, and even its own religious beliefs. The original zealots of the American temple were not priests at all in a literal sense, but philosophers from across the Atlantic who greatly influenced the ideology of America, and perhaps even the original Puritans who founded the distinctly non-British religious views which would shape America.[60]

From the simple idea of Liberty, long before the American Revolution, a quasi-religious revival was born, which was the Enlightenment. This spiritual revival led to the contemporary equivalent of "warrior-priests" from earlier times—the patriots, the zealots, the nationalists of North America—to break away from England and go their own path, as England had broken from the Catholic Church over two hundred years prior. After the founding texts of the Enlightenment from Europe came new founding texts,

---

[60] If we are to take this interpretation, parallels to the Eastern mystery schools which in part formed the bedrock of Greek and later Roman elite culture can be seen. The same is true of the Eastern religion of Christianity forming the religious bedrock of the modern West or the Buddhism of India being foundational for Japanese civilization.

namely the Declaration of Independence, *Common Sense*, the Federalist Papers, The Articles of Confederation, and The Constitution, which put to scripture what was previously an oral or implicit tradition. This era could be said to have ended after the War of 1812, when the avatar of the transition between a legendary founder (priest) and a frontiersman warlord (warrior) was made a national hero, embodied in the person of Andrew Jackson.

As the old priests of the American founding died off, it was still generals and war heroes who became the leaders of the nation, though ones not necessarily related to the founding creed explicitly. In the government, far from the near-direct democracy of today, only the landed were permitted to have a say in the lower house, while the upper house was appointed. These warriors did as warriors do, and conquered their surroundings, as previously discussed. The spirit of this era began to decline after the Civil War, which was symbolically a war between a landed warrior aristocracy in the Southern states, and the newly ascendant industrialized urban bourgeois order that was quickly forming in the North. The Northerners, embracing efficiency and capitalism through industrialization, had little need for slavery, as opposed to the Southern agrarians who adhered to the traditional ways. As the nineteenth century wound to a close, and the Native Americans and other imperial powers were largely defeated on the American continent, there was very little of the warrior aristocratic order left in America.

From here, the age of the merchant in America began. It is ironic, however, that America reached its greatest extent of military might, not in its warrior aristocracy era, but in the age of the middle class. However, this seems to be normal when investigating other empires and civilizations. The height of Roman military might was not during the Punic Wars, nor was the height of English martial power found in the High Middle Ages, nor could we find the apex of Classical Greek militarism in the Archaic era. Interestingly, it was in the closing of the third age that this was often the case.

Inventors abounded in the US, such as Edison and Tesla. The stock market came to be used by a larger audience, eventually leading to the economic bubble of the "Roaring Twenties." The Federal Reserve was introduced to promote artificial economic growth, and later the Keynesian understanding of economics was employed for the same reason, while other rival economic theories were also developed. It was during this time that America became the nation of the middle class and the idea of the "American dream" was popularized. Eventually, the bourgeoisie of the world, often from countries where such a class was repressed, came to America in droves to realize this dream. From this point, items of bourgeois sentiment were the primary societal focus. Not just economic success, but a view of nationalism and the "city on a hill" vision of America as an even further distinct people and nation became the state religion. Intellectualism, along with investment in the arts and universities, grew substantially. It should be noted, however, that this intellectualism was the mirror opposite of the founding idea, as seen in movements such as modern art and socialism.

Finally, out of the World Wars and the societal revolts of the 1960s began the era of the plebeian class in America, which Glubb associated with decline. And indeed, the era in which the modern equivalent of the peasantry has reached primacy is truly the beginning of the end of any empire, to the chagrin of Marx. Rather than valuing enterprise, the ultimate value is equality. When equality fails to eliminate hierarchy, equity is pursued. It is at this point that the empire swings into free fall.

The 1990s and early 2000s was a period in which the inadequacies of the new order were most heavily felt. First was the end of America's foil, the USSR, in 1991, which in a way propped up the American system's bubble by providing an ever-present specter of communism to react to. Later, 9/11 caused a social break with the old order. This was the original "new normal" of the modern era, with the rise of excessive public safety measures, paranoia, and mass surveillance under the Patriot Act, which would later be unleashed in full in a mere twenty years. Finally, the 2008 crash caused another break with the old in the realm of economics and society. This eventually led to the ascendance of economic leftism in place of economic liberalism as the default opinion of the young left, which is a symptom of decay. Soon after, fringe far-left social beliefs were inserted into mainstream left-wing discourse. Less than a decade after the *anti-gay-marriage* candidate Barak Obama was elected president as a relatively left-wing liberal, gay marriage was made legal nationwide, and even the right completely abandoned the issue. Within half a decade of this, child chemical castration became a mainstream left-wing policy, and open pedophilia is simply waiting for opinion polls to swing in the right direction before making its debut on the mainstream political scene.[61]

This is the essence of the age of the fourth estate. It is a time of the supplanting of the old values completely. The first estate (priestly) values of piety and sanctity, the second estate (warrior/aristocratic) values of honor and heroism, and the third estate (bourgeoisie) values of prosperity and meritocracy are largely diminished. Unfortunately, this leaves mostly negative values at the end of the cycle, leading to advanced stages of decline. The terms "degenerate," "decadence," etc. have become cliché but appropriate. When society truly does degenerate to a point in which innocent children are in harm's way, when a civic religion of quasi-satanism emerges within a decade of New Atheism, when men castrate themselves in an attempt to become women, where the mentally sound are the exception and not the norm, and when racial and ethnic suicide is not only normative but considered among the failing society's greatest values—it is at this point that it is no longer about politics but about an eternal good and evil.

At a rapid speed, we are reaching the stage in which the Israelites found Canaan, the Romans found Carthage, and the Spanish found the Aztecs. During this final stage of an empire's existence, indeed at the end of an entire civilization, the degenerated people will often commit child sacrifice and ritual self-mutilation, and worship demonic gods of death such as Baal, Moloch, or Mictlantecuhtli.[62] It is no surprise then that these societies were completely leveled, rather than subjugated. In the case of the Spanish, the destruction of the dark Aztec religion and conversion of the native populace via robust missionary programs was believed to be necessary. In the case of Carthage, the people were annihilated and the land salted. The Old Testament tells that the extermination of the Canaanites by the Israelites was quite literally God's divine will. What great

---

[61] Garrison and Peinovich, "On the Groomer Question."; James Fulford, "Download Ketanji."; Malkin, "Michelle Malkin: GLSEN's Groomers in Plain Sight."
[62] Smith, "Canaanite Child Sacrifice."

civilization who comes after ourselves would not look at what we have become and launch a war of extermination against the satanic entity that we are destined to be in our last days? Perhaps this is not far from the perception that the hungry wolves of Islamic and Confucian civilization have for the aging West.

IV

I have spoken of "civilization," rather than a simple empire. The end of an empire does not spell the embrace of the most extreme trends which I have just identified. The end of an empire is degenerate, decadent, and a pathetic shell of its past self, to be sure. However, an empire dying does not in itself spell child sacrifice and mutilation. This is usually reserved for the end of an entire civilization.[63] Indeed, we are not only witnessing the end of the American empire, but Western (or Faustian) civilization as a whole. The West not only includes the US, but also empires that have already declined and fallen such as Britain, France, and Germany. The fall of America is simply the final part in a cycle that is far older than America.

A civilization goes through the same phases as an empire, but on a larger scale. There are ages of the priests, of the warriors, of the middle class, and of the masses. The era of the priest class is also largely an era of the warriors as well (and vice versa), with the priests respecting the role that warriors play in society. This can be notably seen in the early modern era in the aftermath of the collapse of the Holy Roman Empire. Up until the Peace of Westphalia in 1648, the Catholic Church, alongside the warrior kings of feudal Europe, ruled on an equal though teetering field of power. This was, of course, a long time coming, nearly being accomplished during the wars between the Holy Roman Empire and the Vatican for sovereignty over the realm. There was also the creation of a new church in England in the sixteenth century, a church in which the monarch of England was also the head theocrat.

With the fall of the primacy of the Church, the West saw an age of the rule of kings and the aristocracy, and the emergence of

---

[63] "Human Sacrifices: How Many Were Killed in Aztec Culture?"

absolute monarchy, most popularized by charismatic monarchs such as the Sun King Louis XIV and Henry VIII. This traditional political regime of the primacy of warrior nobles essentially lasted up until the aftermath of the Thirty Years' War, but was truly stamped out in the eighteenth century when a series of revolts instigated and led by the bourgeois class overthrew or attempted to overthrow several monarchies, pushed for reforms, and generally supplanted the warrior aristocracy for power. In the US and France, revolution was successful and democratic republics were installed (with France requiring several more revolutions until they reached ultimate success). In Britain, which was the most important power at the time, the institution of monarchy had been severely weakened since the civil wars and revolutions of the seventeenth century in which the Parliament defeated the Stuarts and instituted a representative government. Indeed, Cromwell has been described as a bourgeois revolutionary, despite being a military commander.[64]

Thus, the West generally entered the age of the merchant class in the aftermath of the Thirty Years' War, Westphalia, and the subsequent revolutions. Even where the monarchy remained intact, the power of money and the middle class could not be ignored, and it was during this time that mercantilism and colonialism abounded. It was a time in which one of the most powerful militaries in the world was that of a corporation—the East India Company—instead of a country. It was the era of the galleon, the slave trade, West Indian sugar plantations, the Dutch poppy trade, and the Industrial Revolution. It is easy to see that during this time there would be discomfort from the last caste, the peasant and worker, due to the harsh working conditions of industrialism. Thus, it would be only a matter of time before socialist groups and unions of solidarity became pronounced, especially in the most industrialized centers of Europe, which led to Marx and Engels writing about the plight of the proletariat.[65]

---

[64] Hill, "Cromwell and the English Middle Class Revolution."
[65] Marx was incorrect in his estimation that the age of the proletariat revolution would introduce the end of history, just as Fukuyama was incorrect that the neoliberal order would institute a similar equilibrium. Marx was close, but failed due to his hubris in his ironic belief in Western chauvinism and White supremacy. Marx believed that the other races, including Slavs, whom he incorrectly lumped in with non-Europeans, were largely incapable of class consciousness, and were therefore

It is interesting to note the relationship of the American and French Revolutions at this time. These revolutions marked the height of bourgeois revolt, which lasted largely until the revolutions of 1848. However, despite the close proximity of these two revolutions, on the scale of their respective empires they have differing significance. The American Revolution was truly the beginning of a new empire, as we have already discussed. However, the French Empire began centuries earlier. Rather, the revolution in France not only failed, but instituted a warrior-bourgeois transitional regime under Napoleon which transitioned from monarch to emperor, only to truly become a stable democratic regime in 1870—eight decades after the revolution began. Here, we can see complications in the cycles of both empire and civilization. Napoleon was not an aristocrat, but a *soldier*, fitting for a transitional period in which a monarchy is overthrown during the bourgeois age of a civilization. Avoiding reductionism, it is no surprise that the French Revolution failed to bring about a Marxist-style total transformation while the American one succeeded, when looking from the perspective of the flow of time of entire civilizations. The French were ahead of their time, needing several decades before they could fully transition from *ancien regime* to the Third Republic.

This era of the middle class began to unravel as the Western world continually extended suffrage to the entire body of citizens, including non-landowners and women. From here, expenditures across the Western world spiraled out of control under irresponsible, high time-preference (that is, preferring less now

---

obstacles to the international workers' revolution. The thinly-veiled implication of Marxist thought is that the Western European would have to be the last man standing and introduce the end of ends. However, the impossibility and insanity of this scenario is obvious. It is also a testament to the bastardization of Marx by modern pseudo-Marxists who conveniently ignore this implicit aspect of his theory. While the idea of extermination is preposterous and evil, it does introduce some nuance into the way Marx actually thought. Far from the radical liberal universalism of today, Marx recognized that an end of history would only be possible if there was but one civilization with minimal differences between its various nations that stood in the ruins. However, the modern leftist has simply cherry-picked the part that he thought sounded correct and worked on the theory that was doomed to fail. The lack of predictive power of Marxism is a stark testament to why progressivism, a particular type of linear history that modern academics still cling to, is an unsound position.

rather than more later) tax and spending policies.[66] The last true vestiges of traditional power in the West were broken after the World Wars, with the democratic powers triumphing over the aristocratic powers such as Germany, Italy, Austria-Hungary, Russia, and the Ottoman Empire. Furthermore, the aristocratic officer class of that time, as was the case of the aristocratic knightly class of Thirty Years' War era in Europe, as well as the patrician class of the late Roman Republic, was largely wiped out. The governments of Europe were replaced by democracies and, when reactive elements arose in the future Axis countries, they were once again destroyed and even further democratized by the dominant democratic sphere. It is only in the final phases that the accumulated resources and power of the late-stage civilization will finally reach the apex and enter a steep decline, and have the dysfunction that we see in America and throughout the West today, which parallels the collapse of classical civilization.

It is interesting to note that America, unlike her mother nations of the British Isles and the Continent, only began existing during the reign of the profane and less-metaphysically-concerned caste eras. America was conceived during, indeed *for the purpose of*, mercantilism. Furthermore, America's birth itself marked the high note of the bourgeois moment of the West and, by popularizing the democratic ideal, in some ways opened the doors to the proletarian age. It is for this reason that the early part of American history, which is a microcosm of the priestly era of America, is not religious at all but rational, profane, modernist, secular, and purely philosophical, though it at times seems puritanical in comparison to today. Due to America's *too humble* beginnings, it is easy to see, not only the ease with which America was further corrupted, but that today America is the ultimate exporter of every corruption imaginable to the rest of the world. We need look no further than the Paris Commune of 1871 to see what is in store for a society ruled by the multitude:

> It was then that the work-shy rabble were in power, and not the
> working class: deserters, criminals and bullies, literary men and

---

[66] Chantrill, "US Government Spending History from 1900."

journalists, with among them, as always, many foreigners: Poles, Jews, Italians, and even Germans. . . . A loose alliance of the large cities (that is, of their lowest classes) was to overthrow and conquer the open country and provincial towns—a notion typical of Latin anarchy.[67]

A similar course of events was of course seen in the Bolshevik Revolution and in our own cultural revolution today, where one only need visit any American city—whether it be the degenerate cities of the West Coast or the once great but now Africanized cities of the Southeast and Great Lakes regions—to find this motley crew of left-wing villains, the locust horde which mans the ranks of the revolution.

V

The easiest way to illustrate the phenomenon of Western decline is through art, which has seen relatively no true innovation since Impressionism, and architecture, which has devolved into building the tallest glass rectangular prism. Artistic music (baroque, classical, Romantic, etc.) is dead, having been replaced by pseudo-art music exemplified most typically by the talentless pop industry. Another example of this trend toward the attempt at differentiation and progress for its own sake, with no transcendent quality, is the "piece," John Cage's "4' 33''" (pronounced "four minutes, thirty-three seconds"), in which an orchestra sits in silence for the allotted amount of time without playing a single note. The orchestra apparently counts the minutes of pauses as accurately as a metronome. Other pieces are just random sounds assorted in an exact way. However, it should be noted that these are sounds and not musical notes. It is no wonder, then, that enjoyment of music has deferred to popular music genres, as the *art* of music is dead. This is only the phenomenon of music. Other forms of art and culture have fallen to similar levels of "deconstruction."

Modern art is an even more ridiculous case study in how far society is willing to go to pull the leg of those unfortunate enough to

---

[67] Spengler, *Hour of Decision*, 126.

stumble across the modern attempt of "artists" to play with the dead carcass of an impossibly lost form as if it were a marionette. It is so much so that modern art has become a *meme* in and of itself, associated with the ugly, obnoxious, and pretentious—essentially an aesthetic *reductio ad absurdum* of progress. Visual art has become a way for rich elites to launder money rather than something containing a message or enriching the human experience, as well as to signal their virtue and intelligence in a real life parody of the "Emperor's New Clothes" story, where the powerful view the "I" of intelligence as more important than true wisdom. One could go so far as to say that the viewers themselves have become the *true exposition art*, an exposition of self-indulgent, arrogant bourgeois society which they claim to disdain while animating the archetype of said society, though neither the artists, nor the adoring viewers are capable of such three dimensional thought. A dot on a canvas or Marilyn Monroe edited through four color filters is not art, nor is the splattering of paint on a canvas.[68] The art of the contemporary West, like the culture it represents, has come to deny the transcendent and the objective. As culture has become the negation of culture, art has become the negation of art, whose only purpose is to deconstruct itself into metaphysical suicide.

Oswald Spengler saw this clearly in 1918, long before the insanity of art and architecture had reached the level at which it has achieved today. After conducting case studies on multiple civilizations, he discovered that this had been the case in every past civilization as well, and the phenomenon of artistic atrophy was one of the canaries in the coal mine of history which could be utilized to gauge the fall of a civilization. The artistic and architectural innovation of Rome had begun to be imported long before Alaric's sacking of the capital, the Magian (Eastern Mediterranean/Persian) civilization has, as of modern times, not produced much for

---

[68] Jackson Pollock, an "artist," whose works consist of slinging various colors of paint onto canvas in no particular pattern, is perhaps the most acclaimed artist of the twentieth century. His painting, simply titled *No. 5* sold for $140 million in 2006—thought to be the most expensive art purchase in history—while his painting *Number 17A* sold for a whopping $200 million. *17A*, being such a masterpiece, was bought by a hedge fund manager, the epitome of high bourgeois elite society, and is not even on display.

hundreds of years, and the West has not produced anything new artistically for over a hundred years while lesser atrophy had set in even earlier than that, despite constant attempts to squeeze every last drop out of the dead golden goose. By continuing to fail at innovation, only creating weirder and weirder art as can be seen today, the artist achieves the opposite of what he or she has intended, forming yet another file in the cabinet of proof that art has died in the West.

There will of course be protest by those sponsors and contributors of the arts who cannot accept this (the modern art museum tourists most likely). However, Spengler's thesis holds its ground both intellectually, as well as in the heart for most healthy people. Recall that Glubb noticed a similar trend, that intellect is the final age of greatness and, since there isn't much more to do, the civilization fights a battle to find the next stage, not realizing that *there is nothing new to find*, resulting in a downward spiral, cushioned by the massive wealth, arts, luxury, and decadence, unable to achieve the previous dynamism of old. There is simply nothing transcendent about modern art, as the spirit has died. It is a cargo cult.

The death of art is so prevalent and unavoidable that even the right, which often understands these principles and intuitively understands the lack of value in modern art, has itself been unable to produce quality art in the modern age up until recently (literally within the past three or so years). The art of the right has been limited to political cartoons and nostalgia-fusion graphic art which produces nothing new and is itself based on the vaporwave movement, which did not even take itself seriously.[69] American culture has become so degraded that visuals as low brow as 1950s advertisements have become idealized by some on the right as representative of true art. It is impossible not to come to conclusions on the quality of art in modern times that has driven those who seek

---

[69] Vaporwave, from the terms "vaporware" and "wave" (i.e. synthwave, fashwave) is an art movement which began as a self-aware and ironic musical and then artistic movement, but has now been adopted in sincerity, usually by the right, due to the undertones of returning to an idealized past. This forms an interesting parallel to the Dada movement of the interwar era, which also became adopted by the masses as a serious movement, though originally intended to be lackadaisical.

beauty to gravitate toward nostalgic images of an already degenerated time. The same can be said about the possibility of the right, which sees itself as the torch-bearer of the West, to improve on an artistic tradition that died long ago. It is telling that the only sector of right-wing art that has appeared on the scene in the past few years that has any true and transcendent value is that which sees the Faustian as something that cannot be returned to, and harkens not to a nostalgic past, but to a future past the fog of war.

VI

I have long deliberated on the question of the actual *force* which guides this phenomenon of degeneration, which can be seen in any and all human organizations and groups. Reminiscent are Robert Conquest's laws of politics, specifically his second law that any organization not explicitly right-wing will eventually become left-wing.[70] While this is obviously the equivalent to our subject but in an expressly political context, the left and right are synonymous with disorder, chaos, and reform on one side, and order, tradition, and stability on the other, respectively.

At long last, I believe that I have come to the correct conclusion as to the profane, visible, and material outward manifestation of the metaphysical concept which has been discussed. I hereby dub the phenomenon the *Guénon Effect*, named after the like-minded theorist on meta-history René Guénon. Specifically, I was inspired by his masterwork *The Reign of Quantity and Signs of the Times* in which Guénon's main thesis is that of the degeneration of quality into quantity, on a metaphysical as well as physical level. Here, I wish to expound on Guénon's theory to explain degeneration leading up through our time.

The Guénon Effect can be summarized as follows. Over time, quantity will accumulate until it can finally supplant quality. When quantity reigns, its essence eventually becomes the new highest of quality in contrast to a new quantity, and so on. In a Hegelian motion from approaching pure quality at the zenith to approaching pure

---

[70] Derbyshire, "Conquest's Laws."

quantity toward the nadir, quality will continue to degenerate until only quantity remains. When the elimination of quality has been achieved, even quantity continues to eat itself into an anti-quality, now approaching a mirror of the zenith, in a supernova of indulgence.

All of this is not to say that there are no elements of the bourgeoisie, or even the peasantry, during the age of priestly tenure, or vice versa, but to point out how the humble worker had little effect in the priestly age of old, while a true priest has little effect in our plebeian age. The Jacquerie peasant uprising of aristocratic medieval France was surely a force, as is the Catholic Church or the House of Windsor in some ways today a force in the egalitarian West. However, there is no denying the reality of the fall from grace of institutions associated with the priest and warrior castes, and the ascendance of institutions associated with the lower two castes. Furthermore, the "fourth estate" forces in the fourteenth century, as well as the early nineteenth, were quelled, while today the Catholic Church does not exert power by traditional functions or appealing to a higher order, but by appealing to the rabble and to bourgeois sentiment. The same can be said for any European monarchy. Opposing castes are indeed operating within the paradigm of their antitheses' age.

VII

Thus, the case has been made that progress is a dangerous myth which has resulted in a naive misunderstanding of the development of technology, ideology, and philosophy through the subversive, malicious, and biased agents in power, whose entire worldview is based on the cyclical history theory being incorrect. If civilization is only progressing toward the edge of a cliff, the deification of progress and, therefore, much that has been taught about history, philosophy, and politics over the past centuries has been wrong. As a result, people's conception of history, from the highest of high Brahmin academics at Harvard to the high school freshman in World History 101, must be learned as it truly is.

Glubb was right when he wrote "Men can scarcely be blamed for not learning from the history they are taught. There is nothing to learn from it, because it is not true."[71] The entire starting point of historical study is wrong, so it is no wonder that it is impossible to "learn from history," as Hegel critiqued.[72] The assumption and the golden cow of history and Western liberal politics, progress and democracy respectively, are faulty bases for society that cause problems which cannot be fixed without addressing the elephant in the room that our most basic and foundational beliefs are fundamentally wrong.

While Glubb, Spengler, Guénon, Evola, and many others write about differing subjects and cycles within the context of cyclical history, and indeed often disagree—such as in the case of Spengler's and Evola's views on the merits of Roman antiquity or Evola's and Guénon's disagreement on the primacy of the warrior versus the priest caste—they provide a groundwork for understanding and future study of the subject. The focus of Sir John Bagot Glubb is shallower, and more for Western audiences in terms of historical pattern-finding. His focus is historically and geographically on a smaller scale: that of empires or nations of people, not giving any mind to collections of empires and peoples within an entire civilization. For example, he focuses on empires like the British or American Empires, as opposed to the broader West of which both Britain and the US are a part. Glubb gives little time to the philosophical, spiritual, or metaphysical, as this is not his field, and his writing was directed toward the layman, making *Fate of Empires* a short and readable introduction to cyclical history.

Spengler's focus, however, was on entire civilizations, which can comprise a number of empires. His work is not focused solely on the "decline of the West," despite the title of his two-part tome, but rather the seasons in which a civilization like the West and other civilizations undergo before disintegration, as well as a comparative angle of the study of civilizations: a factor that is not much heeded in other works of this type.

---

[71] Glubb, *Fate of Empires*.
[72] Pinkard, "Spirit of History."

As for Guénon and Evola, their focus is largely on a far greater picture encompassing the entire human race and is influenced by esoteric knowledge, reading between the lines of mythology, religion, history, and other traditions, though they also wrote on the shorter timeframe of civilizations. Thus, while Spengler does often delve into the metaphysics of a civilization as an organism in itself rather than only a collection of organisms, Evola and Guénon explore practicality, metaphysics, and spiritual/religious subjects, creating a deeper and fuller, if at times harder to grasp, theory of cyclical history.

What is it that we are to do in regards to cyclical history? What are the ramifications of such a theory in politics and society? Glubb naively and with little suspicion of intellectual gatekeeping in academia hoped that someone "would try to establish in some university or other a department dedicated solely to the study of the rhythm of the rise and fall of powerful nations throughout the world."[73] Of course, it has in recent years become clear why this is impossible, as the educational establishment is highly motivated to suppress this mode of thinking, and so this suggestion of direct action must be discarded. But what of his warnings of "signs of the times," as it were, such as the general degeneration of society, to put shortly what was discussed earlier? It does not take an academic rogue to notice that the US is declining as a superpower, though this is usually tainted by vulgarities such as that "China will overtake us" and similar sentiments. Thus, it has only been through neoliberal or neoconservative influence that we may even approach this problem, and even then in an unserious fashion. However, to summarize, Glubb is absolutely correct that the American Empire is on its last leg. For those who espouse the dogma of the "end of history," they will be sorely disappointed to find that not only is the US in full decline, but also that the Chinese boogieman will also likely be in decline soon. With reference to China, it is necessary to return to Spengler.

Spengler does not seem to have any inclination toward any action one way or another. Rather, he was simply a historian and philosopher documenting what he found from studying history.

---

[73] Glubb, *Fate of Empires*, 22.

What we can learn from Spengler is that, as Glubb concurred, not only the American Empire, but Western civilization as a whole is petering out. What will finally extinguish it we cannot fully know, nor can we know its developmental nature: whether the West will slowly fade as Rome did over the course of hundreds of grueling years, or a quick extinguishing with a foreign flag or a foreign race occupying the seats of power. And who will this be? China? Doubtfully. While China rises in power, their culture is just as defunct and dead as that of the West, and has been for some time, in that their birthrates are low, their culture is stagnant, and their economy is built on a house of cards. The same is true of Arab society, which, despite gaining ground in Europe, faces the same fate: a once grand culture whose golden age is many years in the past, having seen their height of culture and power over a millennia ago, and as is evident in that their last great empire, the Ottoman realm, was destroyed a century ago. Spengler personally believed Russia to be the future, though his writings should be analyzed within the context of the time in which they were written. Unlike China, the West, and the Arabs, the Russians have yet to produce a great civilization, in the way that Rome or the British Empire were at one time, and are therefore virgin soil for the next great leap of humanity. Perhaps the modern Slavs have a similar potential as the Goths of late antiquity, whose virile spirit founded the heroic feudal order atop the ashes of ancient Rome.

Guénon and Evola would likely disagree, believing that the last stage of the Kali Yuga (the Vedic term for the final stage within a grand cycle of humanity characterized by greed, lust, betrayal, violence, and ultimately calamity) is upon us, and that the degeneration of society has reached a tipping point; that through Western influence the entire world, to include even parts of the world that have traditionally been uncorrupted by the proliferation of caustic Western culture, has been rotted to the core. Thus, the hope that there will be a resurgence of civilization in the form of Russia, one of the most deeply corrupted empires via Faustian spiritual and social encroachment, is a pipe dream. To the Traditionalists, there is plainly no hope in the physical world for the time being. However, unlike the other two historians discussed, Evola and Guénon have some advice on action in the modern age.

Therefore, we will delve into their suggestions for a modern man who feels lost in the Kali Yuga.

The main takeaway of their approach is that you *cannot* fight cyclical history, because it is an integral part of the universe. Rome had five good emperors (Nerva, Trajan, Hadrian, Antonius Pius, and Marcus Aurelius) in the precise time they were needed the most, and it did not help Rome in the grand scheme of things. Greater men than *you* have tried to divert humanity from destruction and each and every one of them has either failed, or misguidedly facilitated the forces of chaos (consider the American Founding Fathers for example, who were manipulated by the Enlightenment and Freemasonry in particular with regards to equality and universalism). If the tide cannot be stopped, why attempt to save the country, or the civilization, or the world, for that matter? Guénon wrote that it may be a blessing in disguise to be the most degenerated civilization because this means it will be the first to fall, the first to rise back up, and therefore become a leader in the world community and help the world begin again.[74]

For much of his life Evola pursued political action, believing that the Fascist regimes had some potential to be *the ones* to end the cycle and bring back an ordered world of tradition.[75] Of course, he became disillusioned with them for their inability to listen to reason in their lack of spiritual orientation, which they shallowly believed they already had, though this was mostly cosmetic, as Evola recognized. After the Second World War, despite being paralyzed in a Soviet air raid, Evola still had fight in him, writing *Men Among the Ruins*, titled thusly for obvious reasons. He was later taken by the authorities and imprisoned for months, being falsely accused of attempting to restart the Fascist movement in Italy, despite his criticisms of it. After finally being acquitted, it seems that Evola had to face the writing on the wall, and wrote *Ride the Tiger*, which came to roughly the same conclusion that his friend Guénon had decades

---

[74] Guénon, *The Crisis of the Modern World*, 109–117.
[75] However, Evola was critical of fascism, although he praised some aspects of it due to its partial similarity to Roman governance. A major traditionalist critique of fascism is that it is bottom-up instead of top-down; it is not truly oriented toward the divine, nor does it originate from the divine. He held the same critiques of National Socialism. See *Fascism viewed from the Right* and *Notes on the Third Reich* for more on this.

earlier: that it would be best to allow the storm to pass, rather than be swept up by it for no reason other than a false sense of glory. The title "Ride the Tiger" is borrowed from an ancient Eastern expression which postulates that, rather than fighting a tiger head on, it is better to grab on to its back and ride it until it tires itself out, allowing you to strangle it. The analogy in this context should be obvious. The decades of wisdom of these two philosophers should not be wasted, and their advice should be taken into consideration. What is certain is that it is a fool's errand to attack a vicious tiger head on against its claws and teeth rather than to just ride it.

But is there truly no hope? *Ride the Tiger* was written over half a century ago. The culture has continued to worsen since then, to a point which Evola would likely have found unbelievable. The traditions have been destroyed, creating the "virgin soil" that Spengler alluded to in *The Decline of the West.* Guénon's "anti-quality" phenomenon is in full swing and can only last so long. Are we, or perhaps our children, the generation to rebuild not the West, but to create something entirely new and greater than was previously imagined? Will we live to see a new golden age and the ascension of the perennial principles of the ancients? Is it no coincidence that there is a resurgence in the young traditionalists who are primed to become the "Sea Peoples" of the Bronze Age Collapse? Could they be the ones to flip over the table of modern decadent civilization, creating the fertile soil for something new, greater, and heroic? I believe there is merit to these claims, and that to end our fight is a betrayal of the virile spirit which will be necessary if we are to be the phoenix which rises out of the ashes, whether they may be literal or figurative, of the European diaspora civilization. As we increasingly approach this hypothetical golden age, it will become more and more pertinent not to just study the forgotten history of the decline of civilizations, but also the ascension of great peoples, in part so that we can have a set of principles by which society can be rebuilt.

3

THEMES OF THE AMERICAN DECLINE

"One has only to glance at the figures in meetings, public-houses, processions, and riots; one way or another they are all abortions, men who . . . have only heads full of disputatiousness and revenge for their wasted life. . . . It is the dregs of the great cities, the genuine mob, the underworld in every sense, which everywhere constitute the opposition to the great and noble world and unite in their hatred of it."

– Oswald Spengler

I

The moral realm is clearly something which can be accepted by most clear-minded folk as having suffered in modernity. In a way, art itself is part of this subsection of the atmosphere of the society, as it is the decadence of greater society and societal spirit which has largely corrupted art and culture in general. All things cultural in the modern West are incapable of reaching to new heights and "thinking outside the box." Ironically, all culture also prides itself for attempting to go outside the box, *but simply for the sake of doing so.* This is the decadence of modern culture. As a rule, it breaks the rules. The obsession with "theory" and rules, while supposedly transcending order in a pseudo-artistic anarchy of the modern and post-modern artists who peddled their cynical *consumer product* on the streets of New York, is a refutation of the supposed free willed nature of this art. In reality, the anarcho-tyranny of the art scene foreshadowed the anarcho-tyranny of politics. It is this decadence that we mean; the attempt to be different in a "try hard" manner, and its fruits to this day.

This cultural decadence, of which we can use art as a sort of mercury in a "culture-meter," has made its greatest impact in the realm of morality. The secularization of a civilization has weakened the weight-bearing apparatus of the West. The realization that most people really don't care about any higher or transcendent ethos hit the US like a freight train when, seemingly overnight, the norm switched from Christian to the "spiritual not religious" New Age fakery. However, even decades before this, a true transcendental/idealist metaphysical framework was lost from the West. To be a Christian simply meant to be a materialist with a sprinkle of dualism and an invisible friend who might give you good luck at obtaining a promotion or winning the lottery, or getting the girl. It is no wonder that it was so easy to go from apostasy to atheism, New Age, or some other placeholder that leaves a tradition- and God-shaped hole in the collective heart of a people.

Without religion, there is no guiding force. "If you stand for nothing, you'll fall for anything" indeed. In the realm of sexual immorality, this is especially visible. Religion was a great tool for keeping our primordial urges in check. Within a few years of the final death of God, to use Nietzsche's expression, monogamy was already out the window. Jordan Peterson's benign suggestion of socially enforced monogamy was attacked as outlandish.[76] As always, the norm of last week is "fascist." It has gotten much worse since then.

While promiscuity is steeply rising as it becomes normal for young women to sleep with dozens of men, which is damaging to long-term pair bonding, the rate of involuntary celibacy among men is skyrocketing.[77] The spoils are not evenly given. This is already having disastrous consequences. Some men are driven out of desperation to polyamorous relationships, in which their female

---

[76] Peterson, "On the New York Times."
[77] Ingraham, "The Share of Americans Not Having Sex."

partners sleep around with other men. Many, perhaps even most in the coming generation, will never find a wife.[78] Even if they could, many are completely shunning the prospect all together due to government disincentives exacerbating the death spiral of intersexual relationships in the West.[79] Only a small percentage of high-tier men can come out on top in this climate, given the declining number of women who have not destroyed their quality through having dozens of partners, or waiting until they are older and therefore less fertile. And even then, these high tier men are not immune from government intervention. Women will suffer as well. An unmarried man implies an unmarried woman. While women will live large when they are young, they will find it difficult to find a husband later on. As they can afford to have high standards in a polygamous environment such as the modern online dating app world, they will retain these standards. In the end, women will either settle down with someone they feel is beneath them, or avoid marriage altogether, choosing to be a spinster rather than the former option. This will only be solved when polygamy is legalized, popularized, and normalized, which will likely happen in the next two decades, as monogamy in the traditional sense has already fallen out of fashion. Polygamy will then lead to a host of further problems, which is why it is abandoned or limited in civilized societies. The fruits of polygamy are seen in the Middle East and Africa, where much of the young male population is completely out of control, seeking violence.

Even before this rampant heterosexual deviancy and degeneracy flourished, the rise of homosexuals, transvestites, and other sodomites has been gaining traction since the 1960s and 1970s. First it was made legal, then normalized, and then they were given special privileges. Slowly their deviancy is becoming *pushed* on the impressionable youth. Various fake identities have been created so

---

[78] Brown, "U.S. Marriage Rates."; Brown, "1. A Profile of Single Americans."

[79] Especially in North America, women are incentivized to divorce their husbands in exchange for many years of free money in the form of alimony and child support, due to a biased divorce court system which favors women. In contrast, men are thus incentivized to remain bachelors to avoid this fate or, perhaps worse, they put themselves into a powerless, passionless, unhappy marriage until death do them part. This was in large part made possible by no-fault divorce laws. Davis, "How 50 Years of No-Fault Divorce."

that everyone can join in. It is incredible that Barack Obama ran for president *against* gay marriage, while Republicans have since accepted that they have lost on the issue as well as the will to even fight against it. California voted against gay marriage in 2008; now it's legal even in West Virginia and Wyoming by federal decree.[80]

Much of the sexual deregulation is a symptom of declining birthrates, a common symptom of dying empires and civilizations.[81] Beginning with the Silent Generation, divorce became increasingly acceptable.[82] The Baby Boomers exacerbated this trend while simultaneously refusing to have children.[83] The lowest birth rates in the US up until recently were in the 1970s, when the Boomers were of marriage age.[84] Divorce among Boomers meant that Boomer men could potentially scalp the Generation X women in second marriages. Generation X men would do the same to Millennial women and it is likely that the same will occur with Millennials and Generation Z. This is due to the fact that men tend to marry women who are younger than them while women tend to marry men who are older.[85] In a society with a normal birthrate, above the replacement level of 2.1 births per woman, this would not be an issue, as there would be more young people than old and, therefore, less male relationship prospects than women. However, as the reproduction pattern has in some cases completely inverted so that there are more elderly than young, there are more women than men on the dating market.[86] The law of supply and demand easily predicts what will happen next. Women are in shorter supply, giving them a slight leg up. Thus, sexual relations in the West have become centered on women (rather than men as is traditionally the case). Much of the sexual ailments of contemporary society, at least within the sphere of heterosexual relationships, can simply be

---

[80] See 2008 California Proposition 8, as well as the results of *Obergefell v. Hodges*.
[81] "The Julian Marriage Laws." The fact that Augustus had to pass laws on marriage and adultery indicates that there was a huge problem with this in the Roman Empire.
[82] Davis, "How 50 Years of No-Fault Divorce."
[83] Phillips, "No Spouse, No Children." "Almost 20 percent of women in the postwar generation remained childless, most often by choice. The more highly educated the woman, the less likely she was to become a mother."
[84] "United States of America: Annual Number of Live Births per 1,000 Population."
[85] Jacob Ausubel, "Globally, Women Are Younger."
[86] S. Dixon, "U.S. Online Dating Website."

traced back to this seemingly benign first catalyst of a domino effect of epic proportions.

Degeneracy of this sort is common in the later stages of empires and civilizations. Even the stereotypically socially conservative Muslims of the Caliphates allowed this degenerated hyper-Dionysian impulse to overtake them when their empires began to crumble.[87] Simple homosexuality is, of course, in the grand scheme of things only the beginning, as anyone in the twenty-first century can easily recognize. From the acceptance of homosexuality, transvestitism has emerged. From transvestites came maniacal and demonic Frankenstein surgeries to turn men and women into true abominations. From this, the children must not be exempted; all in the name of equality, of course.

And when children are added to the equation of this rejection of all order for the sake of spiting God, how surprising will it be when pedophilia is made legal and perhaps even encouraged? Will pederastic rites by self-deluded monsters in the form of men, who claim to be nihilist materialist atheists, become a staple of life at the end of our civilization? Furthermore, is it already occurring in the dark among the marionette string-pullers? Whatever the case may be, though we may have our suspicions, the floodgates against this chaos will not likely be withheld forever.

II

In terms of the spirit of Western man, it is clearest here how he has fallen. Emasculated, severed from the higher, the Absolute, from any meaning whatsoever, here we can see the true end-project for the life of the ordinary. The Last Man is the only bug which can survive the torrent in the current condition of his surroundings both social and physical. It is only he who can see the obvious lies around him and mold to them. If humans' true strength and worth, according to the materialists, is that he can adapt and overcome any environment, then are we not witnessing in this pathetic skinny-fat

---

[87] Steven, "A Historical Look at Attitudes to Homosexuality."

estrogen-filled man the final "evolution" of humanity that is "adapted man?"

Where is the spirit of modern man? I see none, and it is forgivable to question whether he even has a soul to begin with.[88] If he ever did, it has long been carried off in the wind of this modern gust never to be seen again. It is a fool's errand to attempt to salvage what is unlikely even present. Here lies the true evil of the regime: to kill a man is to commit a sin but, to kill the spirit of a man, let alone the mass of the collective spirit, can never be atoned for.

With the weakening of the spirit, a multitude of further problems has emerged. The bourgeois and now plebeian spirit of our time has resulted in a collective disdain for any pain, suffering, or sacrifice. Is it any wonder that the women of our time, whether their ancestors arrived on the *Mayflower* or have just gotten off the boat, shirk their responsibility to their family in favor of the office cubicle? Childbearing is painful and therefore not chic. Men are hardly different, and they also have their fair share to contribute to the fall of the family. Ernst Jünger most notably recognized this pattern of shirking responsibility and hardship for comfort in the last century; and in the twenty-first it has only been exacerbated in a way where only the blindest *product* of the age could not clearly see this reality before him.

This failure to struggle or even to be willing or capable of true struggle among the masses is a phenomenon which buds its head like clockwork near the end of a society. How can excellence, or even basic functionality, be attained or even maintained without struggle? This seems to be the case in all human institutions, even down to capitalist corporations.[89] Indeed, our empire was ripe, and therefore began to rot, long before most of us were even born. And

---

[88] In Chapter 8 of *Revolt against the Modern* World, Evola writes "The belief that everybody's soul is immortal is rather odd; very little evidence of it can be found in the world of Tradition." Evola, *Revolt*, 47.

[89] Kroc and Anderson, *Grinding It Out*. In the corporate context, even Ray Kroc, the founder of McDonald's, saw this cyclical metaphysics of human organization, and famously said in Spenglerian fashion: "As long as you're green you're growing; as soon as you're ripe you start to rot." The corporate world is littered with the skeletons of once great companies, from Opel and Plymouth cars to the British East India Company.

one might go so far as to say that our empire itself, the United States, is simply a product of the early stages of rot in the Western world.

This, of course, is the true meaning of *decadence* which is so often invoked on the right that it likely sounds cliché, and perhaps is often used as a buzzword. However, that decadence is real and indeed the great *sign of the times*, there can be no denial of. As previously stated, this collective sense of comfort and indeed such universal value in comfort as opposed to honor, duty, piety, and so forth, is among the most common of patterns that emerge in the psyche of an aging race.

Interestingly, John Glubb came to the same, if not a more extreme conclusion on the spiritual nature of decadence, writing that:

> *Neither is decadence physical. The citizens of nations in decline are sometimes described as too physically emasculated to be able to bear hardship or make great efforts. This does not seem to be a true picture. Citizens of great nations in decadence are normally physically larger and stronger than those of their barbarian invaders.*
>
> *Moreover, as was proved in Britain in the First World War, young men brought up in luxury and wealth found little difficulty in accustoming themselves to life in the front-line trenches. The history of exploration proves the same point. Men accustomed to comfortable living in homes in Europe or America were able to show as much endurance as the natives in riding camels across the desert or in hacking their way through tropical forests.*
>
> *Decadence is a moral and spiritual disease, resulting from too long a period of wealth and power, producing cynicism, decline of religion, pessimism and frivolity. The citizens of such a nation will no longer make an effort to save themselves, because they are not convinced that anything in life is worth saving.* [90]

Perhaps this can be seen in the still relatively strong specimens of the US military being completely overtaken in Afghanistan by the

---

[90] Glubb, *Fate of Empires*, 20.

Taliban, who never gave up their fighting spirit after over a decade of ceding the country and burrowing. The mountain men of Afghanistan, though physically weak and without first world means of strengthening the body, defeated the Americans and their puppet government easily when the right time came. Indeed, "they have the clocks but we have the time," as the Taliban fighters famously declared.

A decadent race is incapable of such planning, despite their sophistication and seemingly low time preference in comparison to the barbarian savage. The Mujahideen fighters may have less education, intelligence, and even strength than their adversary, and yet they are able to subliminally and supra-rationally plan, potentially generations into the future. This trait cannot be taught at a university. In *On Pain*, Jünger declared "Tell me your relation to pain, and I will tell you who you are!" That modern civilization's aversion to pain and hardship is one of its most prominent characteristics should tell us all we need to know about both its degeneration and furthermore how much longer it can expect to survive.

III

With this decadence of the spirit come more problems, one of which is the question of fulfillment and caste in the modern age. With the reemergence of late-stage ideals such as "equality," "democracy," and even "equity," the entire ideal of a role has been wholly removed from the equation. Thus, modern man has not only been deracinated, but stripped of his caste, and therefore his purpose. The priest caste has been relegated to become pauper-figureheads, the warrior caste to become the new petite bourgeoisie or mercenaries, the producer class to become the aristocracy, and the peasant with his plebeian view of the world to be a cog in the managerial elite class which directs the vision of the culture. If we imagine the cycles to operate like a clock or calendar, it is as if the entire traditional system has been turned upside-down. Within the system, it is impossible to obtain true transcendent fulfillment as one cannot lie to oneself about his situation and truly be on a correct footing. It is this internal lie that is promoted by egalitarianism. The most distinct anomaly in this rearrangement is the contrast of place between the peasant and the priest. It is here that the satanic, or the upside-down nature of the system is most apparent.

Take the peasant-priest, who is of the lowest moral caliber of all peoples and yet guides society on morality. Traditionally, the peasant, literally *le villein* in medieval France, was to be guided like a child, for to leave him to his own devices would not end well for anyone, including himself, similar to Eve in the Garden. This character is now not only left to his own devices, but is allowed to guide society itself. The priest class of modern America is thus occupied by megalomaniacal characters of the lowest levels of society and propped up by an aristocracy occupied by powerful merchants. These groups are in far over their head and thus are severed from any transcendent societal order on which they would be placed in the correct totem of the hierarchy.

The modern aristocracy, made up of a bourgeois caste of the money-changers, hardly resembles the warrior-aristocracy of old. Yet at the same time the business class hardly resembles that ideal of the hardworking and risk-taking class of producers which it normally should be. Rather, the aristocracy is composed of cowardly little men of sub-par repute but with a knack for a certain pathological cruelty. And thus, Mammon will "become so big and strong that it no longer does its own work but attempts to enslave and rule over the classes it isn't fit to rule, thereby overturning everyone's whole life."[91]

The same disjointed role is true for the natural warrior class in America and the West. If anywhere, the traditional warrior class currently occupies the role of a third estate small business owner and working class tradesman type who is taken for a ride by Big Business/government managerial aristocracy and, on occasion, the roving dregs and hordes of degenerate and common "priests." If a natural warrior is lucky, he will be able to serve in a warrior cargo cult for the Globalist American Empire as a mercenary and bring his toil to the technologically outclassed traditional peoples of the world.

---

[91] Plato, *Republic,* 442a.

The true priests of the West by their nature, the savants and misunderstood geniuses, are incapable of fulfilling their natural role and are actively suppressed by the regime. The only approved role for them is to either be enslaved to the ever-grinding, inexorable march of technological progress in the name of the god of materialism, or to again be enslaved to their inferiors in the task of rationalizing the un-rationalizable through propaganda via the academy and media. Huxley saw precisely this in his fictional character Helmholtz of *Brave New World* who, though a valuable genius, was relegated to the ends of the regime and intellectually stunted to avoid problems. The philosopher becomes the sophist; the priest becomes the social engineer.

The classes are completely disjointed, and thus we are all stripped of our caste: a fate once seen as liberation, but now clearly as enslavement, as all degenerate into *dalits*: the untouchables with no caste. Rather than the bug-like state of all men today, traditional man would fit into and enjoy his role in society. The peasant who creates the sustenance from rain and soil, connected to the land, the merchant, producer, and guild-artisan, whose trade has been in the family within the same four walls for countless generations, the warrior-aristocrat, protector of the people and of his estate, and the priest, securer of salvation, transcendence, and ritual, are sadly ideals long lost to time, never to return to our people within this confined condition.

IV

It is also clear, in defiance of Glubb (who claims that late stage peoples are actually physically stronger than the barbarians), that not only the spiritual but also the genetic quality of Western man has deteriorated after roughly two centuries of poor genetic pressures following the industrialization of the late eighteenth and early nineteenth centuries. As with the spiritual realm, the idea that strong men create good times, good times create weak men, etc., also applies to the physical realm. This biological component should be considered in the decline of civilization.

During the rise of the West, law and order was maintained through brutality against the criminal elements, meaning a large portion of the lowest dregs of society were executed for their crimes and were thus unable to continue their lineage. Furthermore, the elite class was able to reproduce proportionally at a higher level than the rest of society due to cleanliness, the ability to have on-demand wet-nurses, and also the normality of the phenomenon of extramarital affairs which produced bastard children of noble genetic lineage. The high reproductive success of the elites resulted in the peasantry being genetically repacked time and time again with noble genes, though very far removed from their titles and wealth. Despite some mores and taboos within Christian civilization against polygamy and extramarital affairs—something less common in other cultures—the end result was the same. And even with the mores of Christian culture, the Gothic ideal of chivalry paradoxically included and idealized extramarital affairs, notably displayed in the story of King Arthur.

With less environmental pressure due to the Industrial Revolution and increasingly high living standards for the lower classes, the peasantry was able to reproduce in much greater numbers while the elite classes became decadent, and came to suffer their own genetic bottleneck due to hundreds of years of genetic gatekeeping and the resulting inbreeding, which the Church often ignored. Furthermore, the constant wars that on one hand created a strong Europe also decimated the warrior-aristocrat class, especially as warfare became increasingly destructive and indiscriminate. This was foreshadowed in antiquity with the dwindling of the numbers of nobles in relation to the plebeians, indeed the wiping out of entire families, due to centuries of constant external warfare and internal bloody politics.[92] This was a constant discomfort in the late Roman Republic, driving the rise of the equestrian order, because as the patricians dwindled in numbers they were no longer able to supply enough cavalrymen and administrators on their own. This same phenomenon resumed in

---

[92] Estimates for the number killed by Sulla's proscriptions range from several thousand from ancient sources to several hundred according to modern historians. Regardless, it was a large number, and was followed by a relatively smaller yet still extensive proscription by the Second Triumvirate.

the War of the Roses, in which the Tudors came to power by virtue of having not been killed off as many other prominent nobles had. It was intensified in the blood-bath of the Thirty Years' War, in which the Peace of Westphalia was not obtained through victory, but due to all sides involved having slaughtered each other unto total exhaustion. It reached its pinnacle in World War I, in which 17 percent of Britain's officers (who were generally young aristocrats) were killed in only a few years, in contrast to the lower but still staggering 12 percent of enlisted troops.[93] This decimation of the warrior aristocracy, coinciding with a boom in the commoner population, substantially altered the ratio of aristocrats to their subjects. Can it be little wondered at that Western Europe, and especially Britain, have spent the last decades in the grips of a soft peasants' revolt through labor politicking, slave morality, and pacifism that resents everything that is heroic and virile? Who is left who feels tradition as a living reality in their blood and can thus carry on the old order? Very few Westerners, it seems.

A genetically high-quality population requires a bottleneck in which there is great mortality. As mortality decreases, genetic quality declines as well. In all life, humanity included, to merely replace oneself is never enough. Not only is there a move toward the mean, but there is also a slight regression. If parents had two children, their two children would on average be inferior to the parents. However, if two parents had ten children of which only five survived to have children of their own, the survivors would likely be of superior quality, as they would generally be of the top 50 percent of survivability. This prospect is indeed horrific, and it is only a strong people who will be able to face down the horror of this reality as our ancestors did, and how we sadly cannot. Modern parents are overly protective by virtue of how they have very few children. Take for example how modern man trembled in fear of COVID, which had a 99.98 percent survival rate for most age groups.[94] Such people could never endure an actual plague, let alone the traditionally high child mortality rate which was a fact of life until fairly recently.

---

[93] Curry, "How Many People Died in the First World War?"
[94] Roy, "Estimating the Risk of Death from COVID-19."

Two centuries of this genetic program has caused high mutational load in Western populations, especially the first to industrialize.[95] What has followed is all of the negative aspects of the modern world: the loss of religiosity, the mental illness epidemic, physical unhealthiness, low birthrates, and nihilism, among much else. The genetic component is but a part in this equation, working in conjunction with the general spiritual malaise of our time. It is no surprise then that academia has attempted to suppress the field of evolutionary psychology and sociobiology, as the prevalence of these sicknesses, which are in large part caused by genetic factors, is the very environment that allows the modern academy to exist at all, with these "spiteful mutants" (in the words of Edward Dutton) manning the ranks of the pseudo-intellectual class.

V

In governance, the spirit of *égalité* has dislodged the ideals of *liberté* and *fraternité*. With equality comes democracy and with democracy comes the gradual democratization of all things in public and private life. It has long been observed that republics give way to democracy, and then tyranny, as was often the case in the Greek city-states. Furthermore, tyranny has traditionally been equated with the overthrow of the traditional order by the lower elements, such as with the ancient Greek tyrants who were usually installed via a takeover of the conquered pre-Dorian lower class against the ethnic Dorian aristocracy.[96]

The trend toward the lower over the course of history coincides with the rise of democracy as the rule of the lower. Starting as a constitutional republic, the US has degenerated further and further into a democracy and now a tyranny. Despite my critiques of the founding and its inherently liberal conception, the Founders' experiment was much more interesting in comparison with our brute "one man one vote" system of today. The Founders envisioned

---

[95] Lynn, *Dysgenics.*
[96] Sealy, *A History of the Greek City States.*

a system in which the benefits of the right and left's conceptions of governance could coalesce into one government. With monarchical (executive), aristocratic (Senate), and third estate (House of Representatives) branches all represented in this new government, it seemed as if they could potentially achieve the best of all worlds with this masculine republic. In contrast to the tyranny of today, one might be forgiven in describing early America as aristocratic.

Unfortunately, if the vote is given to some, it will eventually spread to others, as people will never vote to restrict their own vote. Beginning as an explicitly White and somewhat conservative order, the vote was limited to landowning White men of good character. This degenerated into simply White men, and then men, and then men and women, and finally it is the felons and those of the worst moral character that are not only allowed but *encouraged* to vote. More and more it is the lowest elements of society which are represented in governance. The modern man, in his arrogance, assumes that the wisdom of the ancients, taken for granted up until the end of living memory, was racist or sexist or some other non-argument characterization which would have been laughed at by our ancestors of higher spirit and stock.

The egalitarian spirit of the late-stage group, in conjunction with the higher time preference and lower intelligence inherited by the dysgenic processes inherent to decadence, creates a high time preference state in which long term goals become impossible. Even at the end of the last epoch and the beginning of our own, the United States was capable of the planning necessary for space travel to the moon, a feat which modern man is now wholly incapable of, and which has not been replicated in fifty years. The crowning jewel of Faustian man's mark on history was a feat which necessitated a somewhat low time preference on an institutional and national scale.

Today this is but a memory, as modern man is of high time preference in all non-frivolous pursuits and only maintains a low time preference in useless endeavors pushed by the powers that be, such as following bread and circuses, waiting to have a family, or continuing education for no apparent reason other than that the TV man said so. Perhaps this is further evidence of the degenerated man's susceptibility to propaganda than any holdout of civilization maintaining low time preference. This paradox (that modern man is high time preference yet delays the progress of his own life) has led not only to the decline in native populations but, predictably, the spread of crime, the lowering of income, and the increase in wealth gaps between a calculating pathological elite and a slave class of the impulsive.

This time preference phenomenon is utilized within democracy in such a way so as that the permanent government is constantly looting the state and even future generations via debt. Hans-Hermann Hoppe has rightly noted the democratic form of the psychology of a politician, which is in the spirit of "what I cannot loot today I will not be able to loot tomorrow."[97] Rather than a sort of Bonapartist dictatorship of hereditary monarchy which can plan a lifetime into the future or even multiple generations, as the Chinese are at least attempting to do now (even if in an Orwellian manner), the democratic West is only capable at best of planning an election cycle into the future. In contrast, hereditary kings and nobles tend to view the realms they rule as property that they will pass on to their posterity, and thus have a strong incentive to care for them, similar to how a landowner of an estate will invariably treat his property better than an apartment renter, who is unsure if he will even renew his lease. This shortsightedness, which incentivizes looting, is the very essence of the dysfunctional democratic ship of state. Nothing can be planned for ahead of time, and thus the only option is to line one's own pockets before crashing into the cliffs. Anything else but cynical favor-dealing in democratic politics is completely absurd and inevitably falls through.

VI

Highly important is the issue of the foreign hordes which invade our lands. This is a common occurrence at the end of empires and civilizations. Most recognizable in history is the case of the Romans, who invited masses of foreigners, most notably Germanic peoples into the empire and made citizenship a frivolity for various reasons,

---

97 Misesmedia, "Hans-Hermann Hoppe: Why Democracy Fails."

the parallels of which can be seen today. Like the Roman Empire, the American Empire is simply folding rather than fighting tooth and nail. This may be another sign that the end of the US is not only the end of its own empire but a definitive end to Western civilization as a major force and culture, much as the fall of Western Rome was a definitive end to classical antiquity and the classical Mediterranean civilization.

The US is inviting these immigrants into the country for a multitude of reasons, the first being compassion among the masses. The *zeitgeist* currently stipulates that not allowing these aliens into our space is "hateful" or some other nonsense. Of course, this is largely propaganda by moneyed interests who have other reasons for supporting the invasion (cheap labor, readymade political voting blocks, personal ethnic preference), though the true motivation of the masses is of this nihilistic libertine "live and let live" mantra that has been adopted by the common man. All other rationalizations for the seizing of our ancestors' posterity is only that: a rationalization for the utterly mad.

The elite consensus, of course, is that mass migration is a good thing. During any other time, even the mercantile phase of the American Empire only a few decades ago, and already situated at the end of Western civilization at its conception, it was simply understood that the adoption of the world's alien masses was a ridiculous notion. It did not need to be rationalized; it just was. This is in spite of how America, born in the degeneration that was the Enlightenment, did indeed invite immigrants, though specifically those from Europe, where the newcomers would already be somewhat similar to the native population in that they shared their religion, race, and culture to an extent that farther flung people do not. This "common sense" of in-group preference is lacking in the late stage, a common sense which continues to be practiced by the very invaders whose level of in-group preference is brazen and shocking (such as in the case of ethnic nepotism), though ignored, by the naive Westerner.

First the invitation was extended toward relatively similar people to the WASP founding stock, peoples such as the Germans, Dutch, and Irish. Then came Southern and Eastern Europeans, and then East Asians (for a short amount of time), Eastern Jews, and yet more from the East and South of Europe. Finally, all race-based restrictions were abolished in 1965. Just as in Rome, when Roman origin was no longer required for Roman citizenship under Caracalla (who himself was half Syrian), the American system saw a similar cheapening. Soon after quotas on origin were abolished, the invitation became an invasion, and the nineteenth century stock, let alone the Anglo-Saxon founding stock, is now a much smaller portion of the overall population, especially in the ancestral and historic cities that they founded.[98]

Business interests support this great replacement for obvious reasons. A constant supply of cheap labor, especially undocumented cheap labor, means that wages become lessened and profits for large corporations rise sharply. Furthermore, the already declining founding population, dying off due to low birthrates, must be replaced for the economy to remain stable. This can be seen in the pro-mass migration types switching from their "workers of the world unite" and "we need a living wage" platitudes to suddenly becoming capitalist economists harping on about the GDP and how what amounts to slave labor is necessary because "no one else will do it." It is a curious flip-flop. Clearly, the peace-symbol-waving "rebels" are in fact unwitting pawns of the system.

Mass migration further exacerbates the loss of culture, i.e. the transition of the population centers from "culture cities" to "world cities." The phenomena of a loss of culture and the invitation of new culture work hand-in-hand with each other. While new cultures are invited to supplement a dying culture, the oftentimes vibrant foreign cultures blend into a drab gray color of nothingness. Chinatown or Little Armenia may have the culture of China and Armenia, of course, but what is the culture of Los Angeles? And even these holdouts are assimilated into global homogenization. Koreatown, Los Angeles is now predominantly Hispanic. The young generation who has never seen culture outside of small hubs within the world city will thus go so far as to claim that Western or White culture does not exist, or even has never existed, spurned by a counterproductive and actively hazardous education system.

---

[98] For more information and specifics on these changing demographics see recent US Census data and also Lutton, "Immigration and Race in America."

The xenophilic masses stroke the ego of these newcomers whose culture is oh-so-superior, by virtue of exotic restaurants and naive idealizations. The narrative is of course spun largely by powerful interests from the top down. The aliens then become the shock troops of the failing decadent elite against its own people who can no longer be trusted because they are possessed by "reactionary" ideology—reactionary only to the extent that defending oneself against an attacker rather than accepting helplessness is "reactionary." The foreign hordes as well as the traitorous natives will replace the heritage of Americans in all aspects of life, including the areas of hard power, such as the police and the military. Eventually, the more virile and healthy foreigners who have often lived in Darwinian conditions in their homelands may simply overthrow the old order, seeing themselves as the true holders of real power: that is, by the sword, as was the case when Rome was sacked by the Visigoths, or the sacking of Babylon by the Medes. The question is whether the foreigners will actually be able to overthrow their masters in the case of the US. More likely, the power structure will use ethnic divisions to keep the discontent at odds with one another, allowing it to maintain its influence for as long as it can—until its empire of dirt is no longer worth administering.

VII

Military effectiveness will experience a complete decline due to outside influences and residues of the dying inner culture, as we can already begin to see by blunder after blunder of Western military power. This was predicted many decades ago by Glubb, and the parallels with the late Roman Empire as lamented by Vegetius are striking.[99] The military, once staffed almost exclusively by the founding and early immigrant stock, largely from the Deep South and Midwest, is now slowly becoming dominated by minority groups. The motivation for military service—glory, honor, serving one's homeland—is no longer the primary motivating factor (not that these ideals were ever as widespread as is commonly thought)

---

[99] Renatus, "The Military Institutions of the Romans (De Re Militari)."

outside of the absolutely most motivated and the naive, although they quickly become disillusioned.[100] As a result, the special operations forces, which currently serve as the backbone of America's declining campaigns, are still nearly exclusively White.[101] The same is true, though to a lesser extent, of the non-special operation forces of frontline infantry.[102] How much longer even this will last under the dual insults of vaccine mandates and "anti-extremism" hysteria remains to be seen. And even if these dual insults were ever rolled back, they will not be forgotten and can always resume.

Outside of combat arms, the enlisted ranks are increasingly dominated by immigrant groups and the lowest dregs of native society, who are there simply for benefits and guaranteed pay. Each passing year, the clock reaches closer and closer to complete foreign or treasonous control. The officer corps is already completely cynical and in bed with the regime; all reactionary elements in leadership have largely been purged over the past three decades.[103] The warrior class is already dead in America, outside of the understaffed special operations troops.

I once had idealistic dreams of joining the military, but every veteran who I spoke to who had recently served strongly advised against it, and all gave similar reasons as to the above. Eventually, and after great effort, they dispelled my naiveté. The myth of the patriotic, incorruptible military is just another delusion that must be discarded if we are to have an accurate understanding of the current situation. That it is one of our most cherished myths means that the importance of discarding it is all the greater, because the regime knows this is something they can still exploit to lure young, idealistic men into doing their bidding. The military of 2022 is not the military of 2016, let alone 2001 or the Korean War.

With an ever-increasing gap in the want of military forces and the traditional warrior stock shunning servitude to an empire which no longer stands for what their forefathers created it for, the military continues to shell out more and more incentives for

---

[100] Keller, "The Top 5 Reasons Soldiers Really Join the Army."
[101] Baldor, "US Military's Elite Commando Forces Look to Expand Diversity."
[102] Peter Curry, "How Many People Died in the First World War?"
[103] "Obama's Military Coup."

recruits. However, the quality troops did not join for money or free college or terrible healthcare service but for heroism, duty, and adventure. No one becomes a Navy Seal simply for free education. Thus, the wretches flood the ranks.

The decadent society, no longer taking seriously its own safety or hegemony, corrupts the ranks not only with racial integration but sexual integration.[104] Both of these top-down choices reflect the preponderance toward social policy rather than actual martial aims. The racial policy, since its adoption after the Second World War, has caused division in the ranks and the formation of racial gangs.[105] With the adoption of women and homosexuals into the military, units become demoralized, less effective, and degenerate.[106] Feuds over sexual dominance destroy group cohesion in what was once a warrior band created to defend the homeland.

An entire warship, the *USS Bonhomme Richard*, was destroyed due to one of these love triangle feuds, and the arson was unable to be stopped due to gross incompetence, causing two billion dollars in damage.[107] Despite every seaman's necessary expertise in putting out onboard fires, the local firemen were called, as the crew didn't know how to stop the fire, and were even further hindered by bureaucratic red tape.[108] In 2017, the *USS Fitzgerald* crashed into a Japanese container ship, killing seven crew members. This crash was caused by low morale and the inability to communicate effectively.[109] In January of 2022 the first female F-35 pilot crashed her hundred-million-dollar plane while attempting to land.[110] As of the Second Edition, this has only accelerated in both military and civilian sectors with planes literally falling out of the sky on a monthly basis.[111]

The adoption of women and homosexuals in the military has transformed the institution from a warrior culture to a hormone-drunk college culture. Women have garnered near-unlimited

[104] Steuben, "The Military's Culture of Careerism."
[105] "Gangs in the Military."
[106] van de Camp, "Not Kinder, Not Gentler, but Ineffective."
[107] Ibid. See also Sailer, "White U.S.S. Bonhomme Richard Arson Suspect."
[108] Steuben, "The Road to Kabul."
[109] "Did the Menstrual Cycle of Officers."
[110] Obafemee80, "$100m F-35 Fighter Jet Crashed."
[111]

power, being able to prostitute themselves for promotions, while having the ability to become pregnant to avoid deployment. Accusations of rape can provide women with omnipotent power in interactions.[112] And this isn't even mentioning the many cases of actual rape.[113]

It is very rare to find a young veteran who will recommend joining the US military as a result of the terrible regime in place. The rapes, sexual and racial integration, and the degenerate culture that followed has produced a bureaucratic office work life complete with Title IX seminars and a whole host of state-mandated social insanity. The last warriors to serve the Empire will not be reenlisting.

Decreasing competence will mean the surrender of the US Empire in the international field, ceding dominance to China, Russia, Iran, and other powerful rivals. This was foreshadowed by the American inability to secure Iraq and Afghanistan and the subsequent overrunning of Iraq by Iranian forces and of Afghanistan by the hibernating Taliban. For decades, the US has followed suit with Rome in transitioning from an offensive empire to one that is forever in decline and on the defensive.

Despite a looming war with the new great power alliance between Russia and China, the US continues to create ideological litmus tests for the military through vaccine restrictions and a war on so-called "white rage." The result will be an army of golems who will be prone to follow the directives of the government in operations against its own people; against the nation that in theory it is supposed to protect. A liquidation of White Middle Americans and staffing with preferred groups in the military and security forces is for precisely the purpose it was used for in Rwanda, Yugoslavia, and Cambodia: the repression of one group in favor of others.

---

[112] Steuben, "The Road to Kabul." "It is now possible for almost any woman to claim that she has been raped, to include even saying that she 'felt uncomfortable.' For example, if both parties were tipsy after dinner and drinks, they could claim they simultaneously raped each other."
[113] Hengest, "Diversity in the Army."

VIII

The end of civilization is also accompanied by ecological disaster, which serves as the final nail in the coffin of the dying race. After centuries of overworking the land and growing the population to the limits of what agriculture is capable of, famine and destruction will inevitably follow. The so-called "experts" already harp on about this, though their ire is misdirected at fake targets such as climate change: an unstoppable foe which is only used to secure more power for the regime. This occurs while true issues that can be potentially solved such as declining water supplies, dwindling farmland, ever decreasing stocks of topsoil, and the use of artificial fertilizer continue unabated.[114] It is also debatable whether renewable resources or even nuclear energy are actually viable without artificial government support.

Both the left and the right in unison ignore the environmental issue. The left pretends to be the guardian of the environment, but spends most of its energy on protecting small unimportant brown fish or species such as the polar bear which haven't been at much risk for years, or invasive wild horses. Furthermore, the left-wing centers tend to be far away from nature, meaning that the ecological fetish is likely unserious to most, who are simply conditioned to care about the coral reef they'll never see or the Russian permafrost melting five thousand miles away. This is not to say that these things are not important, but rather to point out that, to the left, environmental issues are wholly theoretical. They are usually not properly in tune with the actual land.

The right, on the other hand, simply shirks the view that ecology is important. I say "right," though in a dying civilization such as our own, the true right in the proper sense is nowhere to be found near the levers of power. Thus, the ecological ignorance or even disdain from this side comes from the libertarian ethos, the worship of markets, and the quantitative rather than qualitative view of the

---

[114] Most artificial fertilizers are petroleum based and only enrich the plant, but not the soil. Along with causing topsoil to become depleted of its natural nutrients over time, it also means that any issues with oil, such as scarcity and price, are also food supply issues. Barth, "Pro & Cons of Petrochemical Fertilizers."

world: no different from the progressive, only a different side of the same materialist coin.

With the gradual ecological disaster comes gradual decline in quantity available due to supply shortages, which are already becoming more and more common in the developed West. As a result, material quality of life will see—indeed already has seen—a marked decline. However, this will not be as pronounced as the coming food shortages which will end in global famine, deadly pestilence which will attack the malnourished, and war bands which will fill the ensuing power vacuum. With the degradation of material stocks used to produce food, this will be unavoidable, and despite how the global elite are in consensus as to depopulation, there will be no true effort to curb the shortage problem as there was in the days of food panics, when Malthus warned that a population's food consumption cannot surpass its food production.

This is no fluke. Environmental damage is part and parcel of a dying civilization. While the consensus among historians is that environmental catastrophe is hardly ever the true cause of civilizational collapse, it is a great factor in this process, especially in the case of the most complex of societies.[115] Oftentimes, it is the complexity itself in conjunction with an environmental change that creates such conditions. Complexity allows societies to transcend far beyond their normal capabilities, meaning that the larger a society becomes, the harder it falls:

> *When powerful regimes (such as the Third Dynasty of Ur, the late Sassanians, and in the early Islamic period) pursued policies of maximizing resource production, complex irrigation systems were developed that were beyond local abilities to manage and repair. State control was required. When the political realm proved unstable, dangers of salinity increased and the possibility loomed for sudden, catastrophic fluctuations.*[116]

---

[115] Tainter, *Collapse of Complex Societies*, 52–54.
[116] Ibid., 48.

The same phenomenon occurred in Rome, when perhaps the most advanced food distribution system until modern times collapsed in on itself due to agricultural exhaustion. Amenities such as aqueducts, road networks, massive markets, and centralized administration allowed the population within Roman territory to balloon massively. However, once population was able to peak, there was no way to put the genie back in the lamp:

> Hughes indicts the Roman failure to adapt their society and economy harmoniously to the natural environment. This failure was then a major cause of collapse. Deforestation led to erosion, the most readily accessible minerals were mined, lands were overgrazed, and agriculture declined.[117]

The US, like Rome before it, has devalued the currency in a vain attempt to "let the good times roll," made largely possible by the high time preference populace who will vote for whichever political program will continue the prosperity (even if it means pushing off the true costs to the future generation), but more importantly due to the fact that the US dollar has been the world reserve currency for some time. The economically destabilized Western countries will no longer be able to purchase the most important supply of all—sustenance—any more than the Venetians were able to purchase a loyal and formidable military, if environmental and economic disaster hits the West in a historically significant way.

It may be a sad thing that the environment, and indeed everything else within the scope of civilization, will eventually come to a standstill and free fall. However, death is a necessary part of the circle of life. A hard natural reset is the optimal future for all people, as the survivors will be the best that civilization has to offer and will truly be free. In contrast, those in power prefer a managed decline in which the age is continued *ad infinitum* so as that the powerful of today may remain the powerful of tomorrow. This is not to glorify the unavoidable hellscape of starvation, war, and poverty, but to simply point out that there is light at the end of the tunnel, and that allowing the natural progress of mankind through the "end times,"

---

[117] Ibid., 49.

as opposed to the synthetic plans of God-defying micromanagers, is in fact the lesser evil, and not to be avoided. It is imperative that the natural life cycle of the civilization be maintained.

In all aspects, including the complete breakdown of supply chains and civilized society, the cities will be the first to fall. However, the cities will not be the only areas to be destroyed in the process of the death of the West. The cities are already undergoing violence, chaos, and supply shortages. Of course, supply shortages are only for luxury goods now. This is only the beginning. The supply chain of a city is a highly intricate machine that can be completely thrown out of order by a simple prolonged power outage. Power outages will be the least of the urban bugman's problems at the end.

Furthermore, the native White population of urban areas is already on the decrease, as if America were Rome, Byzantium, or Baghdad toward the end of their reigns. This also is only the beginning. White flight has taken the White city population to outlying suburbs of the cities, away from the alienation, crime, and cultural rot which now plague once vibrant communities. However, suburbs are becoming less and less a refuge from the city, and mob violence and lack of police presence is also likely in some suburbs after years of the same chaotic forces at work in the cities.[118] As a result, suburban people will flee to rural localities until the very same effect in the cities and suburbs subsumes these areas as well which—if we are to take the opioid crisis and the feeling of dread and doom permeating much of rural America, as well as the exodus *away from* rural areas by young blood as a sign of the times—may already be here. There is no escape but salvation through collapse. The people's toil will finally have come to an end as their Faustian bargain, to raise a great culture with all that comes with the process toward the end, has indeed come to an end and the once great culture, corrupted into a *fellaheen* people who will never repeat past greatness in the same iteration, may finally rest.[119]

---

[118] Sailer, "White Sergeant Convicted."

[119] *Fellaheen* is a term used by Spengler to denote the degenerate remains of a burnt out or collapsed civilization, no longer acting as a historical force. They often become a peasant caste under a new, virile culture in its springtime. The word *Fellah* specifically refers to the peasant class of Egypt. The reference is illuminating; this peasant caste has lived in their area for thousands of years, largely unfazed by the conquering warriors of Greece, Rome, Arabia, Turkey, France, or England.

PART TWO

THE NATURE OF POWER IN AMERICA

4

Notes on the Cathedral Thesis

"Having never been made steady in their tastes, their feelings, their thoughts, they will be at the mercy of the winds, possessing only illusory joys that will burn them and immiserate them at the whims of others."

– *Léon Degrelle,*
The Burning Souls, *28*

The question of politics in America has often left people wondering who actually is in control. In the last few years it has become abundantly clear that politics is more complicated than just elections and elected representatives. Rather, the outwardly political with its red, white, and blue banners and "I voted" stickers has only one small part to play in the realm of decision-making. The ramifications of this increasingly obvious revelation are disturbing. If "we" are not in charge of "our democracy" then who is? If the outwardly political is just the tip of the iceberg, then what makes up the rest of (or at least the decisive portion of) power? Is it the bankers, Wall Street, and big finance, as the Occupy Wall Street movement claimed? Or perhaps it is the military–industrial complex and other branches of big business whose army of lobbyists certainly influence Washington, and likely not for the benefit of "the people"? There are a multitude of potential answers to this question, ranging from the Illuminati to the CIA. Clearly, this question has puzzled people from every walk of life in society if the suggested answers are so disparate. Here we examine an attempt at answering the question in the context of modern America.

The true answer, according to Curtis Yarvin, is in institutions that until recently hid in plain sight. Yarvin's theory is that the real center of political power is a web of institutions that he has dubbed the "Cathedral." The Cathedral is shorthand for the main outlets of information in America. After following the thoughts of Americans today, what Yarvin found is that their origins are in academia (i.e. the intellectual class of professors and academics), as well as journalism/media, and arguably K–12 education as well. The professor class is the origin of nearly all ideas within the Overton window in the West today, and these ideas are disseminated either directly in lectures or, more often, indirectly through *New York Times* best-selling books, the "mainstream media" (and yes, this includes Fox News), and to children through university-educated teachers. The remaining ideas floating around in the American psyche are truly dissident notions, but there is often also misinformation, due to psychological warfare tactics utilized by greater powers, either the actual Cathedral institutions or the institutions covered under the Cathedral umbrella that are more obvious to spot and are, therefore, pointed out as a false end of the rabbit hole by conservatives and liberals alike. Some of these are the aforementioned big businesses, Wall Street, NGOs, and government entities who, by disseminating information, act as part of the Cathedral. Before proceeding further, it cannot be stressed enough that the Cathedral is not a conscious conspiracy with devious plotting, but more of an organic system that came about from societal entropy.

In a great plot twist, if Yarvin is to be believed, the greatest threat to "our democracy" is unmasked as the very individuals and organizations constantly fear mongering about "threats to our democracy." How can Chomsky claim to be a "dissident" when all of the "people who matter" in America revere him as a saint? How can Van Jones claim to be an oppressed and powerless minority "speaking truth to power" while CPAC in 2019 felt the need to invite him to legitimize their conservative position as tolerant and open to dialogue (a common theme of modern "conservatism")? Examples of this sort of cognitive bias abound in the world of popular

Cathedral figures who control the flow of information and dominate every institution in America, and yet are able to turn around and claim to be the underdog.

People like Chomsky and Van Jones can and perhaps do genuinely believe that they are outsiders (Van Jones however appears to be a cynical race hustler), just as liberals, despite winning every political battle since, well, ever on the long term, believe that we are on the cusp of another "literally Hitler" who will usher in a new American Reich which will spell the end times. Thus, these progressives, the proponents of the new and distinctly post-1789 Western myth of progress, have as of late taken on the label of the "Resistance," a double entendre of the French "La Résistance" who fought against, you guessed it, "literally Hitler," but was also popularized by the themes of the terrible *Star Wars* sequel trilogy. Of course, progressives are not the actual resistance but are rather the foot soldiers of the establishment who are happy to trot out in mass numbers.

For the most part, Cathedral operatives are undoubtedly intelligent, as this trait is all but a requirement to reach their rank. Our two past examples, Van Jones and Noam Chomsky, are both intelligent, and Chomsky could even be characterized as *highly* intelligent. Neither of them is infallible, and both of them believe that they are repressed in some way, despite being two very powerful men in America. Thus, we know that intelligence can be duped into believing things that just ain't so. There is little doubt that many of these thought leaders are genuine, though there are undoubtedly many cynical grifters (political mercenaries who will say whatever needs to be said to make a quick buck) who simply gravitate toward power. Nevertheless, their motivation to stop a counter-revolution is simply that: a useful motivation which causes them and, more importantly, the droves of highly motivated liberal activists, to never slacken in his or her *righteous crusade*. Yarvin refers to this effect as the "Brown Scare" and writes, under his pen name Mencius Moldbug, "we see how the witch-hunter can invert the reality of power and presents himself as the underdog, fighting back against the gigantic and all-encompassing conspiracy of witches. This fantasy is expertly constructed and appears quite real to the casual observer."[120]

I

The Cathedral theory stipulates that the current main power structure in the United States and the Western democratic world is operated through the centers of information, led by the university system, which maintains a monopoly on intellectual thought, most relevantly in the social sciences and humanities but also in STEM fields. The result has been a disaster for intellectual rigor and the health of the collective American mind, along with the "discrediting" of fields that would have otherwise proven useful to humanity such as evolutionary psychology and comparative human population study.[121] The colonization of sociology, political science, and anthropology by the liberal and Marxist consensus hive mind is characteristic of what has been happening in academia for a hundred years.[122]

The now-common phrase in response to the conservative complaint of liberal bias in these and other fields, made popular by comedian Stephen Colbert, that "reality has a well-known liberal bias," demonstrates the sentiment of modern liberals who dominate just about every institution in America. How can science be science when, with the fervor of a puritan, liberals can simply *a priori* reject results which do not align with their worldview? If this is possible and even *normalized* in the sciences, how corrupted are our more subjective academic institutions like the social sciences?

---

[120] Moldbug, *Technology, Communism, and the Brown Scare.*
[121] Welton, "It's Official: Even Hard Science Entering New Dark Age."
[122] John Michael Greer has noted the inevitable skepticism toward the scientific community by the masses due to flaws in the scientific religion. From scam artist doctors, to climatologists who lie about the existence of past theories such as global cooling, to the aristocratization of the intelligentsia as seen in late Roman philosophy, in the later stages of a civilization, science seems to begin to lose its ability to justify its own existence to those plebeians who have been pushed out of understanding by the high priests who have no time for questions of their methods or procedures. Greer, *Dark Age America.*

Take the example of Charles Murray, a political scientist who co-wrote the famous and controversial book *The Bell Curve* with Richard Hernstein, a psychologist. There is no doubt of these two academics' *bona fides* as members of the academic community and, therefore, as part of the Cathedral. And yet, due to the distinctly anti-Cathedral nature of the book, these two men (Hernstein posthumously) were expelled from the Cathedral. Their heresy was to write *one* chapter on racial differences in IQ. Mere knowledge of this objective fact is already enough to turn one into a *persona non grata* in the academic world. They were both excommunicated from the academic world despite both being Harvard men, and thus as inner-academia as one could be. While Hernstein's untimely death right before the book's release saved him from the backlash, Murray felt the full brunt of the left-wing academic world's wrath. The APA disavowed and "debunked" his book and years later the consequences of questioning the unquestionable continue to follow him.[123]

This culminated in a protest against Murray at Middlebury College, where he was interviewed by a professor on a new book, completely unrelated to the aforementioned book he wrote over twenty years prior. The interviewer received serious injuries from the left-wing demonstrators. The escape vehicle was blocked and damaged. The protesters blamed campus security and the car for attacking them first; a very likely story.[124] A similar pattern of blaming others for the violence that follows left-wing mobs has been apparent for decades; though in recent years it has become impossible to ignore.[125] The college acted predictably by "sanctioning" a handful of students.[126] No students were charged with any crime for the assaults and destruction of private property.

This is not a one-time event, however. Nor is this type of activity relegated to the Trump and post-Trump era of political division.

---

[123] Chantrill, "US Government Spending History from 1900."
[124] Piro, "Professor Injured, Students Sanctioned at Middlebury College."
[125] The Unite the Right rally at Charlottesville epitomizes this trend, as the ensuing years of lawfare consisted of radical leftists blaming the defendants for the violence that they themselves had instigated. "NJP Condemns the Travesty of Justice."
[126] There is little to no evidence of any serious punishment by the college of any of the students who participated in the mob that left a professor injured. Piro, "Professor Injured."

Edward O. Wilson, a professor at Harvard University, was another trailblazer who attempted to popularize evolutionary psychology in the academic community, which at the time was referred to as sociobiology. Evolutionary psychology, a field of study that could seriously contribute to science and society, was strangled in the cradle, and Wilson was attacked in print and in public.[127] At one lecture, Wilson was attacked by a group of Marxist-Leninists going by the name *International Committee Against Racism*. One of the protesters poured a pitcher over the professor's head.

An entire book could be written on the instances in which professors have been harassed for thinking for themselves.[128] However, the point of these two examples is simply to illustrate that, for many years, the idea that universities are a place for real debate and dialogue is a fantasy. Rather, for decades, through harassment like what has just been described, or through other means such as discriminatory hiring practices, affirmative action, utilizing application essays, or simply assimilating students into a hive mind where they aren't even aware that there are legitimate alternative viewpoints from the ones that they are taught in textbooks and lecture, the Cathedral has been able to sift out the "bad apples" that might prove to be potential Murrays, Hernsteins, and Wilsons. And, considering the left-right ratio in all Cathedral institutions and especially the university system, they have done a remarkable job in their long march through the institutions.

Science is among the most trusted aspects of modern life. Yet it must be reiterated, if the people who perform the science are partisan, biased, and even untrustworthy, how can science itself be assumed not to be partisan, biased, and untrustworthy?[129] *Reality has a well-known liberal bias.* If you aren't creeped out yet, you should know that in science, and especially social science, there is a replication crisis. In other words, a massive percentage of studies that were once taken for granted cannot be replicated and are therefore useless, and the results of ever more studies are much less

---

[127] Jackson, "The Animal in the Man."
[128] Take law professor John Eastman of Chapman University, who was forced to re-sign after assisting Trump's legal team in the aftermath of Stop the Steal, and many more. Fulford, "Patriot Professor John Eastman."
[129] Clark, "Biased Science Makes Bad Policy."

significant than previously thought.[130] It also turns out that successful replication is often a consequence of having the same researchers attempting to replicate the same study. In other words, *it's the researchers who have introduced bias.* Where do the schools, media, and the universities get their information? From studies conducted through universities. Who conducts the studies? Almost exclusively liberal and Marxist intellectuals and researchers.[131] Why are they liberal/Marxist? *Because reality has a well-known liberal bias.* How do we know this? Because the studies prove it. The problem with this circular logic is as obvious as it is disturbing. There are serious cracks apparent in Western epistemology.

Of course, not all science is hogwash. But this demonstration pokes holes in the *scientism* or science worship of liberals, as well as conservatives and moderates, who have been conditioned to view science as perfect. If a worldview is based on a fallible base, problems occur. Even more problematic is that, while science in theory accepts when it is wrong and restructures itself in accord with newly-proven facts and theories superior to the old, liberal ideology only doubles down and gets more extreme. In two hundred years, liberalism was transformed from meaning abolishing monarchy and replacing it with a balanced republic, the promotion of life, liberty, and property, and the rejection of taxation without representation, to suffrage for every bum and vagrant, to the legalization of child chemical castration, supporting the foreign invasion of the home country by foreigners, and the abolition of the family. If there are any liberal readers who disagree with one of these latter opinions, give it ten years and come back. You will either have miraculously changed your mind through your incredible rationality just as the vast majority of liberals have changed their views to fit the current liberal *zeitgeist*, or you will be relegated to the dreaded "wrong side of history": a reactionary.

Thus, the liberal college system is able to manufacture reality through a corrupted and monopolized scientism which, through centuries of built-up trust in the institution of science, has enabled colleges to graft their opinions onto the very notion of science

---

[130] Yong, "Psychology's Replication Crisis."
[131] Jussim, "Political Biases in Academia."

itself—which, of course, has a well-known liberal bias. This is only one way that college is able to subvert the minds of students and the public at large. As René Guénon rightly pointed out, "it is impossible to separate knowledge from the process by which it is acquired."[132] The postmodern left also pose the danger of spreading their ideology of subjectivism, pushing the view that there is no reality or that it is whatever one makes it: a recipe for demoralizing the people who are gullible or open-minded enough to fall for these word-smiths' notions. And if quantity is opposed to quality, as outlined by Guénon, then the natural outcome of allowing more people into college now is that college as a whole becomes devalued, with the end result being that college graduates are overall significantly less intelligent than in previous years.[133]

Academia is an incredible filter for those who will become a potential influence in society, as just about every person who will have any influence on the life of the American people will be required to attend college and, therefore, have to go through the opinionated college system, where an ecosystem of "diverse" leftist opinions are allowed to be expressed and received. Bureaucrats, businessmen, military officers, journalists, lawyers, elected office holders, K–12 educators, medical professionals, and academics, among others, are, with few exceptions, required to go through this process. Academics and lawyers, perhaps the most vital group in this context, are required to be siphoned into an extra filter of post-graduate education, not necessarily just to better educate them so that they can become better public servants and leaders of the country, but to safeguard all intellectual and culturally relevant fields from potential infiltrators. And if one or two miraculously slip by, they will be too saddled with debt to dare dissent.

Since universities are the central organ of information in America, disseminating information and narratives either directly or indirectly through the media and K–12, they exert the most influence in our culture. These powerful people congregating in

---

[132] Guénon, *The Crisis of the Modern World*.
[133] This has been confirmed by the latest studies, finding that college students today have an equal IQ to their uneducated peers. The difference 50 years ago between the educated and uneducated was over a standard deviation in intelligence.
    See Uttl, Violo, and Gibson, "Meta-analysis."

their developmental adult years among each other pose another problem: the dissolution of the separation of powers intended to prevent rash decision-making in government. How can the class of "important people" all getting their intellectual foundations from the same place (colleges, despite being numerous, all have the same opinion on just about everything) not be a danger to "our democracy?" This is the true danger of universities and why academia holds its position as the head of the Cathedral. Not only does academia inform the lesser nodes of information, such as the K–12 system and the media; it also informs the "important people" who will take the ranks of the official high strata of society, but who don't necessarily qualify as the Cathedral, such as business leaders, Silicon Valley workers, and bureaucrats. This is exacerbated when all the important people in the country are largely attending the same few universities such as Harvard, Yale, and Columbia.[134]

Andrej Łobaczewski paints a picture of the propaganda efforts within the university system. Disturbingly, despite being a student, not at a modern American university, but in a Polish one directly after the Soviet occupation of his country during the Cold War, his testimony is incredibly similar to that which impressionable students are currently subjected to in American universities. Due to the importance of his insight, I quote at length. He writes:

> May the reader please imagine a very large hall in an old Gothic university building. Many of us gathered there early in our studies in order to listen to the lectures of outstanding philosophers and scientists. We were herded back there— under threat—the year before graduation in order to listen to the indoctrination lectures which recently had been introduced.
>
> Someone nobody knew appeared behind the lectern and informed us that he would now be professor. His speech was fluent, but there was nothing scientific about it: he failed to distinguish between scientific and ordinary concepts and treated borderline imaginings as though it were wisdom that could not be doubted. For ninety minutes each week, he flooded us with naive, presumptuous paralogistics and a pathological

---

[134] Wai and Makel, "Why Graduates of Elite Universities."

view of human reality. We were treated with contempt and poorly controlled hatred. Since fun-poking could entail dreadful consequences, we had to listen attentively and with utmost gravity. . . .

The grapevine soon discovered this person's origins. He had come from a Cracow suburb and attended high school, although no one knew if he had graduated. . . .

"You can't convince anyone this way!" We whispered to each other. "It's actually propaganda directed against themselves." But after such mind-torture, it took a long time for someone to break the silence.

We studied ourselves, since we felt something strange had taken over our minds and something valuable was leaking away irretrievably. The world of psychological reality and moral values seemed suspended as if in a chilly fog. Our human feeling and student solidarity lost their meaning, as did patriotism and our old established criteria. So we asked each other, "are you going through this too?" Each of us experienced worry about his own personality and future in his own way. Some of us answered questions with silence. The depth of these experiences turned out to be different for each individual. . . .

You can just imagine our worry, disappointment, and surprise when some colleagues we knew well suddenly began to change their world view; their thought-patterns furthermore reminded us of the "professor's" chatter. Their feelings, which had just recently been friendly, became noticeably cooler, although not yet hostile. Benevolent or critical student arguments bounced right off them. They gave the impression of possessing some secret knowledge; we were only their former colleagues, still believing that what those "professors of old" had taught us. We had to be careful of what we said to them. These former colleagues soon joined the Party. . . .

Analyzing these occurrences now in hindsight, we could say that the "professor" was dangling bait over our heads, based on specific psychological knowledge. He knew in advance that he would fish out amenable individuals, and even how to do it. . . . This knowledge about the existence of susceptible individuals [numbering in roughly 6% of the population] and how to work *on them will continue being a tool for world conquest as long as it remains the secret of such "professors."*[135]

Łobaczewski, at the time a student in psychology, dedicated his life's work behind the Iron Curtain to studying these individuals who are susceptible to regime propaganda. What he found was that a constant of roughly 6 percent of the population, mainly compromised of an assortment of psychopaths, sociopaths, "characterpaths," and those with a multitude of other dark-triad (psychopathy/sociopathy, Machiavellianism, and narcissism) associated pathological conditions, would eagerly join the ranks of the regime. For instance, according to Łobaczewski, the brutal prison guards in Communist Poland had an incredible rate of discharge to insane asylums.

More and more, Łobaczewski's words ring true as the supposed education at even, and especially, the most elite universities in the US and throughout Western civilization teach such biased and unfounded ideas. His note that the professor's "speech was fluent, but there was nothing scientific about it: he failed to distinguish between scientific and ordinary concepts and treated borderline imaginings as though it were wisdom that could not be doubted" is practically identical to modern critical race theory and other such subversive fields which deal not with science or statistics but with "lived experience" (though only of pathological case studies and not the experience of normal people) and psychoanalysis. Furthermore, his description of the small but vocal and pathological minority who become assimilated into the regime is quite prophetic.

The prison psychiatrist Anthony Daniels, writing under the alias Theodore Dalrymple, made a similar observation about child education, in relation to his work with the underclass of the East End of London. He wrote:

Political correctness is communist propaganda writ small. In my study of communist societies, I came to the conclusion that the purpose of communist propaganda was not to persuade or convince, not to inform, but to humiliate; and therefore, the less

---

[135] Łobaczewski, *Political Ponerology*, 25–27.

it corresponded to reality the better. When people are forced to remain silent when they are being told the most obvious lies, or even worse when they are forced to repeat the lies themselves, they lose once and for all their sense of probity. To assent to obvious lies is in some small way to become evil oneself. One's standing to resist anything is thus eroded, and even destroyed. A society of emasculated liars is easy to control. I think if you examine political correctness, it has the same effect and is intended to. [136]

The context of this quote was his thesis that the education system, influenced by toxic ideas in academia, was contributing to the mentally disturbed committing crimes due to the education system's belief in environmental determinism and excusing crime in impoverished communities. Even in 2001, Dalrymple could see clear as day the subversion of the Western intellectual tradition and its negative effects. Clearly, academia is no less sinister in the West than it was under the communist occupation of Eastern Europe. And even before the formation of the Iron Curtain, it was these forms of humiliation tactics—the popularization of what is wrong, evil, and satanic—that caused the German people to react so harshly against the Weimar regime, where much of the same ideology was originally foreshadowed, contributing to the rise of the Nazi regime.

Increasingly, "higher education" isn't just a requirement of the supposedly and slightly important people of society, but a requirement for just about everybody. Fallacious correlation/causation arguments, which gained traction during the Reagan administration, have linked going to college to benefits such as higher IQ, higher income, and less crime. [137] Despite the obvious flaws of this reasoning, for our context, we will look at the cultural, intellectual, social, and political effects that sending almost everyone to college has caused.

First, it must be stressed how unnecessary it is to send everyone to college. It is one thing to require a "liberal education" (in the traditional sense) in the humanities, as a political scientist,

[136] Dalrymple, *Life at the Bottom*, 171.
[137] Emmons, "Education and Wealth: Correlation Is Not Causation."

sociologist, psychologist, economist, or other social scientist needs to have at least a basic grasp of the other disciplines within the humanities. Why then are colleges requiring diversity classes for STEM majors? In fact, why are students entering STEM fields even required to go to college in the first place? To learn, obviously. But are there not alternatives such as qualification courses and certifications that could supplant the wasting of four years, and who knows how many man-hours and trillions of dollars, on a mostly useless education? Why is nursing a profession which requires a degree and all the "electives," "diversity requirements," and much more, rather than simply being a trade? Here, an attempt will be made to answer this question.

The most obvious (but not the most accurate) answer is that this is simply a money grab. More people attending college means more money for colleges, which are not getting any more affordable now that *everyone must go to college*. Therefore, colleges can charge whatever they want (as long as they are still competitive), as their service of providing an education has become non-negotiable. And, while students complain of increasing tuition prices and advocate for free college for all, they have also decided that wasting the tens or hundreds of thousands of dollars on college is a good idea as their undeveloped late teen minds can't properly process that the federally guaranteed loan they used to pay for college will have to be paid back with interest. The time preference of an eighteen-year-old is very high, and especially when under extreme peer and elder pressure. This is not meant to be an indictment of these youngsters, who are often not completely at fault, but of the bankers doling out these oh-so-valuable (and federally insured) loans and the Cathedral professors and administrators who make off like the gangsters that they are.[138]

---

[138] It is easy to understand the rationale of academics in this respect. In some ways, they too are victims of the academic system. PhD students and graduates are often forced to toil for years to obtain lecturing positions. They usually have debt, all the while being forced to accept university positions which require dependence on the university system, thereby subjecting the graduate student to poverty-level exist-ence via stipend payments. Thus, the university system has created an infinite cycle of cynical academics clawing their way to their dream job. This system allows for universities to discriminate against conservatives and dissidents as there are often

However, while this may be the original purpose as colleges have institutional power and a monopoly on a student's access to "higher education" and the "college experience," the more important function of all but coercing an entire population into attending college is that of political control by poisoning a population's perspective of legitimate positions in society. In other words, they are able to guide the Overton window and serve as a sentry to distinguishing right from wrong. Yarvin likens academics literally to *brahmins* or a sort of priest caste which dictates the discourse as if in a traditional society, though with "equality" and other axioms as opposed to an actual god.

Just as well, the normal, "unimportant" people are just as, if not more, susceptible to succumbing to one of the worst intellectual problems of modern liberalism: appealing to authority. In this case, authority is in the hands of the professors, who act as high priests of the Cathedral, graciously delivering their sermon directly to the future pseudo-elite, as opposed to the uninitiated masses who must receive their voluntary brainwashing from the screen. Of course, now that everyone is going to college, students are more like pseudo-elites rather than proper elites, but the psychology is the same. James Lindsey, whose claim to fame was studying the corruption in academia, has called attention to this overproduction of elites. [139] The result of this elite overproduction is a class of what can best be described as "degraded bourgeoisie," those who trained but failed in achieving status as part of the elite, who have become jaded and disenfranchised from modern life, and who often turn to extremism and violence via groups like BLM and Antifa.

It must be stressed that, according to Yarvin, this is not an international or even national conspiracy—it is not a centralized, secret cabal of nefarious people plotting devious schemes. Rather, the Cathedral is a completely decentralized and voluntary movement of people who don't even believe they have power over

---

dozens, if not hundreds, of candidates applying for a meager position. Thus, the filters that universities apply to their candidate pool are inevitably tainted by culture. The most notorious example of this practice is forcing applicants to sign diversity pledges and other items of this sort which will weed out those with any sense of dignity. The "emasculated liars" remark rings true. This is all by design. Fang, "Graduate Student Workers Still Struggle."

[139] "Bourgeois Overproduction and the Problem of the Fake Elite."

the more than three hundred million people of the United States. There is certainly some scheming such as institutionalized discrimination and union activity, though the crafty maneuver to *force* people to pay tens or hundreds of thousands of dollars for their own brainwashing was likely an *accident*. However, all evolution is technically an accident. The difference between a harmful mutation and an evolution, however, is that one is damaging and the other is useful. If forcing everyone to attend college and forcing all students to take useless classes with no purpose other than to provide the school with more funds, or to brainwash students via politically charged coursework, somehow cost the school money or made students more conservative, these activities would be quickly retired from the curriculum. College sports, and therefore the admitting of some genuine morons into elite schools, produce revenue for the school and are therefore useful. Hence, school sports exist. This is in contrast to the authentic school sports of past ages, when student athletes were mostly students and the athlete part wasn't the focus.

The form of the Cathedral is not conspiratorial, but evolutionary. Experiments, and often quite radical experiments, in the schools are tried. Some fail while some succeed. If an experiment, such as illegally using pseudo-affirmative action or illegally swindling wealthy applicants out of the "spot price" of attendance, is useful and successful, it will be utilized. If promoting academic diversity, thereby giving the edge to conservative and reactionary applicants due to their unusual views in the age range of the average applicant was pursued, then the program would likely be canceled. The exception would be a hypothetical cost-benefit analysis which somehow finds that a reputation, in the eyes of the public, as a policy neutral university is of greater benefit to the university than the negative result of allowing a few students with alternative viewpoints into the university.

II

Yarvin's theories are so influential that they merit further commentary. When Curtis Yarvin wrote his Cathedral thesis in the early 2000s, he likely would not have expected in his wildest dreams that a president would call journalists the "enemy of the people" and refer to the media as "fake news." Today, the power of the media is much more obvious than it was then, and the notion that the journalist class is one of the most powerful groups in America is no longer a novel claim. Yet it has remained true from then to now, though it is only now that it is so apparent. In the modern political environment, an epoch which was marked by the announcement of Donald Trump's presidential candidacy in 2015, the media have outed themselves as among the most important direct influence on politics.

The media have directed the culture for decades, however. Surprisingly, children in the United States still learn about the "yellow journalism" of the turn of the century America, which in large part caused the Spanish-American War by peddling a conspiracy theory. Of course, this yellow journalism has existed since long before 1898 and will continue long after today. It has been utilized to manufacture consent and even enthusiasm for multiple wars that the US has been involved in since, such as both World Wars, where the choice to go to war in Europe had been made long before any provocation.[140] In both cases the US had been supplying their future allies before entering the war and, in both cases, the media had been exciting the people for war just as Goebbels or Mussolini had done on the opposing side.

The media are often critical of wars, especially in the case of the wars against communism. In fact it was Americans—liberal Americans—who were largely responsible for financing and running interference for prospective communist regimes such as Lenin's 1917 Revolution in Russia and Mao's rise to fame and victory over the Japanese and KMT in China in the years during and after WWII.[141] It was the New York Times that suppressed the story

---

[140] For example, on September 11, 1941, President Roosevelt gave the "shoot on sight" order against the German Navy, a blatant act of war, three months before Pearl Harbor.

[141] A forgotten chapter in history is that of the "China Hands." The China Hands were American Sinophiles who aided the communists. Perhaps most notably is Edgar Snow, an American journalist who aided the communists in spreading antigovernment propaganda. He also aided in propagandizing his own country by lying on reports to the US on the democratic inclinations of the communists. Indeed, at the

of the Holodomor for Western audiences. During this manufactured famine, Stalin deliberately starved anywhere from one to five million Ukrainian peasants.[142] Professors, and in large part journalists, were responsible for America's greatest enemies of the late twentieth century. It seems slightly too coincidental that the wars in which liberals earned their "anti-war" reputation were uniquely wars against the spread of totalitarian communism, especially the Vietnam War.

During the Vietnam War, liberals in the media blatantly circulated false or biased interpretations of the goings-on at the front—in what could only be described as defeatism—in a war that could have easily been won were it not for asinine rules of engagement,[143] whose faithful implementation was supported by members of the Cathedral.[144] Scrutiny was placed on the American troops while brushing over the atrocities and violations of the rules of war by the enemy, who was often the source of Geneva Convention violations which caused the lashing out by American troops, such as at Mỹ Lai.[145] This is not to excuse atrocities on either side, but to illustrate the one-sidedness of the media in their portrayal of Vietnam as a war in which the US were the objective "bad guys," a view that is now disseminated in the public K–12 system. In the reverse, it was the left which vied for war in 1941 and it was the "far-right" boogiemen who stood against senseless conflict and to this day are vilified by the so-called anti-war left.[146] Furthermore, the left also defended and continues to defend the Rosenbergs, who leaked crucial nuclear weapons technology information to the Soviet Union which allowed them to catch up to the US in nuclear capability.[147] The Rosenbergs, a cell of Jewish communists, were sentenced to death for treason and continue to be martyrs of the radical left. One wonders if the hundreds of

---

time it was common to be taught euphemisms such as that Mao was not even a communist but a simple "land reformer" in American universities, based on China Hand reports.
142

[143] Jesse Beckett, "The Absurd Rules-of-Engagement."
[144] Shimmer Analysis, "Vietnam War: Yes, the Media Did Undermine the War Effort."
[145] Hastings, "The Hidden Atrocities of the Vietnam War."
[146] Gordon, "America First."
[147] Williamson, "Codename: Liberal."

millions of inmates of the open-air prison that was the Eastern Bloc would have been freed from their totalitarian hellscape earlier had the Communist regime not been able to bully the world with its nuclear arsenal.

The left-wing media, of course, did not hesitate to support the Persian Gulf War in 1991 which was supported by perhaps the most notorious institutions of international liberalism on Earth, the United Nations and NATO. After all, Saddam Hussein was a Ba'athist and thus a non-left-wing authoritarian (left-wing authoritarians get a pass), and therefore a "fascist." The reasoning for the war was that Iraq had invaded Kuwait to seize their oil, and that Iraqi soldiers were committing atrocities against the Kuwaitis such as taking babies out of incubators and leaving them to die, a lie formulated by Nayirah al-Sabah, whose claim to be a nurse at the hospital in Kuwait was proven false and who was in fact the daughter of the Kuwaiti ambassador to the US.[148] Not only was this a lie, but so was the supposed nature of Iraq's invasion as being unprovoked. As it turns out, there was evidence that Kuwait was digging under the Kuwait-Iraq border to siphon off Iraqi oil reserves.[149] None of this led the media to criticize the shoddy foundation of the conflict, or the conflict itself. Furthermore, tensions between the two countries were already strained much earlier due to Kuwait's excessive oil drilling, which deliberately affected the Iraqi economy negatively.[150] Rather than spread a nuanced message which could have prevented a war, the media blatantly peddled convenient lies for the public's approval. After all, *Democracy dies in Darkness*. As always, those who really control democracy, the elites, not the people, will always benefit by trotting out an *argumentum ad populi*: manufactured consent.

---

[148] Jack Xiong, "The Fake News in 1990."

[149] Abdulrazaq, "Iraq Lost Its Future."

[150] The claim of slant drilling is contested to this day. However, there is no denying that Kuwait was waging what seemed to be economic warfare on the Iraqis who were attempting to pay off a large debt. Furthermore, the acts of the US and its allies were not to protect a defenseless country, but to protect the flow of oil and thus protect their own economies. This is not to say that the US does not have the right to act in its own interests, but to accuse the media of acting as a propaganda arm for war, working hand in hand with the US government and international finance— hardly an independent institution.

There are of course other cases of the media having the power to make or break a war that is either popular or unpopular with the Cathedral. Take for example the Iraq War in 2003 which used the excuse of Saddam having acquired WMDs, an accusation that has since been all but disproven.[151] How many millions of dollars in CBRNE equipment was procured by the US military from the American taxpayer to counter these nonexistent WMDs, we may never know.[152]

While liberals earned a reputation for being anti-war during the Cold War, this farce cannot be more thoroughly refuted than by their behavior during the Trump years and the following years in which, seemingly, there isn't a military action or sanction that they wouldn't support (except of course on Red China and Venezuela, which have in some ways been pet projects of some Cathedral alumni).[153] One of the greatest neoconservative warmongers of the past three decades, John McCain, went from being labeled a "Nazi" while running against Obama in the 2008 presidential election, to becoming a "principled" liberal icon of the anti-Trump establishment. Similar occurrences have been seen in famous neoconservatives such as George W. Bush, who was also labeled a Nazi during his time in office and who similarly became something of a darling among the anti-Trump movement.

While Trump was undoubtedly strong on foreign policy, he was also a president willing to negotiate. He was the first president in decades to visit China and the first president to directly negotiate with North Korea. However, what Donald Trump achieved that angered the Cathedral was the mostly successful pullout of US troops from combat zones, which Obama had promised throughout his administration.[154] Trump also averted most unavoidable

---

[151] Martin Chulov and Helen Pidd, "Defector Admits to WMD Lies."

[152] It is here that the reader may protest that the war was supported not by the liberals (though many Democrats did support it), but rather that it was the neoconservatives of the Republican Party who were the main driving force. While this is true, it then raises the question as to who are the "liberals" and the "Cathedral" that are constantly referred to here. It would be naive to assume that the neoconservatives and establishment conservatives are not part of this very structure.

[153] See public intellectuals like Bernie Sanders and Noam Chomsky's support for the Chavez regime, and a multitude of others who view China's centralized system as a preferable system.

[154] Holland, "Trump Defends His Syria Pullout."

military action in Syria, a country still controlled by Ba'athists (and therefore fascists in the eyes of the Cathedral).[155] There were also economic interests involving the construction of an oil pipeline from the Gulf States, through Iraq and Syria, and into Turkey to supply Europe, which would cut out and ruin the economy of Russia, as Russia's economy is reliant on oil sales. Russia, of course, is not considered a friend by the liberal world order, as anyone who has watched Western media will know. Thus, the "live and let live" mantra of the left is only a brand utilized to prevent left-wing experiment governments from being accidentally overthrown by the US government. Rather, the left is perfectly fine with warmongering, as long as it serves its ultimate purpose, which is world domination of the Pride flag-waving Globalist American Empire. The intellectual and cultural imperialism of the Western Cathedral is a serious issue which affects all peoples of the world who wish to be independent from liberalism. It is for this reason, the specter of the homogenizing American imperialism, that the Taliban fought and defeated the neoliberal, globalist American empire, to the chagrin of the neoliberal left and neoconservative right.[156]

So far, only the effects of the media on foreign US wars have been discussed, to demonstrate how corrupt the media are with particularly egregious examples which caused great death and destruction. What has been a more important effect for Americans living in peace away from these wars has been the media's influence on the culture war on the home front. It is here that the media has truly been able to mold the day-to-day lives of most people. In a democracy, the people, in theory, are in power. However, the people are ruled by their thoughts, which are created by the culture and information floating around in society. The information and culture in Western and specifically American society are *dictated* most directly by the media (which is largely directed by academia): the main source of information for people day-to-day.

Take the previous example of the Vietnam War again. As incredible as it is that the media were able to rewrite history and

---

[155] In light if the overthrow of the Assad regime by US- and Israeli-backed Al Qaeda terrorists during the lame duck period of 2024, this is especially interesting.
[156] Jackson, "Perspectives on Peace."

influence public opinion on the home front then and up to the present, what is even more relevant, consequential, and shocking is that the media were able to *defeat* the US government, including the military and CIA, as well as those of its allies in Vietnam, by influencing the home front. The US military wasn't defeated by the NVA and VC. They won every battle, but lost the war due to the media, as well as infiltration into bureaucratic nodes of power, an issue that McCarthy risked and sacrificed everything in vain to defend America from.[157] Government leaks, pro-enemy sentiment on college campuses across the country, and demoralization of troops were all effects of a narrative created by the media, in which the US was the antagonist in the war, claiming the war was a lost cause on a people who actually wanted the brutal regime of the North—a regime which proved its brutality and lack of honor by invading the South after "making peace," and murdering thousands of civilians, most notably clergy, a common occurrence of communist insurgencies.[158] By then, of course, the Viet Cong flags waved by students had already been folded up and forgotten. This is not necessarily to promote or disavow America's intervention in Vietnam, but to point out the simple fact that the media is able to choose winners and losers. Defending South Vietnam was clearly an issue the media had no qualms opposing; while for the wars in the Middle East, the media were perfectly willing to promote these wars, and even to lie in doing so. This apparent inconsistency is explained by a consistent loyalty to advancing leftist and neoliberal interests.

Due to the internet, some have hope that alternative media may be able to compete with Cathedral media. However, this phenomenon is now being reined in by the Cathedral. Alternative media has three main problems: the first is that the forces of the Cathedral are closing in on these outlets either through (1) labeling them as "fake news" (which is projection of their own flaws), (2) pressuring either directly (hit pieces, doxing) or (more commonly) (3) indirectly through de-platforming the source through targeting sponsors, donors, internet service providers, and payment

---

[157] See von Hoffman, "Was McCarthy Right?" and Bernstein, "Vindication of Joseph."
[158] See Guzeva, "How the Bolsheviks Tried." and Royal, "The Calvary of Romania."

processors. Note that most businesses are not part of the Cathedral. Rather, businesses and other institutions are usually deathly afraid of the Cathedral and act as its slaves, lest they face the same fate as those who they are forced to punish. This may be seen in the recent promotion of grooming children by Disney due to pressure from mentally disturbed liberal employees, rather than by the executives who wished to stay out of the issue of Florida's anti-grooming legislation.[159] If Jeff Bezos or the other billionaires of today lived in Nazi Germany, he would be one of the most enthusiastic card-carrying members of the NSDAP, because the kingmaker in Nazi Germany was the NSDAP, just as the CCP is today in Red China, as is the Cathedral in the West today according to Yarvin.

The second problem with alternative media is that it is seen as unreliable. Members of the alternative media must make a name for themselves as a credible news source, with no help from any larger institution. Alternative media cannot compete with big media, because big media has the clout, represented by highly regarded publications which have been around for decades and sometimes even centuries. *The New York Times* is frankly a piece of classic Americana. *The Wall Street Journal* is wise enough to tow the Cathedral line, not that it ever was a dissident outlet. These major publications, of course, are seen as reliable because they are part of the Cathedral and cite the right studies, have articles written by the right professors and intellectuals, and make sure not to offend the Cathedral, which runs the show from behind the curtain. Yarvin points out a fact that seems obvious in hindsight, which is that, while always harping on about "speaking truth to power," the Cathedral media will never critique the university system unless it is to complain about universities not being liberal enough (and vice versa), quite reminiscent of late night talk shows' "critiques" of liberal politicians.[160] In the end, people are simply more likely to

---

[159] Malkin, "GLSEN's Groomers in Plain Sight."
[160] This is quite reminiscent of Kaczynski's "system's neatest trick." He explains that the "system" uses the revolutionary rebellious impulses of citizens who sense some-thing wrong with the system, and essentially judo maneuvers them into fighting *for* the system. Rather than fighting against the system, the left fights for *an even more extreme version* of the system, to which the system happily "capitulates." Thus, they

trust and use sources such as *The New York Times* and even smaller subsidiaries such as *Huffington Post* rather than someone's blog or YouTube channel. Truthfully, while the mainstream media spread disinformation and misinformation, this does not prevent alternative platforms from being just as guilty, though likely due to lack of massive budgets for research rather than blatant malice, power hunger, and partisanship. The difference, of course, is that alt media outlets usually don't *intend* to spread false information.

The third problem with alternative media is that, due to the Cathedral not only controlling but *being* academia, the most credible sources (which have already been established as largely tainted) are used by the Cathedral's media. Therefore, it is necessary to either agree with the mainstream media to some degree, or to do painstaking research for less tainted (and often obscure) sources of information, thus competing with the mainstream media's teams of researchers, who have the luxury of having the Cathedral in agreement from the beginning, while also actually being paid. This has been most apparent in the battle against COVID tyranny. Clearly, the information war is an uphill battle.

This is not to suggest that the information war should be ceded. Rather, access to alternative viewpoints and sources is among the most important missions of our generation. It is an uphill battle, but one that can be fought with continually progressing technology and more minds collaborating on alternative media and alt tech platforms. Furthermore, as the media continue to out themselves as untrustworthy, more and more people are turning to alternatives, meaning that the uphill battle becomes less and less steep as time passes.[161,162]

---

act as foot soldiers of the system, all the while maintaining the morale of zealous fanatics, believing themselves to be "speaking truth to power," "standing up to the man," and "punching up," while doing precisely the opposite.

[161] Konstantin Kisin's essay "Why Don't They Believe Us?" paints a highly descriptive and accurate picture as an answer to this very question, putting into words the collective consciousness of the American people who have seen the lies of the media. The Russian collusion hoax, the fake polling data of the 2016 election and Brexit, defending rioters and violent criminals, the COVID flip-flop, all the way to more recent blatant lies have resulted in the American people having enough of the dishonest media.

[162] As of the Second Edition, with the rise of alt media, the issue has become more

122 | THE AMERICAN REGIME

III

The final branch of what Yarvin dubbed the Cathedral that will be discussed here is the K–12 system. Though Yarvin spent more time in his own works focusing on the State Department, which he saw as the internationalist wing of the Cathedral that spreads these ideas abroad, this is beyond the scope of studying power in the US.[163]

The main and obvious takeaway of this system of power is that it is the first of many filters that sifts the wheat from the chaff by breaking down students. Of course, it is not a revolutionary notion to claim that the public school system was invented as a way to create a mass of mediocre citizens through an industrialized education program. It was the Prussians who first utilized this theory in its modern form.[164] The regimented formal stereotype of the Prussian system should give an insight into what modern education truly is, as it was precisely this system that was copied by the US. Rather than making good little soldiers though, as in the Prussian system, the American system is utilized to create an army of "bots" which do what they're told, not for the furtherance of military discipline, but rather to create a safe and efficient environment for the elites of the country. It is no surprise then that students learn nearly nothing of value in the public schools, and what they do learn of value is in such an inferior form that only half of students enjoy or appreciate their education, let alone retain it.[165]

For the most part, the students that do well are the drones, those who can be characterized as midwits or "head girls," who are certainly somewhat intelligent, but not deserving of their status as

---

complicated. However, this does not mean that the issue has disappeared. As the alternative media becomes the new mainstream media, the exact same problems resurface, only through new mediums. The alternative media is largely dominated by a new cadre of mainstream voices masquerading as alternative. Nevertheless, with the democratization of information, the situation has never looked more optimistic.
[163] As of the Second Edition, it appears that this is a point of Yarvin's that directly affected the second Trump administration in its attacks on USAID, a government organization which spent billions in taxpayer money on leftist international fronts. Indeed, Yarvin has gained prominence in these last few years, being recognized as a sort of magus of "New MAGA."
[164] McGuigan, "What Is the Prussian Education System?"
[165] "Are Students Engaged?"

some sort of genius, as their position is gained not by their intelligence but by their conformity, which the school system was designed to create.[166] Thus, these high mark students move on to the universities where they and their mediocre counterparts from all over the country can do their midwit things and, if they're lucky, obtain a midwit job at a bureaucratic organization.

But it is the teachers themselves that the Cathedral issue represents. The great tragedy of the professors, media, and K–12 education is the magnitude of their power, which went unrealized until recently. Indian tradition holds the Brahmin (priestly) caste to be the highest in society, as did most other traditional cultures such as medieval Japan (Japan's warrior caste and what we Westerners would refer to as a priest caste were essentially conjoined), Europe, and the Islamic world. However, where the insight of the Hindus truly comes into play is that the Brahmin class stands in for the head of the metaphysical body of society, from which emanates thought and speech. This is essentially the basis of the Cathedral theory, and Yarvin himself often refers to this Brahmin caste in his works, though he may not have realized the insight which he inserted into them. Thus, the genius of the comparison between ancient Brahmins and modern leftist high priests is that Brahmins are not only priests but the teachers of the society. I bring this up now as it is profound that we have relegated a subsection of the most important and powerful roles of society to NPR-watching wine aunts. It makes some sense in professors, as they admittedly tend to be highly intelligent, corrupted as they may be. But teachers? Simply preposterous. This is, of course, a result of the age of quantity as described by Guénon. Modern society has put preference on a Prussian school system in which everybody must be taught, often beyond their comprehension. As a result, an impossible number of pedagogues must be corralled into the schools to teach an impossible number of children. Thus, society at large suffers due to the lie and assumption of equality.

It should have been obvious that the teachers had more power than personal responsibility, and for decades we were warned by the fringes that the education system taught largely useless

---

[166] McElroy, "A Nation of Workers."

information. "Why do we graduate without the knowledge to file taxes?" for example, is a common theme. Lately, they are ramping up the propaganda in preparation for the students to enter university. Critical race theory seems to be the issue of the day, and has raised the alarms of the populace who are finally realizing the major flaws in the K–12 system and especially the types of people who are involved in teaching.

IV

The Cathedral theory, in many ways, accurately portrays power relations in the modern United States and the West in general. The essential tenets are that (1) the main levers of power are not in the government, corporations, or any other outward body of power, but rather within a quasi-Brahmin caste which has control over the populace by exerting soft power via an "information war" on the masses; and (2) the Cathedral is not a cabal of major media outlets colluding with educational institutions and other outlets of power, but rather a largely unified consensus reached organically over decades by the natural force of societal entropy.

Through this theory of power, Yarvin attempts to solve the problem of social democracy. In modern democracy, power is decentralized and this is assumed to be an absolute good. However, this means that the actual power brokers are out of sight, making it highly difficult to actually pinpoint the source of power. As a result, political movements of both grassroots left and right are unleashed on the incorrect political target, missing the true meta-political source of their grievances. Oftentimes, the true power centers trick grassroots movements to attack those with whom they should ally.

However, the Cathedral theory is far from perfect, as we shall see in the next chapter. It is far less simple than the assumption that the brain of the system controls all the other levers of power, while the other nodes have no influence on the appointment of news anchors, journalists, professors, and teachers. The Cathedral theory often overestimates the intellectual rigor and bravery of professors and assumes that political collusion either does not exist, or exists in such a minimal way so as to make the phenomenon insignificant.

Both of these hypotheses are in fact false, as we shall see. The truth is that, while the Cathedral theory is highly important for future serious political discussion, it is nonetheless a product of its origin. While Yarvin is among the most important people who have popularized the elite theory today, he is limited by how his Jewish ancestry has influenced the way in which he views conspiratorial behavior (Jews have historically been accused of conspiratorial action, and often rightly so). Even the most brilliant of thinkers can still be prone to subconscious biases through no fault of their own. Nevertheless, blatant cabal trickery, insider trading of information, nepotistic plots, and clique takeovers are all a real part of life in the higher echelons of power.[167] While much in the world of power is organic, Yarvin ignores that which is not, likely due to paranoia about "anti-Semitism," as Jews are often blamed for these supposedly organized conspiracies. Yarvin is noteworthy for his criticism of Kevin MacDonald's interpretation of Jewish influence, calling MacDonald (a professor of evolutionary psychology, specializing in the Jewish people) an "anti-Semite."[168] It is ironic that the main point of MacDonald's, that Jewish contributions to science and social science coincidentally tend to shirk any responsibility of the Jewish people for any wrongdoing, or benefit "Jewish interests" in some way (see psychoanalysis, radical leftism, modern anthropology, sociology, and neoconservative Zionism, all to be discussed later on) is precisely what Yarvin is doing by loading all elite institutional blame onto convergent behavior.

This does not necessarily mean that his findings are wrong, but that they are indeed biased and thus limited in some way, however slight. This theory of nepotism and interaction of far-left Jewish subcultures, which Yarvin criticizes MacDonald for acknowledging, is ironically present in the Cathedral theory, as Jews possess great influence over media, academia, and the US State Department.[169] Indeed, Yarvin's main critique of MacDonald is that he has *too much* evidence.[170] Furthermore, convergent behavior and conspiratorial

---

[167] Geraghty, "The Remarkable Apathy."
[168] Moldbug, "Why I Am Not an Anti-Semite."
[169] See Lichter et al., *The Media Elite*. Also, the State Department is currently headed by three Jews: Antony Blinken, Wendy Sherman, and Victoria Nuland.
[170] Joyce, "Jews in the Cathedral."

behavior are not mutually exclusive. Rather, oftentimes the former is a key predictor of the latter. With this being said, while the Cathedral theory's flaws in regards to the highest echelons of power must be recognized, it is also necessary to acknowledge that the theory is probably the best explanation of *low-level* elite behavior. This is because, while the Cathedral may have a limited amount of effect on someone like George Soros, it certainly is predictive of what the hordes of bureaucrats at powerful organizations like the CIA or the writing staff at Warner Brothers have occupying their mind. Yarvin's theory comes from firsthand experience with the low-level elite and, therefore, the theory should be regarded as one which explains their behavior, but is not an all-explaining crystal ball. Essentially, I aim not to "refute" the Cathedral theory of power, but add to its canon and fill in the gaps.

5

ON OTHER POWERS

The Cathedral theory posits that the true source of power in America is represented by the information centers, which control the flow of thought for the majority of Americans. While these groups (academia, the media, and K–12) are highly influential, the assertion that these syndicates are the true center of power is flawed, to say the least. In this chapter, we will explore other nodes of power to examine what mega-entity, if any, is at the top, including a re-examination of the Cathedral entities from a different lens.

I

In tandem with the increasing focus on the media by the right, especially in the post-2015 world, is the scrutiny placed on "Big Tech," a catch-all phrase which includes the major Silicon Valley corporations. Indeed, these seemingly niche corporations have quickly risen to become the most wealthy and powerful organizations in the entire world. Names such as Google, Facebook, Apple, Twitter, Microsoft, and Amazon, are the most prolific of these brands but the roster continues to grow, along with their market share.

First, we can examine Google, which technically has some competitors, though they are all greatly inferior, and most of the mainstream competitors are no better in terms of their agenda for political control. Google, and its parent company Alphabet, controlled by Sundar Pichai, is one of the largest and perhaps the most powerful corporation on Earth, for the reason that its search engine, like the Cathedral, controls the flow of information. They choose what comes up on the first search page, and some websites are impossible to find unless it is directly searched for. For example, the dissident right-wing news site Stormfront is not even on the first page of the Google search engine when typing in "Stormfront." This is an extreme example, though it demonstrates the capability of an information monopoly to determine what search results are found by the average person, who doesn't have time to scour the internet, when they search for things such as "gun control," "Trump," or "Black Lives Matter." The value of Google's siding with the establishment can easily give one campaign the boost it needs over the other. According to research psychologist Robert Epstein, "Given that many elections are won by small margins, this gives Google the power, right now, to flip upwards of 25 percent of the national elections worldwide. In the United States, half our presidential elections have been won by margins under 7.6 percent, and the 2012 elections was won by a margin of only 3.9 percent— well within Google's control."[171] And of course we know that Google has indeed manipulated every election since 2016, as they are censorious on their video platform, YouTube, and actively hide search results they don't like, dubbing it "disinformation."[172] Supposedly, Google provides billions of search results for any given search, and yet you will be hard-pressed to actually be provided more than a few pages of results on Google. Quite fishy indeed, Mr. Pichai. The kicker, of course, is that Google didn't have to spend much on this. They just enabled an algorithm with the press of a button. *That* is real power.

Again, Google also controls YouTube, which has a monopoly on online video platforming, and controls and censors opinions contrary to what they wish to allow on the website. Like Google, YouTube uses an algorithm which often makes videos that counter the narrative impossible to search for. While the videos haven't

---

[171] Epstein, "How Google Could Rig."
[172] Simonson, "How the CDC Coordinated."

actually been removed, as they technically did not violate any rules, they require a separate search engine or a direct link to actually find. For many years, Google's investment into YouTube was seen as a bad one, causing Google to lose millions.[173] However, the point of buying out YouTube was not to gain money, but power, by means of controlling the flow of information.

Facebook and Twitter, two social media platforms that additionally own smaller platforms, also exert extreme influence on politics, culture, and the free flow of information. Facebook and especially Twitter have turned themselves, in our age of technology and internet communication, into the *de facto* public square of free discourse. These soulless corporations do not value free speech and actively target speech of which they do not approve.[174] The algorithm facilitates hate mobs and prevents alternative messages from gaining traction (for example, household name conservative pundits often have far fewer followers than relatively unknown liberal "journalists"; this was later found out to be the deliberate result of the use of bots in the aftermath of Elon Musk's first attempted acquisition of Twitter) and, on the extreme end, the platform doesn't even allow opinions to be shared at all by arbitrarily enforcing purposely vague terms of services up until quite recently with Elon Musk's acquisition.[175] While all Big Tech companies do this, social media giants are perhaps the most dangerous due to their active control of the public forum.

These social media companies pride themselves on having facilitated the CIA-backed Arab Spring and subsequent "color revolutions," allowing the "pro-democracy" rebels to overthrow their governments with the aid of Western communications and networking platforms.[176] It would be foolish to believe that these multi-billion-dollar operations are incapable of overthrowing other governments such as the US government itself. Indeed, they *succeeded* in doing just that in 2020. While they call this assertion a "dangerous conspiracy theory," if it is framed in a positive light, they fully acknowledge it and are proud of their part. For example, the

---

[173] Winkler, "YouTube: 1 Billion Viewers."
[174] Simonson, "How the CDC Coordinated."
[175] See *Jared Taylor and New Century Foundation v. Twitter, Inc.*
[176] "GT Investigates."

regime publication *Time* magazine proudly stated that the 2020 election was "fortified," which appears to be a euphemism for stolen. Molly Ball, a Jewish activist journalist bragged that:

> *Corporate America turned on [Trump]. Hundreds of major business leaders, many of whom backed Trump's candidacy and supported his policies, called on him to concede.... There was a conspiracy unfolding behind the scenes, one that both curtailed the protests and coordinated the resistance from CEOs. Both surprises were the result of an informal alliance between left-wing activists and business titans. The pact was formalized in a terse, little-noticed joint statement of the U.S. Chamber of Commerce and AFL-CIO published on Election Day. Both sides would come to see it as a sort of implicit bargain—inspired by the summer's massive, sometimes destructive racial-justice protests—in which the forces of labor came together with the forces of capital to keep the peace and oppose Trump's assault on democracy.*[177]

Talk about "mask off." This would be quite amusing if the person writing those lines wasn't an untouchable member of the authoritarian regime, instituted by big capital, including the Big Tech platforms. The point is not to reminisce on satanic midwit journalists and their antics, but to demonstrate that corporate America and the media were able to seize the most powerful office on Earth, and people are still focused on ridiculous distractions like the QAnon conspiracy theory (an obvious disinformation campaign likely orchestrated or facilitated by the CIA, similar to the Cheka's "Operation Trust" campaign in the early Soviet Union) or winning "fortified" elections.[178] Clearly power does not lie where those in power would want us to believe.

There are also the online banks which control much of the capital flow in our technological age. The large banks collude with the government to hunt down dissidents such as the January 6th protesters and Canadian anti-lockdown demonstrators, and just

177 Ball, "The Secret Bipartisan Campaign."
178 Sheth and Relman, "Michael Flynn Said."

about anyone who's anyone on the American dissident right has been banned from PayPal.[179] PayPal became even more authoritarian recently, with an acceptable use policy that subjects users to potentially $2,500 in liquidated damages for transactions involving "intolerance that is discriminatory," or "the promotion of hate," or even if PayPal merely *believes* a user has engaged in such activities.[180] Payment processors have a similar function. Corporations such as GoFundMe used online dissidents to gain momentum, while creating an economy where dissidents often relied on such companies for their livelihood. After gaining popularity among the masses, dissidents were thrown under the bus.[181] Other corporations like Visa and MasterCard ban dissidents, while also controlling monopolies or oligopolies, twisting the arm of the American people to their will, at risk of financial trouble, inconvenience, or even ruin.[182] The gig economy has also borne fruits for Silicon Valley power. Corporations such as Airbnb, GrubHub, Lyft, Uber, and so many more ban dissidents, making normal life more difficult for those who would otherwise use and even rely on their platforms.[183,184]

However, as powerful as Silicon Valley is, at the end of the day they are simply services to which higher forces outsource tyranny. Yarvin makes a similar observation.[185] Many, in reaction to the increasing censorship power of Big Tech, prodded Yarvin into acknowledging this problem, which has grown immensely since his original writings on the subject around 2008. His view, which is not inaccurate, is that the Big Tech companies create power, but do not possess it. Rather, power is leaked, and elites acting as power-leeches fight for the power emanated from these corporations. For example, while Twitter and Jack Dorsey might be openly left-wing,

---

[179] Vincent, "Security Experts Blast Bank."; Katherine Fung, "Banks Have Begun Freezing Accounts."

[180] Parker, "PayPal Is Still Threatening."

[181] Taylor, "Would They Let Him Die?"

[182] Greenfield, "A New Color of Censorship."

[183] "Why Michelle Malkin Is Banned from Airbnb."

[184] While visiting DC in 2025, I found that I was at some point banned from Lyft and Uber before I had even made an account and, had it not been for taxis, I would have simply been marooned at the airport.

[185] Yarvin, "Big Tech Has No Power at All."

even if they weren't, they would still have power-leeches attacking them and pushing them toward the left. Twitter in the abstract may not necessarily support BLM, Pride, or any other evil left-wing cause because of moral reasons, but because they know the drill and want to avoid controversy and bad press. This was recently proven correct when a Facebook "whistleblower" (most likely a political operative who infiltrated the company, or a company operative who "leaked" the documents in a controlled manner, though this is but speculation) came out against the company, not for its censorious actions against free speech, but because Facebook *was not censoring enough*.[186] In this way, the Cathedral may still be on a plane above, while the Silicon Valley corporations that control the flow of information are but a platform which supports the Cathedral due to implicit coercion.

Also relevant is the earlier example of color revolutions. Unlike a corporation such as the United Fruit Company or Exxon, Silicon Valley does not have much incentive in and of itself to influence foreign affairs. However, there are plenty of entities which do. The Cathedral has an ideological motive; both neoconservatives and leftists want to see non-democratic anti-globalist governments toppled. On the other hand, the State Department and other security agencies also share the same motive as they serve the interests of Globalist American Empire and support its governing ideology. In the case of the color revolutions, it was indeed these state entities who were the true cause.[187] It is likely that these clandestine government bureaus incentivized or threatened the social media giants to maintain communications in these areas, while if the roles were reversed, such as in the case of a group hostile to the US, the government would incentivize or threaten these same corporations to create a communication blackout, though this is, again, speculation. This is, of course, assuming that both entities are not simply on the same page as is, therefore needing little collusion between organizations. The disturbing revelation, of course, is what this means about the 2020 election. Thus, the government and political movements leech off of Big Tech, while Big Tech yields

---

[186]Washington Watcher II, "Facebook 'Whistleblower' Frances Haugen."
[187] "GT Investigates: US Wages Global Color Revolutions."

relatively little political power as a standalone, but produces great rewards for those who are able to game the Golden Goose.

II

The US government itself is the most obvious character in the play of power and, subsequently, is the most popular one to point the finger at. However, when speaking of "The State," it is easy to become confused as to what is truly meant, since there are multiple categories which can be fairly coined "The State." Among these are the elected and non-elected personnel. On the federal level, the elected are the president and Congress, while the unelected are various bureaucratic administrations, represented by everyone from the moron behind a desk at the DMV to the Director of the CIA—not to mention the Supreme Court. The mistake that most make is to reflexively put all blame on the government and especially the president under the assumption that, as arguably the most powerful individual in the country and representative of the State, he also carries *the majority* of power. This is an obvious miscalculation and a false assumption made by those who know no better. To truly discern where power in the government lies, and if the government itself is even the main source of power in the meta-political realm, it is necessary to dissect along the lines of the aforementioned segregated state apparatuses.

First, and easiest to discount, is the presidency. While the president is arguably the most powerful man in the country, his power is relatively minimal compared to the leviathan which is the modern state apparatus. While the power of the presidency has gradually increased over the years, making leaps under Andrew Jackson, Lincoln, and FDR, the president is still only a small player in the grand scheme of things. The most obvious example of this is the Trump presidency. For all his flaws (and there are many), it is no exaggeration to claim that getting Trump into the White House was at least two back-to-back miracles for the American right: the first being winning the Republican primary and the second being winning the general election. Despite this, without political capital, Trump was unable to do much meaningful work as president and much that he did do would likely have also been done by a Democrat or establishment Republican presidency. The main achievement of the Trump presidency was putting the US embassy in Jerusalem and sending more aid to Israel, both of which only weaken the US abroad via strained relations with the Islamic world, and at home by wasting tax dollars.[188] The Border Wall was downgraded to a Ballard fence and never finished. When it was president versus Congress in a showdown over the border funding, it wasn't Congress that blinked.[189] Even when the most grassroots president in modern history had the legal power to pardon his many supporters who would soon become political prisoners under an authoritarian police state in but a few weeks, he would rather pardon Israeli spies and his Jewish son-in-law's gangster father, not to mention the pardon of rapper and career criminal Kodak Black.[190,191]

This is not meant to be a treatise against Trump specifically, but to point out the obvious with perhaps the best example of the true ineptness of the presidency in the face of hostile rival power nodes. Yarvin came to the same conclusion: that grassroots presidents (and prime ministers) who attempted to work within the system ended up only taking one step forward and two steps back. All they achieved was slowing the inevitable. If Trump, the renegade outsider president, cannot use the presidency to further his agenda, no president can. The disturbing truth is that, at least in presidential elections, even before the riggers and elites corrupted the democratic process, your vote doesn't matter and, according to Robert Michels' Iron Law of Oligarchy, likely never did.

In terms of the presidency, both parties are simply acquiescent to the bureaucracy. The left allows the bureaucracy to run relatively unmolested and simply administers the executive branch, while Republicans usually behave no differently, only toward different bureaucratic branches, especially the military. In the worst-case scenario such as Trump, an outsider president who threw a wrench into the system of operations, the entire system will attack from all

---

[188] Maltz, "U.S. Envoy Ranks Recognition."
[189] Berman, "Trump's Border-Wall Blink."
[190] TOI Staff, "At Israel's Request."; Samuels, "Trump Pardons Charles Kushner."
[191] Of course, he did eventually pardon his supporters—four years too late.

sides or simply hibernate until institutional power is able to overthrow the executive administration that is unwilling to play ball. While there are exceptions of true "great men of history"— those who are able to rise at the right time and bend the state to his will, who emerge every seventy or so years, such as Jackson, Lincoln, and FDR—the general rule remains, and it is scarcely a reactionary who is able to defy it (though Caesarism, the populist reaction and overthrow of a regime, led by a charismatic leader, does occur every now and again).

But what of Congress? Perhaps senators and representatives have some usable power; "Power to the People" and whatnot. Unfortunately, it is perhaps worse here than with the presidency. At least in a presidential election, there is a slight chance that a renegade like Trump can be elected. In Congressional politics, power comes from the plurality and, while it is technically easier to elect a renegade in an individual race in Congress (and especially the lower house) than to the highest office, the chances of a grassroots party takeover is basically impossible, and only has one opportunity every few generations, as a failed swell will be ruthlessly squashed by the establishment.

The democratic ideal, that one's vote counts as much as George Soros' or Bill Gates' vote is an obvious lie. This is not to say that grassroots candidates cannot be elected (however rare that may be) but rather to acknowledge the fact that, if greater interests are the main factor in deciding who represents the people in Congress, then for all intents and purposes Congress is not in power. Rather, those who put the Congressmen in their seats, the men who pay their campaign bills, are in power and, almost exclusively, it isn't the average Joe who is paying for campaigns. To the extent that it is Average Joe donors, it is the firm that advertises and raises money, not those they raise money from, who has the sway. Thus, it can be easily deduced that Congressmen are simply pawns for special interests, whoever they may be.

The final branch to explore is the judiciary and, in this case, it seems that we are finally on to the scent of the origin of power. As shown during the Trump presidency, the US governing system has degenerated more and more into a rule of judges, in which it is these appointed dealers of supposed justice who are increasingly behind the levers of *real* power in politics. Their judgment is law, even when they blatantly act against the law, or Talmudically twist the law into a parody of its former self. Local, state, and federal governments have recently been blocked by thorn-in-the-side judges at record levels, mainly to counter populist policies. Indeed, the judiciary is turning out to be the ultimate broker of legislation today, "legislating from the bench," as it were. The Founders designed the Supreme Court and the lower courts to be a "check and balance" to popular power. However, today it has become an insurance policy to bail out the powerful in a pinch when all else fails. This, again, ties into the myth of presidential power, as the misconception that the president can *just* sign executive orders willy-nilly has been proven to be a one-way street. Rather, executive orders are mainly available as a workaround by the powerful, through the president. In other words, it doesn't work when the executive order is being signed for purposes antithetical to actual power. It was here that Trump was so often blocked for blatantly political reasons, while Obama before him was largely successful.

So then, is the judiciary the real power in government, at least in comparison to the executive and legislative branches? Well, not exactly, as recently seen with Biden being quite willing and able to do his best to circumvent the Supreme Court on lockdown policy.[192] As with the executive order issue, judicial power is obviously a one-way street. But where is it that this street leads? "Cthulhu always swims to the left," yes, but by whose orders and for what reason?[193] It should also go without saying that the judiciary is made up of law school graduates and their lackeys, who have gone through the ringer of Cathedral education, even more so than other elements of the government. The legislative branch isn't much better, with 175 out of 435 congressional representatives being lawyers in the 117th Congress.[194] Why does it seem that the supposed nodes of power are only able to exert the power when it is for a predetermined purpose, and can we really claim that these individuals have *any*

---

[192] Gangitano, "Biden Calls on Employers."
[193] Here I refer to Yarvin's famous axiom, with Cthulhu referring to the forces of chaos and entropy, which seem to always inch slowly ever toward this end, while rarely, if ever, backpedaling toward order and structure.
[194] "Members of the 117th Congress with Law Degrees."

true power if this is the case? Furthermore, despite the Supreme Court being an undemocratic institution in which judges serve for life, they are not immune to pressure applied by the masses acting on orders from those they fear (see the reaction to the overturning of *Roe v. Wade* for example). It can also be reasonably speculated that many SCOTUS and circuit court justices have been blackmailed. While speculation, the Jeffrey Epstein revelations have confirmed these decades-old suspicions in many cases, and the media is perfectly happy to hide scandals of their favorite pawns while making mountains out of molehills when it comes to their enemies.[195] It would also be naive to assume that the Epstein criminal enterprise was and is the only one of these blackmail operations. It was probably just the most flagrant.

We have discussed all branches of the federal government and come out with much wanting in terms of locating actual power. However, let us finally delve back into the executive branch outside of the president: the federal bureaucracy. It would be quite difficult to claim that bureaucrats have no power. The policeman has power over you as he points his firearm at you; the DMV worker has power over you as she takes her sweet time printing out your paperwork, or arbitrarily fails you on your driver's exam; the federal agent has power when he decides whether to target a Black murderer or a White firearm enthusiast, and these are just minor examples of bureaucratic power, in which the decisions of a soulless toady can mean the loss of time, property, or even life for the average American.

However, it goes much deeper than this. A bureaucrat can "lose" or "forget" an important order from Congress or the president, with no repercussions because, remember, these two entities have minimal true power. If anyone in the *de jure* government has actual power, it is ironically the most modest, measly, and unexpected suspect: the bureaucrat has the closest thing to true, unadulterated power. Like the judiciary though, this isn't the whole story, as bureaucrats are easily swayed drones who listen to their superiors. "Losing" an important document that is approved by the "deep state" regime would never be tolerated or ignored. When a Christian

---

[195] Sarnoff, "Jeffrey Epstein Flight Logs."

woman refused to sign paperwork approving of a gay "wedding," it was national news for a week.[196] Power only goes one way, and our mission is to follow the trail, a trail that evidently does not lead to bureaucracy.

Once again, for all the apparent power they can wield, they too are just cogs in the machine. Easily manipulated, the type who enters into administration tends to be a mousy, mediocre college graduate who doesn't ask bothersome questions and is just there to be the system's janitor or janissary, depending on their level of intelligence, neuroticism, and indoctrination. Thus, this type is precisely the target of Cathedral indoctrination and is the most enthusiastic for his or her (probably her) nightly brainwashing via one of the mainstream press publications. This person also greatly values the opinions of his or her former college professors who are regarded (rightly) as their intellectual superiors, and makes sure to catch the NPR podcast on the drive home. The Cathedral wins again when it comes to the bureaucracy. There is, of course, a not-so-typical type in the bureaucracy, the senior officer, who is a completely different animal and should be treated as such.

The leaders within the bureaucracy arguably have much more power than the president or other branches of the state. While the aforementioned petty bureaucrat can theoretically create major ripples in the grand scheme of history, this is mostly an illusion, as this rule is only applicable when said bureaucrat goes along with the predetermined mantra. The petty bureaucrat is also, frankly, a moron in comparison to the heavyweights who manage them. The directors of respective divisions of the government will act ideologically and mostly free from meaningful oversight, all the while being unelected: a great factor in freedom of action for the bureau leader who need worry less about factors that elected officials are constantly battling.

Here again arise some problems. For instance, locating power in the bureau heads assumes these individuals act in a vacuum. In reality, they had to work their way to where they are. Elites don't just magically appear in a president's cabinet. They are chosen, and not by the executive, mind you. Corporations, NGOs, non-profits,

---

[196] Buchanan, "Court Clerk Kim Davis."

PACs, and a whole host of shadowy and not-so-shadowy organizations crawl out of the woodwork to place people where they are needed. Some groups are well known, such as the ironically named Anti-Defamation League of B'nai B'rith, to the only now infamous BlackRock, Inc., a semi-clandestine multibillion dollar firm, or Project for a New American Century (PNAC), once among the most powerful think tanks in the Beltway, and yet a name with which only a small fraction of Americans are familiar. Presumably, these powerful groups and individuals put certain elites behind the levers of power because of an alignment between them. Organizations will appoint likeminded individuals. Furthermore, they can revoke appointment recommendations as well.

The question of government organizations, especially the security agencies, acting as independent entities in and of themselves—without a necessary central brain or leader like a Portuguese man o' war—creates an interesting chicken-or-egg problem that is unanswered by the Cathedral theory of power. To explain this requires a history lesson. A little-known fact is that the postmodern craze in academia, media, and the culture at large can claim its popularization in America to the forerunner of the CIA, the OSS.[197] Similar ideology, or the precursors to such ideology, can also be traced to the CIA-funded Congress for Cultural Freedom.[198] It seems that much of the evil in this world can be traced back to American spooks and the small remainder from foreign ones, but I digress. After the Second World War, the OSS contracted the Frankfurt School philosopher Herbert Marcuse to study the psychology of the political right, hoping never to have to face the threat of fascism again.[199] At the time, the Frankfurt intellectuals, open Marxists, were teaching in American public universities, having chosen Columbia and Berkeley as their place of exile from the Nazi regime, nearly all of them being Jewish refugees.

Would this not prove that the bureaucratic organizations like the OSS/CIA are the true holders of power? This postulation does not

---

[197] Jeffries, "The Frankfurt School: A Timeline."
[198] Harris, *The CIA and the Congress for Cultural Freedom in the Early Cold War: The Limits of Making Common Cause* (London: Routledge, Taylor & Francis Group, 2018).
[199] Kirchheimer et al., *Secret Reports on Nazi Germany*.

pass the smell test, as "responsible" and "in control" are two completely different matters with different implications. The CIA is certainly at least in part responsible for many social trends, subliminal messaging, and the guiding of the culture in a negative direction.[200] However, the CIA and the greater United States intelligence community are not truly in control. The early CIA was, and to some extent still is, notorious for being an irresponsible, unaccountable, and immoral branch of government whose blunders and evildoing are a whole other can of worms.[201] It is no surprise then that they would allow such a radioactive substance as critical theory to poison the American experience. The CIA notion also does not explain *why* the Frankfurt School intellectuals had to be supported in the first place. Why was it that radical leftism, even more radical than FDR's normalization of modern left-wing politics, was rising in popularity in the postwar years, necessitating clandestine intervention?

Like Big Tech corporations and the Cathedral institutions, it is easy to be misled by the undoubtable influence garnered by the state security apparatus. Only by being in control of these entities is the true ruling elite capable of using legitimate force, multi-billion-dollar clandestine operations against their enemies, and multi-trillion-dollar military operations. Through the CIA, the ruling elite is able to influence society; through the FBI, they are able to crack-down on dissidents and rival elites who wander off the plantation; through the State Department, entire nations can be brought to heel under the elite. And yet we have yet to figure out who the true top of the pyramid consists of.

The CIA, FBI, NSA, and State Department, among others, are certainly a *tool* for power. However, no one asks the big question, which is "*cui bono*?" Who benefits from putting such-and-such a psychopath in so-and-so position? Surely someone does. The Cathedral usually benefits, as politics and society almost always move in their direction. The house might not win every game, but play enough and it is a statistical impossibility that you beat the casino. However, even when there is little or no grassroots

---

[200] Carpenter, "How the National Security State."
[201] Gross, "The CIA's Secret Quest."

pushback, the Cathedral *does not* always win. Say what you will about the inconsistencies of the Brahmin class in America, but Noam Chomsky and his sycophants emphatically did not support the Iraq War, nor did they support the bank bailouts in the aftermath of the 2007–2008 financial crisis.[202] The Cathedral has predictive power, but it isn't perfect. To advance further through this web of lies, we must follow the money.

III

To claim that business is in control isn't a new notion. It is so obvious a factor of power that across the political spectrum, only the most die-hard capitalist apologists see nothing wrong with the outcome and rational conclusion of the not-so-free market capitalist system, known in political jargon as the neoliberal order. Despite this seeming-consensus among critics, both sides of the political establishment, regardless of their professed ideology, are proponents of neoliberalism. The left supports global interconnectivity, free trade, open borders, and open markets, while the right wing operates on a hyper business-friendly, ultra-capitalist model which necessitates the same globalism and open borders as the left, to the chagrin of their voter base. While there are many problems with this system, problems that the average conservative unfortunately looks over in analysis due to the reactionary impulse against socialist doctrine, here we will focus on the consequences in the world of political power which has been affected by the free market; specifically, by powerful individuals, corporations, and other organizations who have often benefitted through the quasi-laissez faire economic system.

So far, we have gone through a multitude of entities and found that their respective power alone cannot be explained as the true source of control which can explain how the rest of the apparatus works. Neither the State Department nor the elected official gains much power through their position—or at least, as much as it would seem at first glance. The sad reality is these people are all

---

[202] See Chomsky, "Full Transcript." And Chomsky, "Wars, Bailouts, and Elections."

employees, and they all know it. But by whom are they employed? Simply, everyone in government is a slave to a system greater than themselves. Those who deny this truth are quickly neutralized.[203] Special interests exist on a plane of political existence higher than the politician; i.e. the government has power, but the corporate world is ultimately the one who decides where that power is targeted. While it is true that Big Tech is a part of this network, social media and other similar platforms are hardly the most influential groups in terms of directly exerting political will for the sake of profit. Rather, as was shown earlier, these companies are only important insofar as they play the role of a truly renewable energy source for other groups to leech off of for their own sake. Big tech, for the most part, is a hostage to the system, even if oftentimes a willing one.

Corporations and the ultra-wealthy are powerful. There is no way to get around this. Campaign finance laws or not, they will find a way to wiggle their way into the halls of power. Firstly, and most obviously, they exert their power through buying off politicians. There is a multitude of ways of doing this. Money can create PACs and Super PACs which indirectly fund political causes. They can create fundraisers and use their prestige and wealth, along with the prestige and wealth of their friends, to create war chests for their preferred politicians. And these are only the most outward methods of political finance.[204]

Money can also buy think tanks, political, social, cultural, etc. organizations which can have major meta-political impact. This includes the Cathedral organs. For example, if some so-called "philanthropist" wants to promote mass immigration into the US for the purpose of driving down wages and driving up profits in his company, there is nothing stopping him from buying politicians, think tanks, NGOs, and even universities via simple positive/negative reinforcement through the dollar. These

---

[203] Consider how retaliation against whistleblowers would seem to be the norm and not the exception: Melissa Goodman et al., "Disavowed: The Government's Unchecked Retaliation."
[204] Take the supposedly incorruptible Alexandria Ocasio-Cortez, who was given a $35,000 ticket to the Met Gala. Presumably someone paid for that ticket. Expensive dinners are perhaps the most notorious type of under the table *quid pro quo* in the political world. Nelson and Brufke, "AOC Slapped with Ethics Complaint."

universities teach generations of future elites, these NGOs lobby governments, and these think tanks pick the president's cabinet. Ultimately, it was a small clique of intellectuals and philanthropists who guided the Bush presidency into the Iraq War, due to their predilection toward Israel.[205]

An example of the power of money in American politics is the famous "military–industrial complex," made up of a multitude of major well known military contract companies such as Lockheed-Martin, Boeing, Raytheon, Northrup-Grumman, General Dynamics, L3, and many others collectively worth many trillions of dollars. It is their God-given right (apparently) to bribe the government via campaign donations, and is it any surprise that they use this to advocate for war, militarist policies, larger "defense" budgets, and hawkish elected and appointed government officials?[206] It is obvious then why the US has such a hawkish foreign policy and by far the largest (and among the most inefficient, as seen in Afghanistan, even before the Taliban takeover) military budget on Earth, outspending all the other great powers combined. This policy is, of course, completely compatible with the intellectual Cathedral and think tank hegemony between the neoconservatives on the right and the imperialistic proselytizing strand of liberalism that now most properly describes the Globalist American Empire. Before the imperialism of the modern left, the military–industrial complex was also consistent with the similar virus of the Wilsonian millenarian project, which met its demise in Vietnam and was replaced by the New Left liberalism that we have today.

Big pharma is another name that is thrown around. Quite rightly, the finger points to these crooks as the source of the problem of the medical industry and its infamously high prices in the United States. Perhaps the most significant factor in the Medicare problem in the US is not the fact that the US relies on a privatized (though less and less so) medical coverage system, but that the medical corporations lobby the government to limit the amount of doctors artificially, driving down the supply and increasing the demand for medical

---

[205] I am of course referring to the neoconservatives, most of whom are Jewish Zionists (with a minority of heretical Christian Zionists), who are responsible for the "special relationship" between the US and Israel.
[206] Dan Auble, "Capitalizing on Conflict."

care.[207] It would be foolish to believe that these shady characters are not the true drafters of any and all healthcare legislation. Furthermore, the medical industry has made many billions of dollars off of the COVID-19 vaccine and lobbied the government to prevent the American people from having the ability to sue in cases of the rushed vaccine having negative side effects such as paralysis, death, and heart problems.[208] The media might be pressuring the public to take the "vax," but who is it that's pressuring the media? Is the Cathedral in power, or is it the money that talks? Considering that the major networks are all sponsored by Pfizer, the main vaccine peddling corporation, the latter seems more likely.[209]

When it comes to the health of Americans, the food and farming lobby is also a major influence. Much of what is wrong with the country today can be traced back to the major food producers. Far from the family milk farm that we imagine when we think of a farm, the true producers of what we eat and drink are food factories, where the health of the product (plants and animals) and the consumer are usually ignored.[210] There's good reason for the near-extinction of the family farm. It is by design. Lobbyists and the FDA work hand in hand to write regulations which are nearly impossible for small, natural, organic, healthy food producers to keep up with.[211] The FDA is also sure to use an outdated food pyramid which prioritizes profitable foods that aren't necessarily healthy in such large portions, such as carbohydrates.[212] The death tax, intended to

---

[207] There is a similar phenomenon in an artificial shortage of doctors. "Because the number of residencies is tantamount to the final number of doctors, the federal government has enormous leverage over the number of new physicians that enter medicine each year."
"But the number of new residencies for which the federal government pays has not budged in twenty years. In 1997, Congress passed the Balanced Budget Act, a bipartisan effort to cut back on spending. The act put a cap on the number of annual residencies CMS would support, and froze the funding at 1996 levels." Benjamin Wofford, "We're Devastatingly Short on Doctors. Why Doesn't the US Just Make More?," Washingtonian, April 13, 2020, https://www.washingtonian.com/2020/04/13/were-short-on-healthcare-workers-why-doesnt-the-u-s-just-make-more-doctors/.
[208] Liu, "Pfizer to Become $100B Behemoth."; Sigalos, "You Can't Sue Pfizer or Moderna."
[209] Nevradakis, "'Brought to You by Pfizer'."
[210] del Prado Alanes, "What Is Factory Farming?"
[211] See Salatin, *Everything I Want to Do Is Illegal.*
[212] See the 2020 film *Fat Fiction*

redistribute a percentage of wealth from the wills of the rich, has been used to force families to sell their farms, often in the family for generations, to large multinational corporations owned by investors who will never visit the farm and have no care for the health or livelihood of people who they see as cattle themselves.[213] The FDA, in partnership with both the food industry and Big Pharma, is perhaps the most notorious example of the famous "revolving door" lobbying scheme in which executives and high ranking bureaucrats tap in and out of the ring to change the regulatory environment to suit their patron industry's needs.[214] However, this phenomenon exists across the board.

Big tech can be mentioned again, not because of any specific influence, but simply as a corporate interest. Politics aside, it is in the interest of Big Tech companies to maintain their monopoly in their given field. Even if YouTube was still apolitical, or Twitter, or any other platform, it would have every incentive to attempt to eliminate any alternative, either by tugging at the strings which the alternative relies on such as payment processors or internet service providers, or by simply buying out the smaller subsidiaries. Microsoft is an example of a company that has bought a large portion of the tech companies, such as Skype and Mojang. Facebook, Amazon, Apple, and Google (FAAG) are some of the largest public offerings on the stock market and among the biggest lobbying spenders in Washington.[215] Power to censor or no power to censor, FAAG can drop cash on elections to get what they want. For the time being, people like Mark Zuckerberg have nothing to worry about, no matter how many times Republicans in Congress feign righteous anger and subpoena them to the Capitol. Even when Musk was considering acquiring Twitter, the reaction by the government was to investigate him for unrelated business dealings.[216]

Does this mean that we have triangulated true power in the form of business interests? Not necessarily. While profit and greed are among the greatest motivating factors known to man, they aren't *the* greatest factor. Since what James Burnham dubbed "the managerial

---

[213] "Estate Taxes Are a Threat."
[214] Lupkin, "A Look at How."
[215] Romm, "Amazon, Facebook, Other Tech Giants."
[216] DaSilva, "Elon Musk Is Being Investigated."

revolution" of the twentieth century, even corporations are very much like the government, in that they are made up of a massive bureaucracy.[217] Furthermore, the people who run the companies, such as CEOs, presidents, VPs, CFOs, COOs, and other board members are often not the owners of said company, and even if they do have a stake In the corporation, they are not the owners of a substantial percentage of the company due to the company's sheer size.[218] Thus, even the corporate rulers are not necessarily shareholders with something to lose, but high-level bureaucrats, which is to say, employees.

While the corporate theory seems the most obvious, it actually holds less predictive power than the Cathedral theory. Often, those who defend the corporate theory, often those of the left, will claim that corporations pursue the appearance of virtue signaling due to cynical profit seeking. However, as is clear from the resulting loss of millions or even billions of dollars in revenue by many corporations and even Christian nonprofits and church organizations pursuing these policies, this explanation does not hold water. There is a motive which transcends profit that we have so far failed to triangulate.

IV

While business funnels the majority of money in politics, there is also something to say about non-government organizations, a catchall term which includes nonprofits, charities, ideological organizations, think tanks, and political associations specifically built for lobbying and activism. This includes everything from Black Lives Matter to the Catholic Church. Business may control the majority of capital, but the influence of invested, motivated, and often fanatical interests that are not necessarily always tied to business should not be underestimated.

While the systems of thought control known as the Cathedral, comprising the media, academia, and the K–12 system are also

---

[217] Burnham, *The Managerial Revolution*.
[218] Jensen and Murphy, "CEO Incentives."

technically NGOs, their influence is much more drastic in nature than others, in the same way that Big Tech or the CIA is not just a business or intelligence institution, respectively, but a source of power which leaks and can be tapped into by other actors and institutions.[219] NGOs act in a similar manner, not as simply an NGO but rather as an outlet of mass psychosis. Consider the educational unions.[220] The National Education Association is the most powerful union in America, being made up of public school teachers.[221] Their main goal is to protect these educators, which has made it difficult to fire teachers, thus reducing the quality of education in the infamous American education system.[222] They also push for ever-increasing teacher pay and benefits, resulting in exorbitant costs to the taxpayer for increasingly poor child outcomes.[223] They are a major lobby for the Democratic Party, and it is no surprise that teachers vote overwhelmingly for the Democrats.[224] It is notable that the NEA as well as the American Federation of Teachers are ardent defenders of critical race theory being practiced in classrooms, despite overwhelming condemnation from parents.[225] Furthermore, the teachers' unions advocate for mass migration and other leftist items which have nothing to do with teaching.[226] With the toxic culture created in schools by the unions, alternative viewpoints are less and less to be found. Unsurprisingly, the university lobby is no different. The University of California is a top donor in national elections to the Democratic Party.[227]

There is also the Israeli-Jewish lobby, which advocates on behalf of the state of Israel, and to a lesser extent the Diaspora Jewish people in the United States and around the globe. Similar to the

---

[219] Technically media are usually characterized as businesses, outside of a few outliers, while public sector K-12 is part of the government. However, the ties of the K-12 system with unions and other NGOs makes K-12 particularly more relevant to the subject of NGOs than other bureaucracies, which as we have already established, has relatively little unadulterated power.
[220] Hartney, "Teacher Union Power in California."
[221] Anderson, "30 Most Powerful Unions in America."
[222] Bovard, "Teachers Unions Have Always Been Terrible."
[223] Ibid.; "Teachers Unions."
[224] Burke, "Unions Double Down."
[225] Ibid.; Emmons, "BREAKING: Biden Admin Mobilizes FBI."
[226] "Immigration," American Federation of Teachers.
[227] "University of California," OpenSecrets.

military–industrial complex, they also tend to be war hawks, at least where the Middle East is concerned.[228] Thus, it is no coincidence that the Arab world is the focus of US military entanglements today. A destabilized Arab world is more often than not a safe Israel, at least as far as the lobby is concerned:

> The lobby ... includes think tanks ... as well as officials who work in universities and other research organizations. There are also dozens of pro-Israel PACs ready to funnel money to pro-Israel political candidates or to candidates whose opponents are deemed either insufficiently supportive of or hostile to Israel.... In 1997, when Fortune magazine asked members of Congress and their staffs to list the most powerful lobbies in Washington, AIPAC came in second.... A National Journal study in March 2005 reached a similar conclusion placing AIPAC in second place (tied with AARP) in Washington's "muscle rankings."[229]

The Israel lobby is largely responsible for the American foreign policy that has ended in much bloodshed for US forces in the region, especially young White men from the Midwest and Southern states.[230] The Beirut bombing in 1983 which killed 241 US military personnel as well as 58 French soldiers was caused by US forces being stationed in the area to aid Israel, while 9/11 was for the most part directly caused by Arab Muslim frustration with the American policy of all but unconditional support for Israel and Israeli treatment of the Palestinians, a hotbed issue for the entire Arab world to this day.[231] Jewish-Israeli lobby agents in the neoconservative movement, in correspondence with the highest levels of the Israeli government, fabricated evidence of WMDs in Iraq, taking advantage of the anti-Muslim sentiment in the US in the

---

[228] Alper and Cooperman, "10 Key Findings about Jewish Americans." Take how a "large majority of U.S. Jews (82%) say caring about Israel is either 'essential' or 'important' to what being Jewish means to them."
[229] Mearsheimer and Walt, The Israel Lobby and U.S. Foreign Policy.
[230] "American War and Military Operations Casualties: Lists and Statistics."
[231] "Bin Laden: Palestinian Cause Prompted 9/11."; "Full Text: Bin Laden's 'Letter to America.'"

aftermath of 9/11.[232] It was this evidence that was used to justify the 2003 Iraq War.[233]

The Israel lobby's influence on the US government forces the President, Congress, or both to actively go against official US policy when dealing with Israel, such as providing little or no punishment for using US-supplied weapons for war crimes and mass killing of civilians, the accumulation of an illegal WMD stockpile, and colonizing the occupied territories via illegal settlements. Furthermore, the lobby's influence causes explicit anti-US action by Israel to be swept under the rug, such as spy rings, the attempted bombing of the US embassy by Israeli agents in the Lavon Affair, the attack on the USS *Liberty* which killed 34 US Navy seamen, the likely stealing of American nuclear material for the sake of building their own illegal nuclear arsenal, the selling of American weapons and technology to China, and the aforementioned disinformation of WMDs in the early 2000s.[234] Under normal circumstances, many of these actions would be acts of war. However, due to the "special relationship" with our "greatest ally," they are ignored.

An extreme example of a lobby is Black Lives Matter, which uses not only money but political violence to obtain their goals. Like many nonprofits, BLM uses a brand name which sounds innocuous to goad the public into support. Through sympathizers in every institution, organizations like BLM are able to turn donations into a tithe for major companies who matter-of-factly factor in such contributions into their cost analysis.[235] This type of parasitic lobbying is the tendency of a plethora of nonprofit lawfare and supposed civil rights groups. Transgender and homosexual lobbying groups, the ADL (a Jewish lobby which is viciously anti-European), the SPLC (anti-White and pro-immigration), and a multitude of other groups have become so entrenched and institutionalized that they easily garner legitimacy, and are openly

---

[232] Chulov and Pidd, "Defector Admits to WMD Lies."
[233] "Full Text: Bush's Speech."
[234] "Jeffrey Epstein Was Blackmailing Politicians."; Roberts, "Surviving Sailors Break Their Silence"; Cohen, "Israel's Stolen Nuclear Materials."; "Report: Israel Passes U.S. Military Technology to China."
[235] McGregor and Jan, "Big Business Pledged."

used in collaboration with local, state, and federal governments.[236] While these groups have money to spare toward lobbying, they also affect government action via working as a mini-Cathedral by partnering with police departments, public schools, and corporations (notably with CRT lecturers being paid hundreds of thousands of dollars to speak to corporate boards on leftist issues).[237] Through subsidiary media, they slander dissidents and, due to their entrenched legitimacy, politicians and corporations either believe them or at least pretend to. Through networks in the left-wing sphere, these groups are able to organize astroturfed mass protests which are intended to break out into violence, intimidating businesses and individuals who might stand in their way, as well as legitimize the views of the powers that be, whoever they may be. The civil rights groups get notoriety, power, and even a little time to blow off some steam, while others in power benefit by silencing their political opposition. Black Lives Matter is only the newest iteration in a rich history in the US of astroturfed lobbying groups that Capitol Hill uses as a proxy for political violence and human capital.[238]

Think tanks are a major source of political influence as well. Consider, for instance, the Project for the New American Century, a Jewish neoconservative think tank and part of the Israel lobby which was highly influential in Republican Party politics of the 1990s and 2000s, despite the relative obscurity and unpopularity of their ideology among the Republican base. Indeed, no one outside the political elite calls himself a "neoconservative." As Sam Francis put it, "who can imagine a Marine wading ashore at Tarawa with *Reflections of a Neoconservative* in his pocket?"[239] This elite group architected the Iraq war, five years before it happened, in 1998.[240] Some, such as Paul Wolfowitz and Richard Perle, were Jewish-

---

[236] Hamilton, "30 To Watch, They Say."; Peinovich, "Leader of Jewish-Zionist Group."; Howard, *The Transgender–Industrial Complex*.
[237] Krikorian, "How Labeling My Organization."
[238] Such as the civil rights and anti-war movements.
[239] Francis, *Beautiful Losers*, 93.
[240] Vaa, "Project for the New American Century."

American Zionists, while others, such as the infamous John Bolton, seem to simply love war for its own sake.[241]

Other think tanks such as the Heritage Foundation (today perhaps the most influential think tank in Republican Party politics), the Hoover Institute, the American Enterprise Institute, and the Cato Institute seek to control the flow of information that is allowed within the Overton window of conservative politics. The Claremont Institute and the Federalist Society act as gatekeepers in conservative politics as to who may be eligible to be appointed toward a position in the judiciary, based on a fanatical and rigid fidelity to the *word* of the Constitution.[242] While not *necessarily* a negative, this prevents conservative activist judges from sitting on the bench who would be loyal to the *spirit* of the Constitution. This gives the left a monopoly on activist judges, who are notorious for their lack of fidelity to the spirit of the Constitution, which frequently crosses over into thinly veiled hostility against the original intent of the Founding Fathers, most demonstrably seen in the hatred that liberal lawyers have for the Second Amendment.

The Democratic Party and liberals also have think tanks, many of which are heavily funded by George Soros, such as Human Rights Watch, the Open Society Foundation, and the Bill Gates-funded Center for American Progress. Think tanks are able to present and legitimize ideas to the American political class, the media, and the public. Ideas outside the box that are not endorsed by a large think tank are usually considered "fringe" by polite society. Furthermore, think tanks and NGOs swap money like a casino with the Ford Foundation donating to Open Society who then funds Black Lives Matter, who then funnels money toward a CRT education program, whose founder will donate to the DNC, and so on and so forth.[243]

---

[241] However, like most establishment warmongers, Bolton has never desired to actually wage war firsthand. He used a student deferment during Vietnam to dodge the draft, and then after graduating college enlisted in the Air National Guard to avoid combat. These types invariably have the souls of merchants, not warriors.
[242] SCOTUS nominee Robert Bork epitomizes these types. Despite his supposed erudition, he claimed that he was unsure of the Ninth Amendment's meaning (which clearly protects the numerous un-enumerated rights reserved to the people), as if it had an inkblot over it that made interpretation impossible. He was not appointed.
[243] Gaspard, "Why Open Society."

Everyone, of course, gets a big tax write-off for all this "nonprofit philanthropy," by the way.[244]

As seen by the incestuous relationship between supposed *non-government* organizations and the government, these NGOs can often be seen as unofficial or unacknowledged government entities. They are the "black ops" of political action, as the government cannot be blamed for government-sponsored action by proxy. No different than with corporations, the government will outsource political action to these groups to legally circumvent the law. Certain NGO entities are openly part of the fold of the US government, especially the most notorious and flagrant groups such as the ADL, SPLC, BLM, Antifascist Action (Antifa), Hope Not Hate (in the case of the U.K.), and AIPAC, among others. Thus, it is helpful in understanding current events and the American regime to imagine institutionalized NGOs as government entities.

Are NGOs in power, then? Not all NGOs are even institutionally supported, let alone in control. The pro-firearm lobby is, of course, institutionally suppressed, although the NRA has come to operate as controlled opposition to undermine the more strident alternatives, such as the GOA or 2A Society.[245] Some NGOs are more powerful than others. The World Economic Forum is technically an organization that is not part of the government. Is a cabal of organizations an NGO? When we think of NGOs, we think of large but national or sub-national-scale entities and, in these terms, as said previously, institutionalized NGOs can be seen as no more than a branch of government. Furthermore, the government does not hold true power, and so these normal NGOs cannot be said to hold the actual power.

NGOs also don't appear out of nowhere. It requires capital injection to get them going, whether that is from corporations, the government, or other NGOs. It is clear that the major corporations pay tithes to institutional NGOs, and one might go so far as to say

---

[244] Piper, "The Charitable Deduction."

[245] It should be duly noted that the NRA never donated a single cent to Kyle Rittenhouse's legal defense fund, despite their vast financial resources. However, they did tweet the text of the Second Amendment shortly *after* his acquittal was announced, albeit without even saying his name. With NGO friends like these, who needs enemies like the FBI, BLM, and Antifa?

that they are being extorted. However, as is clear from the inability of groups like Antifa and BLM to organize when the elite does not wish them to, such as after the Kyle Rittenhouse verdict, or Blacks protesting COVID lockdown restrictions, it is clear that corporate media and social media are much more influential in creating political violence than the NGOs themselves.

V

Now, it is time to temporarily put on our tin foil hats, because it is impossible to talk about power in the United States, and indeed all over the world, without discussing genuine conspiratorial national and international organizations, as well as their out-in-the-open plans, nefarious or otherwise. These reside on a spectrum that ranges from what we could call out in the open on one side, represented by the World Economic Forum, to the highly secret and shady, such as the people who lurked around with the late sex trafficker Jeffery Epstein.

The World Economic Forum is most prescient today due to the "Great Reset" agenda which was rolled out at the Davos conference in 2021. The famous line that "you will own nothing and you will be happy" rang shockwaves around the world in reaction to the flagrant openness of the elite agenda to institute a neo-feudal order of serfdom for the vast majority of people on Earth. Such a statement would have been regarded as an Alex Jones talking point by the masses the day before the conference, and indeed some still believe the Great Reset to be an unfounded conspiracy theory due to the mass psychosis created by the Cathedral media. It is doubtless that, not only is this plan popular among the elite, but that it is already beginning, as evinced by the push toward a renter economy, not only of houses and leased cars, but even of appliances such as washers and dryers. The investment company BlackRock, which manages nine trillion dollars in assets, plays a part in this saga through purchase of rental properties, pricing families out of the ability to afford a home, often by offering double digit percentage points above asking price at auction.[246] This is only one large, notorious company participating in a common practice. Furthermore, the COVID-19 lockdowns were perhaps the most obvious example of collusion and conspiracy, unless it's a coincidence that the end result was a) millions of small businesses closing down to be replaced by mega corporations, b) the normalization of antisocial behavior, staying indoors, and the destruction of brick and mortar retail to the benefit of Amazon and similar package-to-you companies, and c) impossibly high stock market values benefiting the rich, despite rampant unemployment and a completely thrashed economy.

While it is an old conspiracy dating back to at least the 1940s, the long march through the institutions by the Frankfurt School philosophers is far from irrelevant today. Curtis Yarvin's main theory was the Cathedral theory of the control over information. However, the university system, K–12, and media didn't have as much independent power and weren't as malicious and subversive before the arrival of the Frankfurt mafia to the US. The ability of these characters to rise to the top was not an accident. They had help through state sponsorship by the OSS in the 1940s and later on they were helped by the rising Jewish hegemony in academia.[247] This hegemony in the 1920s allowed for the pseudoscientific Boasian school of anthropology and Freud's psychoanalysis to take the intellectual world by storm due to a history of intellectual prowess of European or American Jews in subjects ranging from the aforementioned to the hard sciences, plus a cunning in-group preference which resulted in intellectual nepotism that allowed ideas to gain more popularity than their merit deserved.[248]

This crack group of intellectuals inspired and was inspired by radicals who advocated for a "long march through the institutions" such as Antonio Gramsci, Saul Alinsky, and Rudi Dutscke.[249] The KGB was also notorious for aiding these types in other countries such as India, and the KGB defector Yuri Bezmenov's testimony to

---

[246] Creitz, "BlackRock, Other Investment Firms."
[247] Jeffries, "The Frankfurt School: A Timeline."
[248] See Cochran et al., "Natural History of Ashkenazi Intelligence." and MacDonald, *Culture of Critique.*
[249] Kilpatrick, "The Long March."

America implied that Russian intelligence was working an active psychological operation on the US during the civil rights era, when subversive ideas such as those of the Frankfurt School were rampant, and many secret communists were embedded in Hollywood and the State Department.[250]

Furthermore, a large number of prominent wars that the US has been in were caused by conspiracy, or at least heavy collusion. The Mexican War was caused by a plan to goad the Mexican Army into firing on US forces in disputed territory along the Rio Grande, giving President Polk the excuse to invade and accomplish Manifest Destiny by seizing the Southwestern states. The Spanish War was caused by the famous "yellow journalism" of the media that falsely accused Spain of causing the destruction of the USS *Maine* by mining Havana Harbor. However, it is likely that the boiler of the ship simply exploded. This allowed the US to seize Guam, the Philippines, and Cuba. The US invasion of Iraq was justified in large part by a search for WMDs that did not exist.[251]

The US entered the Great War in large part due to the sinking of the Lusitania, a passenger ship loaded with arms from the supposedly neutral US to the Allies, long before the Zimmerman Telegram.[252] The Germans warned that the ship would be sunk due to its cargo of weapons, but this was ignored by the US, who used the passengers as human shields and then human sacrifices to gin up pro-war attitudes among the populace.[253] President Wilson ran as an anti-war candidate and would need the support of the electorate to go to war.[254] In the Second World War, a similar situation occurred in which President Roosevelt was supplying the Allies and agitating the Japanese with trade restrictions while claiming to be neutral.[255]

---

[250] This communist conspiracy was of course the catalyst for Joe McCarthy's House Un-American Activities Committee. Now, the Cathedral education system and media paint McCarthy as a kook, and "McCarthysim" today is synonymous for "witch-hunting," despite the fact that most of the accused were later found to be KGB assets after the fall of the USSR. See Roberts, "McCarthy Was Right."

[251] Chulov and Pidd, "Defector Admits to WMD Lies."

[252] Buchanan, "Behind the Sinking of the Lusitania."

[253] Ibid.

[254] "He Kept Us out of War."

[255] See the Lend-Lease Act; "Japan, China, the United States and the Road to Pearl Harbor."

It would also be naive to believe that elites who often meet at young ages at elite universities such as Yale and Harvard do not connive with each other for personal gain. After all, collaboration through networks is precisely the point of attending such a university. It likely has a part to play in how an ingrate like George W. Bush, member of the Skull and Bones secret society at Yale, could become the president, following in the footsteps of his father and fellow Bonesman.[256] Many presidents have also been Freemasons.[257] Other rich and powerful people are members of other groups such as Bohemian Grove and the Bilderberg Group.[258] There are doubtlessly numerous groups evermore secret than the former. While it would be unwise to get lost in the woods on unconfirmed theory, the Wikileaks Pizzagate scandal, the disturbing art of the Podesta brothers, the Haitian orphanage connection, and the vast network of household names involved in Satanism and sexual trafficking does not exactly prevent the imagination from running free.[259]

It would seem that shadowy organizations have copied an old technique of elite university hazing in which an initiate would be forced to do something incriminating to guarantee loyalty to a group, which could then theoretically use the information as blackmail. That ensures that the initiate cannot reveal the doings of those with whom he is in the group, as they could do the same to him. In the case of Jeffery Epstein, a man who had connections to Israeli intelligence and the rich and powerful of the US, celebrities, business magnates, and politicians would be offered underage girls.[260] The interaction would be recorded and the subject would ever be a pawn. However, we may never know exactly who Epstein worked for, as he allegedly committed suicide in jail while the cameras in his cell were "malfunctioning."[261]

There is also much truth to the Cold War conspiracies. During this time, many radical activists and organizations were funded,

---

[256] Cain and Borden, "20 US Presidents."
[257] Ibid.
[258] Blumberg, "The Bohemian Club."
[259] Smithee, "Pizzagate."; Kassam and Powell, "'We'll Steal Your Soul.'"
[260] Ky, "Jeffery Epstein Was a Mossad Spy."; Howard et al., *Epstein: Dead Men Tell No Tales*.
[261] Voytko, "Surveillance Video."

trained, and otherwise aided by international communism through the Russian KGB, the Cuban DGI, and the Polish UB.[262] Benefactors of these agencies included groups such as the Weather Underground and various Black revolutionary groups such as the Black Liberation Front, which attempted to blow up the Statue of Liberty in 1965 with foreign-supplied explosives smuggled through Canada.[263] The communists of course intended on weakening the US, and they succeeded; the death of Western civilization will surely be in no small part due to the contribution of Warsaw Pact intelligence agencies subverting Western institutions through these spy rings.

Yuri Bezmenov, a famous KGB defector, famously laid down the roadmap as to how his former agency would subvert and "demoralize" foreign governments.[264] The communist world would use Cuba as a forward operating base for operations in the US and the Americas, where they would train American radicals, often students, in how to commit acts of terrorism or enhance political riots in their home country.[265] Radicals were trained in camps and supplied weapons and thousands of dollars in cash to contribute to their operations.[266] In Europe, similar occurrences were documented such as with Baader–Meinhof in Germany and the Red Brigades in Italy, among many other groups.[267]

While this is a fine history lesson on the Cold War, it goes deeper. The USSR died in 1991, but the domestic subversive groups and terrorist organizations that it spawned did not. An idea does not need a state. People in the Weather Underground and Black Liberation Front didn't fizzle away like the communist-controlled governments and their intelligence apparatuses did. Rather, they simply went underground. These revolutionaries and their progeny are your professors, your journalists, your corporate executives, politicians, judges, military officers, bureaucrats, and FBI agents.[268]

---

[262] "Fact Sheet: Cuban Support for Terrorism."
[263] Mitchell, "The Journal of Counterterrorism," 30–34.
[264] Offensive Freedom, "KGB defector Yuri."; Nicholas Marshall, "FULL INTERVIEW."
[265] Seger, "Left-Wing Extremism."
[266] "Fact Sheet: Cuban Support for Terrorism."
[267] Lockwood, "How the Soviet Union Transformed Terrorism."
[268] See "Students for a Democratic Society (SDS)" on Influence Watch.

You might know of one by the name of Barack Obama.[269] Oh, how ironic that these students of domestic terror organizations, funded by the KGB, will call you, yes *you*, dear reader, a terrorist, simply for questioning such an unenviable situation. As George Carlin said, "It's a big club, and you ain't in it!"

VI

While Yarvin's theory of political power is doubtlessly relevant and has predictive power, he underestimates the influence of the "other powers," namely business, NGOs, conspiratorial groups, and the government. With this context, we can get to the bottom of the system that has controlled the US since at least the ascendance of the New Left in the 1960s. Needless to say, those who most people consider to be in charge, namely our various elected officials, are in reality puppets dancing within the smoke and mirrors of a magician's routine. Rather, there is a sandwich effect, similar to that described by Samuel Francis, which is squeezing the American people from two sides simultaneously.

We can accurately characterize two separate but intertwined elites: a right elite and a left elite. The right elite is characterized by business interests (i.e. the economic right) while the left elite is characterized by social progressivism (i.e. the social left) under the tutelage of the Cathedral, NGOs, and the bureaucracy. Both sides utilize conspiracies (the preparation of the GWOT on the right and the 2016 election Russia hoax on the left). While they focus on different aspects of politics, they are both aligned. However, while in theory there should be a relative multitude of disagreements, they usually ignore them for a harmony on the major issues. The left focuses on social issues that coincidentally help big business, while big business panders to the progressive left, or at least allows them to run amuck, cutting their losses that they can surely afford if a brick flies through their corporate window.

The elite left has already been explained for the most part in the last chapter. To recap, the Cathedral controls most, if not all, means

---

[269] Klein and Elliott, *The Manchurian President.*

of information and intelligence by their monopoly on the university system, K–12, and mainstream media. As a result, the default message which holds the most *a priori* acceptance by both the laity and the high priests is the information from the TV man and subversive academics. This results in a constant uphill battle with legitimacy. The K–12 and university systems act as gatekeepers on legitimate knowledge, forming a gauntlet through which prospective private and public bureaucrats must run if they wish to have any chance of success in the rat race. The K–12 system educates future elites in their most impressionable years, while academia acts as the sophist gaslight factory in which they can prove "*scientifically*" that up is down and vice versa. The media serves as a retainer to condition the New Man, preventing escape and free thought. Indeed, NPR and NYT don't tell you the truth; *they tell you what is convenient for the prospective elite to truly believe.* If you want a prestigious job, the most important thing to do is believe what prestigious outlets say. Furthermore, the Cathedral institutions act as an intellectual bioweapon, attacking the commons through memetics which are difficult to extinguish and are self-perpetuating. It is easier to stamp out people than an idea.

The Cathedral is a whip for the elite left, influencing thought on foreign and domestic policy, philosophy, and *modus operandi* in general. However, it also influences the elite right in the business world. Major companies have been drifting to the left for decades, and during the Trump presidency, the last vestiges of the elite right who even bothered still supporting the Republicans, such as Walmart and McDonald's, threw in the towel and went "woke," embracing an ideology that even Obama rejected in the early years of his presidency.[270,271] This may seem counterintuitive, until one realizes that the supposed "leftism" of the modern left is in reality just radical liberalism, a worldview that is precisely aligned with the neoliberal late capitalism of the American corporate world.

---

[270] See Brown, "Woke Walmart Trains Staffers." and Dave M., "My McDonald's."

[271] As of the Second Edition, the strategy has somewhat changed. Rather than corporate America "going woke," they are joining the Right, but bringing with them many of the same subversive ideas that they always had, such as transhumanism and techno-feudalism. This phenomenon has been dubbed "putting the woke away" (i.e. boiling the frog).

Company after company, boardroom after boardroom fall to the societal cancer and they lose little. In fact, the negative effect on efficiency that diversity introduces into the business world is counteracted by the inability of diverse workforces to unionize effectively.[272] Women's liberation means more workers and more hours, as does mass migration. Higher minimum wage simply means small businesses are run out of business, unable to afford the wages demanded not by the employees but by the government. On top of all of this, the government uses carrots and sticks to ensure corporate compliance through DEI initiatives. .

On the other hand, the elite right also affects the elite left to an extent. The left will always advocate for some sort of communism or hardcore socialism, at least on paper. However, as has been shown by the complete inconsistency between classical Marxism and the political schizophrenia that passes for political philosophy that we see today, the left has completely abandoned any semblance of traditional leftist idealism characterized by orthodox Marxism, the anticolonialism of Vietnam and Angola, and the union movements in the West. This lack of true ideals and an embrace of what seems to just be childish consequentialism and striving after power for power's sake has led the left to align even intellectually with those who would normally be their greatest enemy, indeed the enemy of humanity. I am of course referring to big business and conspiratorial conniving by the ultra-rich in the aforementioned secret societies and international forums.

This is not hard to prove. It is not difficult to find supposed libertarian socialists, communists, anarchists, and other aligned ideological factions marching in lockstep with the most heinous mega-corporations, internationalist governments, and NGOs.[273] Across the globe, from the Irish pro-free speech protesters outside Google headquarters in Dublin, to Pride parades in the US sponsored by JPMorgan Chase and recruited at by the CIA, the

---

[272] See Peterson, "Amazon-Owned Whole Foods." and Taylor, "Diversity or Standards."

[273] The left has time and time again betrayed their supposed ideals. Whether it may be pacifist types advocating for total war with Russia or supremacy of Big Pharma during the COVID lockdowns, it is abundantly clear that the modern left abides by their revealed preference for simple will to power.

grassroots right, center, and even common-sense left can expect to be attacked by left-wing maniacs, with the protection of the elite right and left represented by business interests, the state, NGOs, and the media.[274] In the reverse, corporations aid the elite left by censoring, de-platforming, and un-personing their mutual political enemies. Clearly, the days of left-wing protests like those against the WTO in 1999 or even Occupy Wall Street are relegated to the dustbin of history.

On social issues, it is no coincidence that the elite right and left are in agreement on heinous ideas such as the transvestite transition industry.[275] The left aid themselves and the economic right through legitimizing insane ideas, fabricating studies in favor of the chemical castration of children.[276] The left help themselves because they have an obsession with the genitals of children, while Big Pharma and the insurance industry gets to cash out on expensive operations and drugs, using people and even children as human guinea pigs for testing harmful hormones which would be otherwise difficult to test on voluntary subjects.[277] The government also wins because castrated non-binary eunuchs are the perfect janissary class, which does the bidding of all of the above for free. We see this in the incredibly high rate of these types in state-sponsored paramilitary organizations such as Antifa and Black Lives Matter.[278] Furthermore, on paper the economy will improve due to lessened birthrates, which is used as a justification to increased immigration to make up the population difference, leading to higher immigration. Less babies and more adult-aged immigrants means more workers and consumers per capita. The government further benefits from population replacement as native US citizens rightfully feel entitled to a say in the goings-on in government, while in contrast immigrants are simply grateful to be

---

[274] Bova, "J.P. Morgan Is Celebrating Pride."; Chibbaro, "CIA Hands out 'Gay' Recruitment Brochure."
[275] Fox News even hired Caitlyn Jenner as a contributor and commentator.
[276] Howard, *Transgender-Industrial Complex.*
[277] Ibid.
[278] These groups are de facto sponsored, given how law enforcement is purposefully ineffective against them. See van de Camp, "Know Your Enemy: Antifa."

in America. Thus, immigrants are more complacent.[279] Women's liberation also aids the economy by lowering birthrates and increasing workers per capita.

The COVID lockdowns are another example of an issue that would normally seem to be counterproductive to all parties involved, and yet has been embraced all around. Indeed, the left began as the most ardent defenders of an open economy, while the grassroots right embraced a short lockdown on immigration and a shutdown of international traffic, especially from China.[280] The left attacked this as racism, and politicians like Nancy Pelosi even encouraged Americans to go out and interact with Chinese people as much as possible.[281] What a far cry late 2019 was from the summer of 2020. The opposite is true now, of course. Big business embraces lockdowns as it runs their small business competitors into bankruptcy, Big Pharma makes billions of dollars from taxpayer-funded subsidies along with surging antidepressant sales, liberal foot soldiers are able to live out their fantasies of harassing whomever they believe to be their inferiors, left-wing organizing continues while conservative protests are selectively suppressed due to being "super spreader events," and the media get the ability to control the narrative and stamp dissidents into submission by hounding any citizen or organization into compliance through a combination of programming, peer pressure, and coordination with the state, liberal foot soldiers, and corporations.[282] Academia has also gained greater influence as science-worship, if we can even call this New Age cult "science," has become the new mandated civic religion. Of course, like with the medieval Catholic Church, the laity is not allowed to interpret theology. That job is reserved for the legions of sycophantic high priests in the media and academia. Those rogue priests who preach heresy are excommunicated. An orthodox CNA is more reliable than a heterodox surgeon according to this strict emphasis on dogma.

---

[279] Though it seems that when immigrants become involved in politics, they are al-most exclusively far-left, such as Ocasio-Cortez and Ilhan Omar, with the exceptions mostly being of the tepid "free markets and nation of immigrants" RINO variety.
[280] Houck, "Open Borders Caused the Covid-19 Pandemic."
[281] "Nancy Pelosi Visits San Francisco's Chinatown."; "Italian Residents Hug Chinese People."
[282] Malkin, "Covid-19, Catholics and Illegal Alien Charities."

The state is perhaps the biggest winner in the COVID fiasco. Currently, the state is working on making it impossible to even exist without the vaccine, all the while conditioning the masses into normalizing a Soviet-esque "snitch culture" and dehumanization via mask mandates, which are proven to make people more compliant to orders and more willing to dehumanize their fellow man.[283] Clearly, the supposedly "anti-authoritarian" and "watchdog" left has always been a power trip grift. As long as the corporations, media, and state allow them to feel important and superior, everything else flies out the window. Through this, the elite right and left have essentially addressed the longstanding grievance between themselves over the issue of authoritarianism. The right gets just about everything it wants while the left obtains some influence and the ability to indulge in lowly power fantasies.

Perhaps the greatest contention between elite left and right that has been settled is the subject of war. Traditionally, the New Left of post-1968 America has been anti-war. On the other hand, the military–industrial complex is obviously in favor of wars. There has been some middle ground, such as the overlap of Jewish support for the Democratic Party and neoconservative elements in both parties, which supports a heavy-handed approach to defending Israel from its neighbors in the Middle East.[284] Basically all Republicans and many Democrats, including most of their representation in the Senate, supported the 2003 Iraq War.[285] In recent years, in reaction to Trump's anti-war version of Zionism, the traditionally anti-war elite left have become much more sympathetic to foreign intervention. Interestingly, this is *despite* a growing anti-Israel streak within the new left.[286] Antifa members volunteer for communist Kurdish militias, the media cry crocodile tears over Trump's attempted pullout of the region, and everyone pretends to believe that Syrian president Bashar al-Assad is an evil tyrant who

---

[283] "Masks Are Dehumanizing."
[284] Giraldi, "America's Jews Are Driving America's Wars."; Kampeas, "Meet the Leading Jewish."
[285] Jonathan Cohn, "Iraq War at 15."
[286] "Some 2022 Left-Wing Candidates." Additionally, anti-Israel sentiment is growing in general among the youth: Silver and Fagan, "2. American Views of Israel." 56 percent of 18–29 year-olds have an unfavorable view of Israel, versus 27 percent for 65 plus crowd and 41 percent of the population overall.

must be replaced by yet another failed State Department quisling like former Berkeley professor Ashraf Ghani, president of the Western puppet regime in Afghanistan before the fall of Kabul. This coalescing consensus on foreign intervention is exacerbated by the notorious left-wing identity in the State Department, the purging of the US military officer corps of reactionary elements, which began as early as the 1990s but came to a head under Obama, who placed primarily left and right elitists in power, and the outward left-wing messaging that has taken the international US government by storm in recent years.[287] This includes BLM murals and Pride flags being flown on US embassies around the world, and the subversive injection of leftist indoctrination into foreign countries such as Afghanistan, before the Taliban retook the country and put an end to the Globalist American Empire's social imperialism.[288] It also helps the left elite in their decision that they are no longer fighting communists anymore but rather anti-globalist nationalists.

VII

There is a question as to who has the greater influence between the Cathedral and the business elites; the elite left versus the elite right. Yarvin's theory clearly postulates that it is the Cathedral which holds true power. However, I clearly disagree on this, as it ignores relevant information about the business sector. On the other hand, some, mainly in the right-wing socialist/third position school of thought, believe that it is the elite right who is in true control, using the elite left as a tool. While the true answer is somewhere in between, it seems clear that more influence and power stems from the elite right, if that term is taken to mean international finance, than from the elite left.

The Cathedral creates culture, influences thought, changes minds, and serves as the central brain of society. However, it is not independent. Can anyone really argue against the fact that the

---

[287] IBD Editorial Board, "Obama's Military Coup."; Steuben, "The Military's Culture of Careerism."; Quinn, "'The Department of Woke.'"
[288] Hankinson, "A U.S. Embassy Should Fly Only One Flag."; Mott, "Woke Imperium."

corporate donors could have any academic's proverbial head on a plate within twenty-four hours?[289] Universities rely on funding. Much of this comes from the government (which is also largely controlled by corporate power), but also from big business and "philanthropists" themselves. The fact that the curriculum is what it is today is not a testament to the professors' supposed rigor, as they surely believe, but simply because roadblocks by higher powers were put into place for those who went against the interest of the moneyed elite. Thus, I agree with the traditional approach to elite theory, that the information organs are simply a tool allowed to exist by those truly in power. The Cathedral is not the true power base.

The emergence of critical race theory proves this fact. CRT is a "discipline" with no merit, but which pushes a highly simplistic worldview, and bedazzles audiences with a full thesaurus of lingo and misused social science jargon. Thus, it seems deeper and more complicated than it actually is. What CRT really is the institutionalization and canonization of a sophomoric and intellectually lazy theory that coincidentally supports all that the power elite support. It was not by academic rigor, but by ideological alignment that such an inane lens for understanding the world was capable of gaining traction. Only someone incapable of basic reading comprehension or the inability to discern correlation versus causation, or just as likely a bad faith actor, is capable of supporting such a concept, and, as anyone who has attended one of their recruitment universities knows, there is a constant stream of dark triad actors and affirmative action students who are willing to fit this mold crafted by the elite for the sake of astroturfed fame, recognition, and grant money. Despite being obviously unacademic through and through, and especially to the critical eye of a college professor, academia is still beholden to CRT whether they like it or not. Not even tenured professors dare to constructively criticize this sacred cow.

People like George Soros and Bill Gates are actively funding radical organizations like Black Lives Matter because it benefits

---

[289] As of the Second Edition, in light of October 7th and its aftermath, this seems to be incontrovertible. The academic class is held on a surprisingly tight leash.

them in some way.[290] There is a misnomer among the mainstream right today that these capitalist moguls are somehow "communists" or whatnot because they support communists. Rather, they are good capitalists manipulating the Cathedral and those of the failed elite class who believe themselves to be ahead of the curve. In reality, these foam-mouthed fools are being guided by the capitalists with the foolish pipe dream that "we will hang them with the rope they sell us," as many a communist has remarked, when, in reality, they are being tricked into doing the bidding of their mortal enemy *ad infinitum.*

It is no different in the actual Cathedral institutions. Furthermore, it is for this same reason that think tanks and universities simultaneously promote Austrian and Chicago school economics alongside neo-Marxist social ethics. The left attacks business by throwing pebbles to which only small businesses, the dreaded petit bourgeois *kulaks,* will be susceptible, while the true elite are able to escape relatively unscathed. All the while, the right's mainstream representation, the GOP, is derelict in its duty to its constituents, preferring to run interference for Fortune 500 companies.[291] The corporations own the media and they, specifically the Rockefeller clique, write the curriculum for public schools.[292] The universities are funded by philanthropists who are tapped into a similar worldview.[293]

To a large extent, the Cathedral does have an effect on the elite right. They and their children attend these universities and are in large part influenced by professors, despite how these professors themselves are largely controlled stooges. They surely get much of their information on current affairs from the media that they control. Furthermore, while the higher-up elites don't send their children to public schools, the curriculum of the private boarding

[290] Perazzo, "Black Lives Matter."
[291] Hood, "Betrayal: American Conservatives and Capitalism."
[292] This began from the very start: McElroy, "A Nation of Workers."
[293] Philanthropy in general has gone woke: Westhoff, "How Philanthropy Is Fueling American Division." See also Graber, "Woke Foundations."

schools is ironically often *more* insane than that of public schools.[294] There is certainly some symbiosis where both affect the other.

There is also undoubtedly something to say of convergent behavior in the elite class. In large part, much of what we are seeing is a result of the natural life cycle of an empire and civilization, and the groups within them. Entropy is clearly a major player in guiding the march of history. However, this is by no means evidence that there are no conspiracies or collusion hidden and not-so-hidden, which are formed by unions of elites with the goal of unifying their efforts toward a greater goal, which goes well beyond the mere societal entropy of the cathedral theory.

---

[294] Ludwig, "Wokeism in Private Schools."; Sharp, "Parents of Kids at New England."; Sand, "Elite Private Schools Go Woke."; Sibarium, "Why Private Schools Have Gone Woke."

6

The Elite

"We Jews, we, the destroyers, will remain the destroyers forever. Nothing that you will do will meet our demands and needs. We will forever destroy because we need a world of our own."

– Maurice Samuel,
You Gentiles, 75

Clearly, the "elite" concept is complicated as they have still remained elusive in our analysis thus far. We have generally identified elites, but have not yet found our way to the top of the pyramid, if there even is one. While each of the previous theories discussed thus far explain much, none of them explain everything, and thus must be considered not as incorrect, but incomplete. It has been determined that there are two main portions of the elite which, in recent times, have coalesced into one elite which attacks like a pincer from both left and right. Furthermore, we have identified that it is largely capital and the Cathedral in conjunction which determine power, though capital has at least a slight advantage. Thus, we may finally be permitted to delve deeper into other elements of the elite, such as the general profile of these elites and their motivations.

I

There are six main competing theories presented by the neo-reactionary movement on the nature of the elites that attempt to describe how the elite enact policy which then reaches the masses. Some posit that (1) the elites are simply incompetent and the result is seemingly pathocratic rule. Others believe that (2) all things in the world are controlled by a single cabal which guides all society from the top down and is always, or at least is almost always in control of world events. The third view is that (3) the Cathedral sets a *zeitgeist* which is subliminally adopted by all institutions and thus has ultimate power to guide society. Fourth is the idea that (4) profits are the guide and thus corporations have ultimate power which they use to further themselves indefinitely. Fifth is the idea that (5) the elites, for whatever reason, are actively sadistic and malicious and use their power specifically toward the end of tormenting their subjects. The final theory is that (6) the managerial/bureaucratic class holds organic control as the pontifex between capital and the masses. We will have to explore all of these individually and find which, or what combination, is accurate about the elite in the current era.

Elite theorists like Burnham would posit that it is the managerial elite who are currently in control, after wresting power from a previous, less degenerated elite, the Anglo "robber barons."[295] While we live in an age that can be *spiritually* characterized as the age of the fourth estate, following the age of the merchants, the workers are not actually in control of the material plane. While it is true that the bureaucracy of both the public and private sector are the most numerous elite class, and makes the majority of on-the-ground decisions to administer the regime, they are hardly the ones calling the shots.

However, the fact that bureaucrats are not in complete control does not negate the fact that they are petty elites who have power, regardless of how much or little. And, it is true that the bureaucracy is completely incompetent in virtually any organization which has grown to a large enough scale, and often inefficiencies abound even

---

[295] Burnham, *The Managerial Revolution*.

in small organizations. Furthermore, despite how the bureaucracy will inevitably be the least intelligent and therefore the most likely institution to commit blunders, stupidity cannot potentially explain failures in more sophisticated, and thus intelligent, hierarchies.

Within the media and university system, propagandists are quite capable of acting in a counterproductive manner toward their goals. It is often the idea-makers that enrage the public and create backlash, leading to growth in the opposition which they were tasked with destroying. Businesses can also commit blunders, such as supporting harmful political causes, thereby alienating customers and losing profits. However, the theory of incompetency relies on the idea that the incompetency of elite institutions is a public negative and that the institutions are controlled by benevolent actors who wish to help, but are unable to. This is obviously not the case and, so far as incompetency is concerned, the life of the average person is *improved* by elite incompetence as he or she has less of a meddlesome pathological system to worry about in his or her daily life. As for "woke" corporations, support of left-wing ideology is not a failure on the part of the corporate board, but a calculated power play.

The Cathedral view is more believable. As discussed previously, while the Cathedral does not necessarily stand at the top of the pyramid (though Yarvin himself would disagree), if one exists, it is still heavily influential on everyone, from the average Joe watching the news, to the future corporate executive attending Brown University. However, while the Cathedral is certainly a mode of creating culture and priming the public for agendas, the professor, educator, and journalist class are not in control of society, as they, like the bureaucrat, are completely replaceable and interchangeable. Those who are unwilling to spout off their lines can easily be exchanged for someone who will. They are cogs in the machine in the truest sense. The Cathedral theory admittedly has extremely high predictive value. What the universities and media push tends to be enacted only a few years later by the government. It can be surmised that the nodes of communication and information are by far the most effective way of controlling the masses toward the bidding of the elite, despite the fact that the

Cathedral elites are not necessarily directing where their information should lead from the top.

We have already come to the conclusion that, of all the powers discussed, it is corporations, or rather international finance which is a sort of "meta-corporation," which hold the most power. Thus, it would only be natural that profit incentive is the major guide of society. According to this frame favored by the left, all action is based on the accumulation of wealth by those who control the means of production. While wealth accumulation is certainly among the great factors, it is not the be-all end-all.

The theory of profits as a guiding force can be surmised simply as capital is power or $C = P$. However, this theory neglects the fact that capital is not an end in and of itself, but is a means toward an end, which is power. Thus, it is the will to power (W) by capital that equals power, $WC = P$, with will to power acting as a force multiplier to capital, and vice versa. Those with the will but without capital cannot hope to obtain power, and the reverse is also true. Obviously, the possession of a will to power is easier to obtain than the financing required to subject others to this will.

The factor of will to power shines light on how resources are not the only factor in play. Those with money, especially oligarchs with more resources than they know what to do with, turn resource into influence. As a result, the predictive power of profit is only so accurate. There are an ever-increasing number of cases in which global capital/finance comes together to push an agenda that is contrary to their supposed economic incentive. The truth is that, due to the bureaucratic takeover of big business, corporations often act in accordance with the social agenda of powerful moneyed interests, now under the guise of what Klaus Schwab has called "stakeholder capitalism."[296] Despite the fuzzy language which evokes the image of a sustainable business model that takes into account the environment and the best interest of the consumer, stakeholder capitalism is in reality an obvious ploy for power. Again, when enough capital is amassed so that oligarchs can afford to lose large amounts of wealth in pursuit of power, power will be pursued and profits will become secondary. Take for an example how

---

[296] Schwab and Vanham, *Stakeholder Capitalism.*

Twitter employed large numbers of employees who, in the wake of being fired by Elon Musk, seem to have mostly acted as political commissars instead of productive employees. Profit is a large part of the equation, but it can only explain the emergence of power via capital, but not the wielding of power by those who have amassed it. Furthermore, as the economic situation of the pandemic has shown, because the moneyed interests are interconnected with each other and the government, it takes little effort to racketeer off of the world monetary system, which is free to print however much money is needed to keep the system that is too big to fail afloat. In a world where such an important organ of power is captured, money becomes more and more abstract, with the tradeoff that legitimacy in the monetary system decreases.

Some believe that this is all the work of a single cabal of elites. However, as has been discussed at length, the nature of the elites is highly complicated, with web upon web of influence stacked one on top of the other, while also resembling a sort of hierarchy with the Cathedral and capital roughly at the top, all being influenced by various conspiracies and collusions which push and pull in one direction or another.

Thus far, we have remained relatively consistent in focus on the Western elite and indeed the cycle of Western civilization. However, in this world there is more than one so-called "cabal" of elites. It is clear that the Chinese, a rising star in world politics, have their own elite class unified under the Chinese Communist Party. It would be remiss to deny the power and influence that these elites have, which may explain many of the actions made by Western governments to the benefit of China.[297] It is no secret that China operates spy rings and is fully capable of blackmailing politicians and using women to snag state secrets, such as in the case of Congressman Swalwell.[298] The Russians also have an elite which are distinct and oftentimes at loggerheads with their counterparts in the West.

---

[297] Morgan, "It's Time to Ban Chinese Students."; Williams, "FBI Director Wray Says."; Bhagat, "Outsourcing Manufacturing to China."
[298] Phillips, "What We Know about Rep. Eric Swalwell's Ties." We also know that top members of Congress from both parties were briefed by intelligence officials in 2015 about suspected Chinese spies trying to infiltrate Congress.

Within the Western elite, there are also disagreements, seemingly minor as they may be. Up until recently, the elite left and right continued to maintain major differences in doctrine. It was only in the post-2015 era that the elite class fully buried their hatchets, realizing that, despite some differences, they could not allow populist energy funneled through rogue elites, in a potential Jouvenelian middle-low versus high uprising, to usurp their power.

Even in spite of this, there are still under the surface cliques and disagreements. Within the US government there is a schism within the Democratic Party, between the Clinton and Obama factions, for control. There is also a debate as to whether the American people and the people of Western nations can continue on the current track of humiliation and destruction, the route favored especially by Jewish power and their urban liberal proxies, such as pushing transgender surgery on impressionable children (as outlined in *The Transgender Industrial Complex* by Scott Howard), or whether it is necessary to allow for the built-up pressure to be expelled via the pressure valve of a seemingly major win, such as a milquetoast Republican victory in a presidential election, so as not to kill the golden goose that is the productive White bourgeois population. Should the lockdowns, vaccine mandates, and repression continue, or is it time for some slack in the line before the final blow? There was also up until recently the conflict between the State Department neoliberal types on one side, and the hard left, mainly academic elites and capitalist elites on the other, as to whether the US should continue its imperialism and thus treat China as a threat to the Western order. That lasted until China made their decision for them by distancing itself from the West. These are some of the major questions that those in power wish to settle.

Of course, this paints the picture of a cabal that agrees on just about everything, only with some minor squabbles over how to accomplish it. To this, the conspiracy frame is largely accurate, as practically all rogue elites have either been defeated or assimilated through concessions. We have already discussed this concept of a relatively recent right-left elite coalescence.

The theory of managerial/bureaucratic control runs starkly against this top-down elite perspective and was the first step toward the theory of a Cathedral. It is apparent from Yarvin's writing in *Unqualified Reservations* that Yarvin was largely inspired by Burnham, who famously wrote on this bureaucratic takeover. It logically follows that, if the bureaucracy is largely in direct control, and if it is further controlled by the "filters" that are used on them via the Cathedral as discussed in the fourth chapter, it would make sense to point to the Cathedral as central to power. However, as has been demonstrated, the Cathedral is largely an organ of moneyed interests, while the managerial sector is at best guided by pure *zeitgeist* and at worst by the information institutions, thus diminishing the extent to which the bureaucratic option can be considered.

In recent years it has become clear that the institutions are united in deed and act in a way that seems to harm the people whom they swore to represent, resulting in the earlier hypothesis that the institutions are simply incompetent (as opposed to willfully evil). Are the elites simply incompetent? That depends on who we consider elites. Whether it is the government, the Cathedral, NGOs, the bureaucracy, corporations, or a web of conspiracies, all of these people or groups are elite in their own way. It is just a matter of ranking which has more control over the others. It is doubtless that each has some effect on all the rest but some are greater than others. However, when *all* outcomes are specifically detrimental to White America, Western/European civilization, and historical Christendom (and the few exceptions pose basically no threat to the power structure as seen by society's continuous leftward drift), some further thought is merited in regards to this radical proposition that the oligarchs are not sleeping at the wheel, but crashing the ship and leaving no survivors *purposefully.*

Andrzej Łobaczewski, a Polish psychologist who worked under the communist regime, became convinced after years of study on the ruling elite of his country that the elite class was seriously mentally ill, especially as regarding dark triad traits (psychopathy/sociopathy, narcissism, Machiavellianism), which resulted in the brutality of the Polish communist regime.[299] Łobaczewski surmised that this was not just a trait of communist regimes, or even authoritarian regimes generally, but of all political

---

[299] Łobaczewski, *Political Ponerology.*

programs, including in supposedly benevolent ones like the US. His theory was perhaps confirmed as, not only was his work on what he dubbed "political ponerology"—literally the study of evil in politics—impossible to publish in his home country for obvious reasons, but also suppressed in the US when he immigrated.[300] It would seem that those psychopaths, sociopaths, and pathological narcissists inhabiting the US regime were intimidated by the theory that governments are occupied by the psychologically disturbed. This may explain the prevalence of sexual predators and especially pedophiles within the halls of power, as psychopathy and pedophilia are highly correlated.[301]

The logical conclusion to this theory of pathocracy is disturbing. If those in power are actively using their power in a sadistic way on those who they are sworn to protect, and if this is an institutionalized prospect, pathological individuals are able to collude and collaborate with fellow sadists, creating an exponential effect of misery. One pathocrat in the bureaucracy can potentially cause mass destruction, no different from a lone wolf terrorist. But thousands of them at the reins of the most influential positions in our institutions will cause untellable destruction that only an army of insurgents is capable of. The pathological angle is in line with not just the conspiratorial frame, but also the idea of convergent belief systems (like the Cathedral), and both appear to have some veracity. That the pathocratic theory of power is able to encompass both the cabal and convergent theories of power, which each separately have a great deal of explanatory power, points toward this theory being the most complete, and therefore strongest, theory discussed thus far. However, it too is incomplete. What if, for example, it is not just generic sadism against mankind in general, but something else such as ethnic animus, which is sometimes at work among the elite?

---

[300] "Ponerology: the Science of Evil," systems thinker.
[301] The FBI has had a number of scandals regarding pedophilia, as well as others: Calhoun, "FBI Agent Who Investigated Sex Crimes."; Simmons, "Sex Offender Typologies."

II

It is impossible to definitively discuss power in the modern Western world, and especially the United States, without reference to Jewish power; a taboo topic by no accident. The elite are largely mental cases, this is true, but many simply act in this manner to the extent that single-minded ethnic interest is viewed as pathological by the majority ethnic out-group. We cannot continue this discussion without the acknowledgement (and evidence) that the Jewish element in America controls every major institution, largely even the military, as the fight against the globalist stranglehold slowly gives way in even the most traditionally reactionary institution.[302] With great intelligence, especially in the sectors that translate to power, and an extreme in-group preference not shed since their days in the *shtetl*, the host nations of this small but highly effective Jewish minority were simple work for such an ancient and experienced people.[303]

Their in-group preference acts in a two-pronged way. On the one hand, nepotism is the most obvious advantage. On the other, viciousness is a benefit in the political realm, as long as it is paired with intelligence. The seemingly pathological behavior (take supporting open borders in their host country for example) held nearly universally by the Jewish people against their naive racial adversary thus aids in their takeover. This supposed insanity is usually not out of any *literal* mental issue but out of ethnic conflict which is viewed by the majority ethnic out-group simply as madness. Thus, the tiny Jewish elements and the equally tiny element of dark triad actors among the other non-Jews may be able to enmesh with each other, creating a pathocratic community of rulers.

In the US, Jewish control is easily demonstrable. Whether control lies with the moneyed interests (which we have found largely to be

---

[302] For example, David L. Goldfein was Chief of Staff of the US Air Force from 2016 through 2020, and virtue signaled about Unite the Right and George Floyd. See Kampeas, "US Air Force Commander David Goldfein Retires." Interestingly, following his retirement, he joined the investment firm Blackstone. See Weisgerber, "Former Air Force Chief Goldfein Joins Blackstone."

[303] Cochran et al., "Natural History of Ashkenazi Intelligence." For a study of Jewish legalism, see Wexler, "Jewish Word."; MacDonald, *Culture of Critique*, xxx-xxxvii.

the case), the Cathedral, the bureaucracy, or the elected positions of power, matters less in the context that all of these levers of power are populated by the same characters. In terms of moneyed interests, Jews make up roughly one in five of the richest people on Earth despite being 0.2 percent of the world population: a hundred times their representation.[304] Traditionally, banking and real estate have largely been in the hands of Jewish families as well, as Jews obtained a head start in the Middle Ages, when usury was illegal among Christians.

Furthermore, Jews are the wealthiest ethnic group in America, and Reformed Jews are by far the wealthiest subgroup. In spite of Asians and especially Indians being ranked as the highest paid ethnic groups in the US (annually earning $85,800 and $119,000 per household respectively),[305] Modern Orthodox and Open Orthodox Jews rake in a whopping annual $158,000 and $185,000 respectively.[306] In contrast, the average income in the US is around $60,000.[307]

Not only do American Jews have large salaries, but this compounds into static wealth which can be used in the pursuit of influence. This political influence is easy to see. *All* of the top six most influential DNC contributors in the 2020 election were Jewish.[308] Before the populist uprising in the GOP, the Republicans were also largely in Jewish hands, with major backers including Paul Singer, Isaac Perlmutter, and the late Sheldon Adelson, among others. The Jewish control of RNC donations resulted in the

---

[304] Gallindoss, "Jews Make-up 19%."
[305] Budiman, "Indians in the U.S. Fact Sheet."
[306] Sales, "5 Key Takeaways, Some Surprising."
[307] Flynn, "25+ Essential Average American." As of 2022 the average personal income in the US is $63,214, and the median personal is $44,225
[308] Debenedetti, "Ranking the Most Influential."; Ben Zion and AP, "Jewish Donors Prominent."; "Jewish Billionaire Seth Klarman's Fund." Before proceeding further, I must clarify what I mean by "Jewish." Among themselves, Jews do not count someone as Jewish unless their mother is Jewish. Metaphysical and cultural matters aside, someone who is half Jewish from their father's side is just as biologically Jewish as if their Jewish blood came from their mother, and thus I do not differentiate between maternal and paternal lines. Additionally, for purposes of this book, if someone is a quarter Jewish or more, but displays Jewish behavior, they will be counted as simply Jewish. This is similar to how most people think of Obama as simply Black instead of half Black. The Ashkenazi Jews have already existed as a hybrid race for centuries, and yet continue to maintain a distinct Jewish identity.

Republican Party focusing on the issues which Jews find most pressing: aid to Israel, aggressive foreign policy in the Middle East, and pro-big business policy. It is also apparent that Jews fight above their weight class in terms of political donation, being more active as individual donors than their gentile peers, even when controlling for income.[309] The necessity of courting the Jewish community is a lesson which anyone involved in politics has come to understand quickly.

Jews have also been largely in control of the Cathedral institutions. "Twenty-five percent of Ivy League school professors are Jews," noted Dr. Seymour Martin Lipset, professor of government and sociology at Harvard University, an overrepresentation of roughly 1200 percent in 1971.[310] As early as the turn of the century, Jewish immigrants flooded the Ivy League. "Just 7 percent of Harvard's enrollment in 1900 was Jewish. By 1909, it was 10 percent. Six years later, it rose again to 15 percent. And in 1922, it was 21.5 percent."[311] This mass movement of such a heavily cohesive and alien group into one of America's most prestigious institutions led Harvard's president, A. Lawrence Lowell to call for a gradual limit on Jewish enrollment in 1922.[312]

The University of Pennsylvania found in 2010 that 20 percent of the student body was religiously Jewish *alone* with a further unspecified number of atheist and agnostic Jews to add on.[313] It is not a rare occurrence in the Ivy Leagues for ethnic Jews to outnumber Whites.[314] Ron Unz concurred, finding that from 2007–2011, Jews numbered approximately equal to non-Jewish Whites in the Ivy League, though the phenomenon did not translate outside the Ivies.[315] Furthermore, Jews are overrepresented by a factor of roughly 3.5 in terms of high ability students in the Ivy League, while non-Jewish Whites are in fact discriminated against when factoring

---

[309] Sharon, "US Jews Contribute Half of All Donations." They also provided 25 percent of the RNC's cash in 2016.
[310] "Harvard Professor Says 25 Percent."
[311] Shapira, "Before Asian Americans Sued Harvard."
[312] Feldberg, "Anti-Semitism in the U.S."
[313] See Telushkin's article for a tone-deaf lamentation of Jews becoming slightly less grossly overrepresented since then. Telushkin, "The Vanishing Ivy League Jew."
[314] Durocher, "White Nationalism Explained with Charts."
[315] Unz, "The Myth of American Meritocracy."

in academic ability.[316] Despite complaints among Asians of Ivy League discrimination, when factoring in Jews as separate from White, the only ethnic group that is discriminated against when controlling for academic ability is in fact Whites.[317] This naturally leads to an inference of corruption and gatekeeping of the elite roles in America.

The saturation of Jews early in the last century within the elite universities of America meant that these same Jews would go on to occupy important positions of power, especially in academia. Due to an extremely high in-group preference in the Jewish community, this was further compounded over four to five generations through nepotism and oftentimes open hostility to the host population.[318] As a result of Jewish control of academia, the majority of institutionalized sources must be processed through an implicitly or explicitly pro-Jewish bent. Furthermore, later Jewish immigrants, such as the Frankfurt School intellectuals and a whole host of other radical minds in line with the general Jewish radical subculture, have found comfortable homes in the American academic system. The implications for the Cathedral theory of power should be obvious, that is, that the convergent behavior in academia and the media is more precisely convergent Jewish behavior writ large, or at the very least, has a strong Jewish flavor to it.

Without exception, the Jewish spirit in America and the West in general has been adversarial to the European order, by agitating for costly wars, racial intermixing and conflict, immigration, anti-Christian secularism, and replacement level non-White immigration. Even at the turn of the century, there was discontent as to the subversive and radical nature of the Jewish immigrants, largely from the Russian Pale, a not unfounded concern.[319] Within two generations, the Jewish spirit which had ensconced itself in the American culture, especially among the impressionable young, had taken the entire nation by storm. Largely inspired by Jewish

---

[316] Ibid.: "Non-Jewish whites are by far the most under-represented group of all, despite any benefits they might receive from athletic, legacy, or geographical distribution factors."
[317] Ibid.; "Discrimination in College Admissions."
[318] See "College Guide Search," Hillel International, for a list of disproportionately Jewish colleges, which tends to suggest nepotism and strong in-group preference.
[319] Zollman, "Jewish Immigration to America."

intellectuals such as the Frankfurt clique, Noam Chomsky, and a whole rabble of lesser-known characters, the New Left was born out of the hectic 1960s and the ensuing home front sabotage of the Vietnam War. Of the major organizers of the Berkeley Free Speech Movement, most were Jewish students, the children of the relatively new Jewish elite class. Of the main representative organization of the New Left, the Students for a Democratic Society, and indeed the rest of the student movement of the 1960s, the entire program was simply Jewish leftist subculture writ large. On this subject, MacDonald writes:

> The Jewish "contraculture" continued to sustain a radical, specifically Jewish subculture into the 1950s—long after the great majority of Jews were no longer in the working class (Liebman 1979, 206, 289ff). The fundamentally Jewish institutions and families that constituted the Old Left then fed into the New Left (Liebman 1979, 536ff). The original impetus of the 1960s student protest movement "almost necessarily began with the scions of the relatively well-to-do, liberal-to-left, disproportionately Jewish intelligentsia—the largest pool of those ideologically disposed to sympathize with the radical student action in the population" (Lipset 1971, 83; see also Glazer 1969). Flacks (1967,64) found that 45 percent of students involved in a protest at the University of Chicago were Jewish. . . . Jews constituted 80 percent of the students signing a petition to end ROTC at Harvard and 30–50 percent of the Students for a Democratic Society (SDS)—the central organization of student radicals. Adelson (1972) found that 90 percent of his sample of radical students at the University of Michigan [where the SDS was founded] were Jewish, and it would appear that a similar rate of participation is likely to have occurred at other schools such as Wisconsin and Minnesota. Braungart (1979) found that 43 percent of the SDS membership in his sample of ten universities had at least one Jewish parent and an additional 20 percent had no religious affiliation. The latter are most likely to be predominantly Jewish: Rothman and Lichter (1982, 82) found that the

*"overwhelming majority" of the radical students who claimed
that their parents were atheists had Jewish backgrounds.* [320]

Some decades after the initial subversive movements, the Students
for a Democratic Society would eventually form a terrorist faction
known as the Weather Underground, which carried out a bombing
campaign in protest against the Vietnam War. The founder of this
group, Jewish SDS alumni Bill Ayers, was hunted down by the FBI
for his terror campaign after the accidental Greenwich Village
townhouse explosion, perhaps the most cliché event in American
radical history, in which some of his friends, including fellow Jewish
Weatherman Ted Gold, mistakenly set off the bomb they were
working on, killing three in total. While on the run, Ayers bombed
the NYPD, the US Capitol, and the Pentagon. [321] All charges were later
dropped and Ayers became a college professor and friend of Barack
Obama, who began his political career in Ayers' living room. [322]
Ayers helped raise Chesa Boudin after his parents robbed an
armored car as part of their Weather Underground activities.
Boudin went on to become a Soros-funded district attorney in San
Francisco, facilitating the complete destruction of law and order in
the city by kneecapping its law enforcement. [323]

From the Weather Underground would form the May 19th
Coalition (M19CO). [324] Despite being a "Black Power" organization
whose name was derived from the birthday of Malcom X, the
founding members were three Jews (Kathy Boudin, Judith Clark, and
David Gilbert) and one White (Elizabeth Duke). In 1983 the M19CO
went on a bombing spree that included the famous US Senate
bombing as a target. A total of eight high-level targets were attacked
from 1982–1985. Susan Rosenberg, fellow Jewish M19CO member
and key architect of the Senate bombing, was captured two years
later, but only spent sixteen years in prison after her sentence was
commuted by Bill Clinton in his last day in office as president. She

---

[320] MacDonald, *Culture of Critique*, 76–77.
[321] In his 2001 memoir, *Fugitive Days*, Ayers brags that he helped blast NYPD headquarters in 1970, the U.S. Capitol in 1971, and the Defense Department in 1972. See
also Murdock, "Obama's Weathermen Pals."
[322] Smith, "Obama Once Visited '60s Radicals."
[323] See Smith, "Parents Guilty." and Smith and Stimson, "Meet Chesa Boudin."
[324] Thulin, "In the 1980s."

also took part in the M19CO orchestrated prison break of Assata Shakur, a Black terrorist who was serving for life plus twenty-six to thirty-three years for murdering a police officer. Assata Shakur was never returned to custody and resides in Cuba to this day. The three Jewish leaders of the M19CO also took part in an armored car robbery, in which they killed two police officers. All three will be out on the street by the time this book is published due to Jews ex machina in politics. Boudin has joined the ranks of the Cathedral as a professor at Columbia University, a top State Department feeder school and famously the place of tenure for the Jewish Frankfurt School in exile.[325]

As in any stratified ethno-religious caste system, the law applies differently between the *shudras* like you and me and the *brahmin* like them. Furthermore, it is apparent that radical American Jews are all the more willing to side with Black criminals and even ghost-form terror groups for Black criminals, such as M19CO, as an alternative to assimilating into White society, consistent with the international findings from twentieth-century Europe and even ancient squabbles they had with White Christians, Arab Muslims, and Imperial Romans.[326]

The second-wave feminist movement of the 1960s and 1970s was also essentially Jewish. Of the three major "White" activists there was a clear Jewish influence. Betty Friedan (born Bettye Goldstein) and Gloria Steinem were both Jews. Even more telling, however, is the third activist, Germaine Greer, was not Jewish but had an "intense longing to be Jewish," and "felt Jewish."[327] Greer lusted for Jewish men, went so far as to learn Yiddish, and even for a time fabricated Jewish heritage.[328] This philo-Semitism would make little sense to someone uninitiated in the true power dynamics of post-War America. Indeed, this peculiar elite behavior is all too common, as charted out by Kevin MacDonald, also appearing in the fields of psychoanalysis, anthropology, sociology, and mainstream politics.[329]

---

[325] See Toosi, "Ivy League Grads."
[326] See Roesenau, "The Dark History." and Evola, "Judaism in the Ancient World."
[327] Germaine Greer, *Daddy, We Hardly Knew You.*
[328] Ibid.
[329] MacDonald, *Culture of Critique.*

Today Jews continue to be a staple of radical left-wing politics, which dictates all culture in the United States via the elite right and left, as previously discussed. From well-known academics of the left such as Noam Chomsky to fringe online debaters, Jews, especially secular ethnic Ashkenazi Jews from major metropolitan areas, dominate across the board in the left-sphere of American politics. Like the M19CO, far-left organizations such as Black Lives Matter, Antifa, the ADL, the SPLC, and Antifa's legal arm the National Lawyers Guild are predominantly Jewish, especially in positions of leadership, even when the organization is expressly dedicated to Black issues.[330] In fact, Susan Rosenberg, the aforementioned radical, currently funds BLM through her charity Thousand Currents.[331]

Jews also control the media portion of the Cathedral. While academia is simply largely Jewish, and the institution often retains a Jewish atmosphere and culture due to Jewish dominance, the news media is a whole different animal. The following companies, supposedly ethnically neutral and certainly not seen as Jewish institutions, are as Jewish as a Synagogue. The Hollywood movie industry itself was founded by a collection of Jewish immigrants. *Every one* of the five film studios that really started Hollywood (Metro-Goldwyn-Mayer, Warner Bros., Paramount, Fox, and RKO) was founded by Jews.[332] Furthermore, Robert Lichter, a Columbia University researcher, found after randomly polling 238 journalists from the major news networks that 59 percent were Jewish.[333]

With such staggering representation in the media, it seems odd that labeling the media as a whole as it simply is, a largely Jewish institution, is met with such outrage from Jews and liberals, unless of course it is said in an approving way by a bragging Jewish

---

[330] MacDonald, "Are These Antifa/ BLM Riots a Jewish Coup?"; Quinn, "Suing the SPLC."; MacDonald, "Black History Month Special."
[331] McKay, "Behind Susan Rosenberg."
[332] Metro was founded by Marcus Loew, Samuel Goldwyn, and Louis B. Mayer (all Jews), Warner Bros. was founded by Harry, Albert, Sam, and Jack Warner (all Jewish), Paramount was founded by William Wadsworth Hodkinson, Adolph Zukor, and Jesse Lasky (a gentile and two Jews), Fox was founded by Joseph Schenck, Darryl Zanuck, William Fox, and Spyros Skouras (two gentiles, two Jews), and RKO was founded by David Sarnoff (Jewish).
[333] Lichter et al., *The Media Elite*.

comedian. Like White replacement, it is only okay to mention it when doing so approvingly. With control of the media, a certain demographic of people is able to control the thoughts of the masses. A media culture dictated by a different group of people will obviously alter the way in which we see the world. Indeed, it is no surprise that Jews (the second most liberal demographic in America, only behind Blacks) have formed an overwhelmingly liberal media apparatus, as was done to academia (which was actually slightly conservative leaning before the 1960s).[334]

The legal system is a strange creature and difficult to label, as it encompasses not just the formal judiciary as a branch of the government composed of judges and their courts, as previously discussed, but also the lawyers who clamor before judges, the schools that produce lawyers, and by extension judges, the entities that fund lawfare, prosecutors, and the academic scholars (almost exclusively law professors) who influence judicial decisions from ivory towers. As already mentioned, lawyers must spend even more time in an academic environment at law school, and so it is little wonder that the legal profession, while technically separate from the Cathedral, is unusually intertwined with the Cathedral (specifically academia) and its Jewish character. This Jewish character is even further exacerbated by the Jewish tendency toward argumentation, hair splitting, and "creative interpretation" of rules that frequently crosses over into bold dishonesty. That these lawyering tendencies are built into the Jewish psyche is evident in the complex ways they have found to circumvent their own laws, such as by having tasks done by a non-Jewish person or automated timing mechanisms to circumvent their rule against working on Saturday (with work even encompassing such *de minimis* acts as flipping a light switch). That Jews are overrepresented in law can be seen by how the Supreme Court was for years one third Jewish when Ginsburg, Breyer, and Kagan were on the bench, and the numerous other Jews who occupy positions

---

[334] "8. U.S. Jews' Political Views."; Jon A. Shields, "The Disappearing Conservative Professor." As late as 1969 about one in four professors were at least moderately conservative, according to survey data collected by the Carnegie Commission on Higher Education.

within the court system at all levels. Wikipedia, at least at the time of writing, has a page listing them all.[335]

But the greatest way that the Cathedral and legal systems are intertwined in a Jewish tapestry of power is in the law's use of citation to scholarly publications. Attorneys and *amici curiae* briefers will frequently lean upon these publications for both purely apolitical matters, such as contract law, but especially for constitutional and criminal law, in which they provide the intellectual ammunition for bad faith, subversive positions to be advanced in the courtroom by attorneys and *amicus curiae* briefs, and then ruled upon into law by treasonous judges.[336] While scholarly journals are not as strong as previous court cases for citable legal authority, their influence should not be underestimated. Every subversive legal doctrine had its first case which established it, and these first cases invariably lean upon scholarly articles that first articulated their subversive ideas and lent them a veneer of respectability. In no other academic field do Cathedral professors have such a direct, concrete, and continuing impact on the real-life practice of the profession that their academic field is supposed to prepare students for (as an aside, while law students do most of the grunt work for law review publications, it is the faculty who ultimately direct their course). The top four most cited legal authors in America are Cass Sunstein, Erwin Chemerinsky, Richard Epstein, and Eric Posner, all Jews.[337]

Furthermore, lawfare is one of the most highly preferred weapons of powerful Jews. Not only do they seem to have a natural knack for it, but they know that it is very likely that a fellow Jew, or at least someone who is seen as a friend of Jews, will be on the bench.[338] The Jewish George Soros has used his wealth to appoint prosecutors who he knows will target lawful Whites while excusing anarchists and African criminals, and for good reason.[339] Jews and their allies also know that legal fees are exorbitantly expensive, and

---

[335] "List of Jewish American Jurists."
[336] For example, in *Shelley v. Kraemer* which struck down racially restrictive property covenants.
[337] Leiter, "Top Ten Law Faculty."
[338] Root et al., "Building a More Inclusive Federal Judiciary."
[339] Alexander, "George Soros-Backed Groups." One in five Americans lives under a Soros-backed prosecutor. See also Daley and Ross, "Meet the Progressive DA."

thus rich Jewish individuals and entities have a distinct edge in a "pay to win" system against middle and working-class White individuals and entities that don't have a sufficient fund for legal fees.[340] Even without Jewish influence, this is simply an inherent flaw in any legal system that allows a party to spend any amount of money on lawyers. Spengler observed that "It is symptomatic that no constitution knows of money as a political force; it is pure theory that they contain, one and all."[341] Rich Jewish activists simply hastened the legal system toward its rational conclusion.

Given the nature of the legal system, it is unsurprising that it worked in perfect harmony with the legislature to enshrine a legal framework to enforce the latest of America's foundation myths, the civil rights movement. The legislature may have passed the Civil Rights Act, but it was the legal system that used that Act as a supporting branch to enthusiastically spin a comprehensive web of case law, instead of limiting, if not outright overturning, that Act as unconstitutional, as any sane judiciary should have done, as was lucidly demonstrated in Christopher Caldwell's *The Age of Entitlement*. This new case law undermines older, more primordial rights, both express and implied, while being careful to not go so far as to openly and honestly abolish them, although they might as well have in many cases, especially so in the case of freedom of association.[342] Meanwhile, an entire list of new "rights" that are wholly repugnant to our history and traditions, such as abortion and gay marriage, were spun out of the ether by unelected individuals, and then not just enshrined as equally important as the old rights, but actually having higher precedence—ironically not in spite of, but because they were newer, as discussed in Chapter 1.

---

[340] Allen, "The *Sines v. Kessler* Lawfare Litigation." See also "NJP Condemns the Travesty of Justice."; "You Still Have to Bake the Cake, Bigot."
[341] Spengler, *Decline of the West*, 372.
[342] For example, *Shelley v Kraemer* struck down racially restrictive property covenants.

III

Over the last two thousand years of the Common Era, the Jewish race has participated in a unique role in the antagonism against European Christendom. We need not delve into two thousand years of history, as the past hundred or so years suffices enough for painting a picture of how the Jewish race views its European adversary. Thus, the cruel nature of the ruling elite is unsurprising in the wider context of their behavior in the modern era alone, once we understand that the elite is disproportionally Jewish, as will be discussed in further detail. To understand this seemingly pathological behavior, it is necessary to provide historical context as to the conflict between Jews and their White hosts in Europe and America.

While Jews such as Karl Marx were central to revolutionary movements, including those of 1848, the year in which he wrote his manifesto, the seminal moment of the modern Jewish theme was the Bolshevik Revolution of 1917, which has served as the lodestar of Jewish social behavior up to the present. Not only was the leadership of the Bolshevik Revolution largely manned by Jews, philo-Semites, men married to Jewish women, and other alien groups, but the Jewish population within the Russian Empire nearly universally supported either the Bolsheviks or Mensheviks, a slightly less radical group with similar aims.[343] The revolution ended purposefully in the deaths of millions of White Russians, the historic enemy of the revolting minority groups who compromised the revolutionary vanguard.[344]

During and after the revolution came the waves of terror, in which millions more were executed arbitrarily by the lowest scum of society, empowered by the aforementioned groups. And a generation after the revolution subsided, even worse terror followed. The Jewish Yagoda, director of the NKVD, exterminated the White Ukrainian population through deliberate starvation, in which as many as ten million Ukrainians perished.[345] The NKVD

---

[343] Quinn, *Solzhenitsyn and the Right*, Chapter 8; Frantzman, "Was the Russian Revolution Jewish?"
[344] Riga, "The Ethnic Roots of Class Universalism."
[345] "The Number of Holodomor-Genocide Victims."

famously utilized Jewish staff to commit the purge, knowing they had little sympathy for the historically anti-Semitic Ukrainian population.[346] It is no surprise that the Holodomor genocide of Ukraine is not common knowledge, and is largely ignored by Cathedral media and educational establishments.

During the Russian Revolution, similar uprisings occurred in Germany and Hungary. The interwar German uprising was led largely by the Polish Jew Rosa Luxemburg, in what became known as the Spartacist Uprising, which attempted and failed to overthrow the government and institute a communist government. The Hungarian uprising was led by the Jewish Béla Kun, who also failed after international intervention.

In the US, the revolution was much more subtle. As previously stated, the Jewish elite were already institutionalized by the 1960s. However, there were several decades of Jewish influence before this soft revolt, subversion, and overthrow of the old American order was achieved. Among the American strand of Jewish rebellion were the famous left-wing anarchist thinker Emma Goldman, along with Ethel and Julius Rosenberg and David Greenglass (three Jewish communist spies who gave the USSR the schematics to the atomic bomb in the aftermath of the Second World War). Other Jewish immigrants and their descendants went on to play important roles in radical organizations such as the IWO and the CPUSA.[347] The Jewish People's Fraternal Order (JPFO), an American Jewish Congress affiliate with membership that peaked around fifty thousand members, was considered the financial "bulwark" of the CPUSA.[348] Indeed, radical politics in the US since the turn of the century has been completely dominated by Jews. One need look no further than Bernie Sanders, a caricature of this type of radical, who went on his honeymoon in the USSR and was a member of an anarcho-syndicalist *kibbutz* in his youth.

Influential Jews in the social sciences such as Franz Boas spent much of their time during American Jewry's early beginnings poisoning American culture with subversive pseudoscience, which

---

[346] Quinn, *Solzhenitsyn and the Right*, Chapter 9.
[347] MacDonald, *Culture of Critique*, 69.
[348] Ibid.

had the express effect of weakening the White cultural immune system.[349] Franz Boas, a Jewish socialist who came to America during the migratory period, is considered the founder of modern anthropology. A political radical, Boas's egalitarian philosophy and unscientific axioms have turned anthropology into a crypto-leftist institution. The result was the downfall of Darwin (and ideas which would reemerge as evolutionary psychology only after decades of suppression), and the ascendance of left-wing philosophy in these fields.[350] Even today, Jews and leftists in academia defame evolutionary psychology as "pseudoscience," seeing it as a challenge to their worldview, now that it has been resurrected years after the interwar period. Well-known Jewish critics of sociobiology and evolutionary psychology in the academic world include Stephen Jay Gould (paleontology), Richard Lewontin (evolutionary biology), Leon Kamin (psychology), Steven Rose (neurobiology), and Jared Diamond (history) of *Guns, Germs, and Steel* fame. This has of course been a grave blow to social science throughout these decades in which evolutionary psychology was forgotten. Only recently has the field been re-popularized, though it is still relegated to the fringes of academia. That evolutionary psychology is ultimately shunned almost entirely for its anti-egalitarian political implications, and not for its credibility, is a strong indication that it is correct.

Boasian anthropology can be characterized by its emphasis on nurture over nature and a typical leftist obsession with the *tabula rasa* outlook on human nature:

> An important technique of the Boasian school was to cast doubt
> on general theories of human evolution, such as those implying
> developmental sequences, emphasizing the vast diversity and
> chaotic minutiae of human behavior, as well as the relativism
> of standards of cultural evaluation. The Boasians argued that
> general theories of cultural evolution must await a detailed
> cataloguing of cultural diversity, but in fact no general theories
> emerged from this body of research in the ensuing half century
> of its dominance of the profession (Stocking 1968, 210).

---

[349] Albrecht, *"Take Your Choice*, Part II."
[350] MacDonald, *Culture of Critique*, Chapter 2.

Because of its rejection of fundamental scientific activities such as generalization and classification, Boasian anthropology may thus be characterized more as an anti-theory than a theory of human culture (White 1966, 15). Boas also opposed research on human genetics—what Derek Freeman (1991, 198) terms his "obscurantist antipathy to genetics."[351]

This philosophy of anthropology is highly reminiscent of post-structuralism, critical theory, and postmodernism, which would later embed themselves in Western universities, mainly by the Frankfurt School academics and existentialists who were also predominantly Jewish (Martin Buber, Lev Shestov, Gabriel Marcel, etc.).[352] This line of thinking, in which everything disagreed with is simply deconstructed, forming anti-theories rather than theories, continues to be the primary mode of so-called "philosophy" today in Jewish-controlled academia, likely a product of Jews' general disdain for White European Christian society. Clearly, distractions from "anti-theorists" such as "find the gene" and semantic games around jargon and terminology are not a new phenomenon in dishonest debate among the socialist left, and specifically the Jewish leftist subcultures (i.e. the fallacious arguments made from authority by the likes of Jewish academics like Gould, Lewontin, etc.). This subversive ideology was also noticed by the famous Christian writer C. S. Lewis:

The practical result of education in the spirit of [subjectivism] must be the destruction of the society which accepts it.... There are theoretical difficulties in [this] philosophy.... However subjective they may be about some traditional values, [they] have shown by mere act of writing ... that there must be some other values about which they are not subjective at all. They write in order to produce certain states of mind in the rising generation, if not because they think those states of mind intrinsically just or good, yet certainly because they think them to be means to some state of society which they regard as

---

[351] Ibid., 24.
[352] See Bowden, "Marxism & the Frankfurt School."

desirable. It would not be difficult to collect from various passages [of their writings] what their ideal is. But we need not. The important point is not the precise nature of their end, but the fact that they have an end at all.[353]

From German-Jewish-American anthropologists at the turn of the century, to British schoolmasters in the 1930s and 1940s, to cosmopolitan postmodernists in the post-war era, this line of thinking, now common in American universities, is nothing new.

Take the Boasian disciple Margret Mead's famous study *Coming of Age in Samoa*, which is a favorite of the modern left due to Mead's conclusions that Western Christian notions of human sexuality are harmful social constructs.[354] In contrast, the girls of Samoa were supposedly highly independent and promiscuous but settled down later in life. Decades later, researchers went back to Samoa, tracked down the interviewed girls, and found that they were just pulling her leg in a big village inside joke on the gullible Western woman.[355] In reality, sexuality is highly regimented in Samoa, and the intactness of a bride's virginity is valued just as much as, if not more than, in previously studied societies, from India to America.[356] The radical left continues to defend this study to this day, citing a multitude of sophistries to claim that the Samoan girls were lying in their old age.[357] Furthermore, the effect of the subversive conclusions that a) our views on sexuality have no transcendent essence but are rather social constructs and b) that in *some* primitive societies women are promiscuous in early age and settle down later, not only says more about the cosmopolitan "scientist" Mead's character than anything relating to the Samoan culture, but also the intentions of the socialist egalitarian Boasian worldview toward the masses who, it is no surprise, would soon after adopt such harmful and purely synthetic and subversive views on sexuality. The critics blame the Samoans' conversion to Christianity

---

[353] Lewis, *Abolition of Man*, 67.
[354] See Donovan, "Misrepresenting Masculinity."
[355] See Shankman, "The 'Fateful Hoaxing' of Margaret Mead." and Appell, "Freeman's Refutation of Mead."
[356] Wiker, "Anthropology Afoul of the Facts."
[357] See Talbott, "Sex, 'Lies' and Videotape." and Shankman, *Trashing of Margaret.*

as a source of the Samoans lying, an implicit critique of Christianity, which may shine light on who it is that is interested in defending Mead's conclusions.

With outlooks based on pseudo-scientists such as Boas and his student Margret Mead predominant in academia, it is no surprise then that Charles Murray, author of *The Bell Curve*, was berated and ran out of the Cathedral despite being of the Cathedral.[358] Not only did his meticulously researched book on the effect of IQ in America fly in the face of and essentially disprove the axiomatic sacred cow of post-Boas anthropology, sociology, and taken-for-granted views on social science at large, but he went so far as to attack the greatest sacred cow in modern social science: the refusal to make a connection between race and IQ.[359] As we recall from the Cathedral chapter, the result of his questioning of the axiom of a *tabula rasa* was met by condemnation for simply being the messenger of a work which said little that was not already known by a large percentage of actual intelligence researchers. Of course, the only ethnic group who has been able to claim that *their* higher intelligence is based on genetic factors are the Jews themselves.[360] To the credit of the consistency on the modern left, a virtue that is quickly dwindling, even this has become the target of radical left-wing politics.

The march through Cathedral institutions continued with the Frankfurt School academics, German-Jewish exiles who fled to the US during the Nazi regime, and who introduced their subversive philosophy to America. Sanctioned by the American Office of Strategic Services, their services were used to counter reactionary ideology during the Second World War and beyond.[361] After this,

---

[358] See Scholl, "'The Bell Curve' 20 Years Later." and Sailer, "'You Have to Tell."
[359] Herrnstein and Murray, *The Bell Curve*, 269–386.
[360] See Bret Stephens' infamous *New York Times* article citing IQ statistics and the higher intelligence of his group. However, in recent decades, the viral and independent quality of the memes originally sowed in the early 1900s have sprouted up and become uncontrollable. Today, even Jews are unable to speak in the open of their higher intelligence, due to it being heretical to the ideology originally created by Jews themselves. The article has since been edited to be free of reference to statistics which are claimed to have come from a study by a supposed "racist." Stephens, "The Secrets of Jewish Genius."
[361] Jeffries, "The Frankfurt School: A Timeline."; Bew, "Marxists and the Office of Strategic Services."; Morelock, "Introduction: The Frankfurt School and Authoritarian Populism."

they were set loose on American academia. Their ideology can be characterized as a distinctly Jewish synthesis of Marxism and Freudian psychoanalysis, two philosophies that were started by and are consistently dominated by Jews.[362] The main contribution of the Frankfurt School to the subversion of American political-social-philosophical thought was the pathologization of basically normal behavior among Whites, while excusing it among non Whites and especially Jews. As MacDonald writes:

> Jewish interests are . . . served by the Frankfurt School ideology that gentile concerns about losing social status and being eclipsed economically, socially, and demographically by other groups are an indication of psychopathology. As an exceptionally upwardly mobile group, this ideology serves Jewish interests by defusing gentile concerns about their downward mobility, and . . . Jewish organizations and Jewish intellectuals have been at the forefront of the movement to eclipse the demographic and cultural dominance of European peoples in Western societies.[363]

As we already know, the modern left in America can trace its ideological roots exclusively to Jewish and adjacent sources from the beginning to mid-twentieth century, and Jews largely fund the political process in the US. They are also the main contributors to modern supposed "conservative" thought as well, partly explaining why the Republican Party has been so impotent in enacting legislation that would aid its White, Christian base, in favor of pro-Jewish legislation.

The neoconservative ideology which dominates establishment party boss Republicanism is wholly of Jewish manufacture. The Jewish intellectual who is credited with founding neoconservatism, Irving Kristol—father of Bill Kristol—found his origin in the New York Intellectuals, a clique of nepotistic Trotskyist Jews of mediocre talent who used their in-group preference and connections in the

---

[362] Bowden, "Marxism & the Frankfurt School."; Newman, "Frankfurt School Weaponized US Education."
[363] MacDonald, *Culture of Critique*, 209.

intellectual world to artificially rise in esteem.[364] Thus, neoconservatism originated from the mind of a far-leftist rather than the traditional conservative pedigree, which was dominant within the White American right up until the 1950s and 1960s. This new ideology would attempt to defend conservative positions from within a liberal framework, and continues to haunt and undermine conservative politics to this day. Unsurprisingly, the neoconservatives are hardly conservative at all. Rather, their movement was a reaction against the growing anti-Jewish, anti-Trotsky, and pro-Arab actions of their once beloved Soviet Russian experiment.[365] The neoconservatives are essentially an outside infiltrator group which subverted the conservative movement in the US by utilizing the GOP for their own aims: hawkish foreign policy (especially as regards the USSR pre-1991 and the Islamic world post-1991), corporate welfare and deregulation, and mass migration.[366]

The other side of the modern mainstream neoconservative movement, libertarianism, is also a Jewish political movement. Modern libertarianism was largely introduced to the United States by Jews such as Ayn Rand, Murray Rothbard, and Milton Friedman.[367] Libertarianism is an ideology designed to tug at the individualistic spirit of European man. The effect is that Whites are encouraged to shun collectivism and working together toward common cause on explicitly racial lines, while outside groups which libertarianism does not appeal to are able to band together for their

---

[364] This group strategy is extremely common in Jewish-dominated industries. In Hollywood, there is an obvious in-group selection of Jews, for example, with an extreme animus toward Whites and Christians. But there is no discernible reason why Jews in particular would be so overrepresented in entertainment, to the chagrin of those proponents of the "Jewish meritocracy" school of thought. By subtly gatekeeping an infiltrated industry, Jews can invite more of their brethren in. This is human nature, no different than immigrants advocating for chain migration so that they can help their family reunite. However, Jews have an in-group preference that can be described as uniquely extreme, and utilize this toward obtaining critical mass in an industry. This pattern repeats itself over and over again. The case of the New York Intellectuals is among the most flagrant and well documented, as there is, in this case, an actual paper trail of Jews citing and promoting other Jews who were members of the New York clique. See Connelly, "Christmas Special."
[365] Zuesse, "Neocons Hate Russia."
[366] Buchanan, *Where the Right Went Wrong*. See also the review of the book in Publishers Weekly. See also Giraldi, "America's Jews Are Driving America's Wars."
[367] Krinsky, "Libertarianism, Jews, and the Future."

racial interests. This leaves White people at a disadvantage through a sort of "poison pill" disguised as implicit White identity. It is no surprise that the vast majority of libertarians are White men.[368] Of course, these ideas of individualism and classical liberalism are hardly genuinely of the right, as was discussed in the first chapter. Furthermore, libertarianism is still evidence of an "othering" of outcasts in self-exile, where they critique outside society, and also reject traditional order often in favor of libertine chaos, as seen most notably in *Atlas Shrugged*.

In the case of Ayn Rand especially, libertarianism is an antinomian force through and through. Rand's "Objectivism" ideology is one that promotes an extreme individualism, which has been a theme of Jewish intellectualism on the left, historically. This libertarian-Objectivist ethos of a rugged individualism, which is far more extreme than the traditional pioneer and cowboy ethos (in that there is no mention of responsibility accompanying liberty), has been adopted by the largely Jewish-dominated modern right, and it is unsurprising why.[369] While Rand is often seen as a figure of the right, it is frankly difficult to see why. It is also ironic that while she was an enemy of "racism" and a proponent of individualism, like her fellow Russian-Jewish anarchist immigrant Emma Goldman before her, she surrounded herself nearly exclusively with fellow Jews. And while Ayn Rand is truly a woman of the left, she became highly influential in the neoconservative order, though this did not prevent her from being openly hostile toward her conservative proponents. Reagan described himself as an "admirer" of Rand while former House Speaker Paul Ryan was highly influenced by her in his youth and made all his interns read *Atlas Shrugged* decades later when he became a Republican congressman.[370] Rand did not reciprocate these views toward her largely Christian conservative admirers, who she believed, in proper Jewish elitist fashion, to be

---

[368] The First Edition was much more sympathetic to libertarianism, seeing it as an attempt by well-meaning Jews to assimilate into the Anglo-American tradition of classical liberalism and rugged individualism. This was likely influenced by the author's nostalgia of his former libertarianism, and seeing libertarians as fellow travelers. In reality, this is yet another example of Jewish self-othering and subversion of the host culture.

[369] Ibid.

[370] Caldwell, *The Age of Entitlement.* 100.

medieval, saying in a speech that "The appalling disgrace of [Reagan's] administration is his connection with the so-called Moral Majority and sundry other TV religionists who are struggling, apparently with his approval, to take us back to the Middle Ages, via the unconstitutional union of religion and politics."[371]

Libertarian moral ethics, as opposed to the traditional ethics of not only liberty but also sanctity, loyalty, etc., have become utilized in a subversive way in recent years. The "live and let live" mentality of libertarianism currently pushed on the Republican laity is used to allow the heritage American stock to rationalize many detrimental changes that they see occurring around them, such as drug use, mass migration, and sexual deviancy. The false idea that libertarianism is a far-right ideology has also had a clear reverse psychological effect, in which many genuinely right-wing people are trapped in a libertarian dead end with no way to escape. One moment it is a far-right ideology to its followers, when so desired, and the next it is a centrist ideology, taking the "best of both worlds" of right and left.

We can see this also in the Intellectual Dark Web, which has grown to prominence on the New York Intellectual model. Nearly to a T, the IDW has copied the NYI as a largely Jewish panoply of left-wing intellectuals disenfranchised with the left, thus infiltrating right-wing thought-space, and subsequently subverting it.[372] While not all IDW members are Jewish, most of them are, and have risen to fame by interviewing each other on podcasts, artificially snowballing each other into fame, or using already well-known intellectuals to propel relatively unknown academics forward.[373] And like many Jewish movements, the head man is a gentile while the supermajority of the secondary figures are Jewish.[374] The front

---

[371] Ibid.

[372] For example, Jews like Steven Pinker, Sam Harris, and Bari Weiss pull the same trick as neocon Jews like Irving and Bill Kristol in courting the right, gaining its trust, and then turning on it in favor of their true innate liberal views that are incompatible with the salt-of-the-earth Americans they are trying to cozy up to.

[373] MacDonald, *Culture of Critique*, 211–221.

[374] Miessler, "A Visual Breakdown." "During the research I started noticing some weird stuff about this supposedly hateful IDW group of Harris, Weinstein, Rubin, and Shapiro. Namely, *they're all Jewish*, and yet a number of them are often labeled as white supremacists and even neo-Nazis."

man of the IDW is the gentile Jordan Peterson, while the other key figures such as Sam Harris, Ben Shapiro, Lex Fridman, Bret and Eric Weinstein, Bari Weiss, Dave Rubin, and Steven Pinker are Jewish. This IDW, like the neoconservative movement, is a clear gatekeeping operation which aims to prevent disenfranchised young White men from becoming racially conscious, which is why Peterson is useful to the establishment.[375]

The result of Jewish control of modern institutional political theory and philosophy is that all viable political possibilities through legitimate means are Jewish solutions. Not only are both parties funded largely by individual Jewish donors, their corporations, and their NGOs, but the Overton window of ideology is in all aspects simply separate fractions of a Jewish *weltanschauung* whole, and this Overton window is indeed gate-kept by Jewish and adjacent academics, journalists, donors, and party officials.[376] Thus, it is no surprise that since the solidification of Jewish control, while the West let its guard down to this un-assimilable people in the aftermath of the Second World War, and the ensuing philo-Semitism that swept the Christian world, it has become *de facto* illegal to be a true man of the right in the West, as the traditional right-wing view of the world is inherently antithetical to Jewish hegemony, since the genuine right wing advocates for, among other things, homogeneity and traditional Christian and/or European social ethics: political ideas which the Jewish community of the West seems to have chosen as their most existential foe.

IV

It is clear from the data and historical record that Jews not only sit behind the levers of power, but also hold an adversarial role in the West to the native nations. As will be discussed, Jews are disproportionally overrepresented in elite institutions, such as the Cathedral and big business. Some might say that this is mere

---

[375] Price, "Conservative YouTube Content."
[376]

coincidence, or proof that Jews are simply more successful by some innate trait of their genetics or culture. To the contrary, their overrepresentation is at times so great as to be comical, if it weren't so tragic, and the policies that these institutions push are almost exclusively hostile toward the interests of Whites and Christians. Indeed, the Jews are a radical people whose *volksgeist* is explicitly contrary to, and to the detriment of their hosts, as they support communism and other subversive elements within social science and the broader culture. With this in mind, understanding that Jews are generally not the plucky, kind, and gentle characters they portray themselves as in their film industry, we can further discuss modern ethnic hatred of Whites by Jews, and why Jewish control of every major institution is a highly disturbing scenario for their racial enemies, who simply wish to live in peace.

It is demonstrable that Jews are largely not just nominally left-wing or cosmopolitan simply out of a genuine belief, but due to a deep-seated animosity toward European Whites and Christians, which consequently translates into support for destructive political aims explicitly with the intention of harming their enemies. Josh Lambert's (a Jew) statement in *Haaretz* (an Israeli newspaper) that "Brilliant actors like Larry David and Sarah Silverman [both Jews] are challenging America's powerful religious, family-friendly culture and asserting their Jewishness by glorifying obscenity" is sadly simply to be expected in the Diaspora Jewish community.[377]

It is telling that Jews vote for the Democratic Party in America by margins higher than any other ethnic group besides Blacks, and run a left-wing anti-White media machine.[378] Furthermore, Jews are the primary political donor class for the Democratic Party, pushing a no less radical anti-White agenda.[379] Jews also support affirmative action while other White ethnic groups do not and, when polled and the question is reframed to point out that Whites will be hurt by affirmative action, Jewish support *increases*, while other ethnic groups polled, even Blacks, decrease to a minority, showing that not

---

[377] Lambert, "'Dirty Jews' and the Christian Right."
[378] 71 percent of Jews identify with or lean toward the Democrats. "8. U.S. Jews' Political Views."
[379] For a list of prominent Jewish donors: Kampeas, "Meet the Leading Jewish Political Donors."

only does the average Jew support preference over Whites, but that many actually see the detrimental effects toward Whites as a *net positive*.[380] Jews are also the only ethnic group which both believes in affirmative action but is also simultaneously against the policy for White women.[381] Western Jews are also notoriously among the greatest backers of non-White immigration into White countries.[382] Traditionally, Jews have supported immigration in the US, hoping to secure an existence for their ethnic kin who were in danger in Europe in the early to mid-twentieth century.[383] However, immigration of other out-groups also serves the Jewish Diaspora in two additional ways. Firstly, diversity causes the host society to weaken, as more and more divisions create cracks in the social fabric.[384] This lessens competition against Jews. Secondly, immigration causes pluralism, meaning that minority status becomes less stigmatized as the majority group dwindles from supermajority, to simple majority, to even minority. For Jews, immigration is a no-brainer, as it potentially increases the Jewish population, while weakening and displacing the host population. Earl Raab, a Jewish activist confirmed such suspicions:

> *The Census Bureau has just reported that about half of the American population will soon be non-white or non-European. And they will all be American citizens. . . .*
>
> *We [Jews] have been nourishing the American climate of opposition to bigotry for about half a century. That climate has not yet been perfected, but the heterogeneous nature of our population tends to make it irreversible—and makes our constitutional constraints against bigotry more practical than ever. (Raab 1993, 23).*[385]

The idea of America as a diverse country and a "nation of immigrants" was also largely a Jewish conception. The first major

---

[380] "Release Detail," Quinnipiac University Poll.
[381] Ibid.
[382] Kevin MacDonald, "Understanding Jewish Influence III."
[383] Ibid.
[384] "Leaked Amazon Document Shows."
[385] MacDonald, *Culture of Critique*, 244.

piece of pro-immigration American media of the modern era, the play *The Melting Pot*, which popularized the description of the US as a "melting pot," was written by a Jewish immigrant Israel Zangwill, seeing its first release in 1908. Of course, the greater Jewish community had no intention of melting into said pot. As for the famous pro-immigration inscription on the Statue of Liberty, "Give me your tired, your poor,/ Your huddled masses yearning to breathe free,/ The wretched refuse of your teeming shore," this was not originally inscribed on Lady Liberty, but was later attached by one Emma Lazarus, a Jewish immigrant supportive of bringing her people to the US due to the Russian pogroms. Even the phrase referring to the US as "a nation of immigrants," typically credited to then-Senator John F. Kennedy, originates from a book by the same title commissioned by the Jewish Anti-Defamation League of B'nai B'rith. And it was the Jewish Toronto mayor Melvin Lastman who popularized the phrase "diversity is our strength," now a common catchphrase utilized as an axiom by Jews and the left to further White replacement as, of course, diversity by necessity means less White representation.[386]

The Hart-Celler Act was a similar occasion of Jews pushing immigration. The act ended America's strict immigration policy, leading to the mass migration which continues today. The act was proposed by Phillip Hart, the grandson of Irish immigrants, and Brooklyn Jew Emmanuel Celler. Celler spent much of his long fifty year career in Congress pushing immigration.[387] Within a year of Celler entering Congress, the immigration restrictions of 1924 were passed, notably fought against by the then-freshman congressman.[388] The destruction of immigration controls several decades later, which he and Hart promised would have no effect on the country's demographics, naively believed by the still gentile-controlled government, would transform the US from a 90 percent White outpost of Europe to a banana republic teetering ever closer toward complete demographic replacement.

---

[386] "Melvin Douglas Lastman."; Goldsbie, "Coat of Many Mottos."
[387] "The Great Replacement," *American Renaissance.*
[388] Ibid.

Along with mass permanent legal migration, Hart–Celler naturally facilitated illegal immigration, because foreigners no longer stuck out from the native population like a sore thumb, and the new legal immigrant communities were happy to help their illegal brethren enter. The mass permanent illegal migration that was made possible by Hart–Celler was combated in what is now Democrat-controlled California, which was once a bastion of Republican politics before the great non-White migration, where the people voted in a landslide to prevent illegal immigrants from accessing taxpayer-funded resources such as welfare and public schools.[389] Even the now Democrat-controlled state's population knew that enough was enough. Unfortunately, the Jewish district court judge Mariana Pfaelzer knew better than the peasants over whom she had power in her unelected office, striking down the law as being in violation of the Civil Rights Act which, as has been discussed, essentially overthrew the true American Constitution, replacing it with a foreign one that made such previously unthinkable court decisions possible.

A similar occurrence was seen in the late introduction of non-White immigration into our mother country across the pond. The first wave of non-White immigration into the British Isles was made by a passenger ship that was intended for troop transport after the Second World War.[390] In a genius plan for profit, advertisements in Jamaica were made and followed up by Black Jamaican inhabitants.[391] Incredibly, the U.K. government seems to not have even been aware of this immigration until they arrived in England. The HMT *Empire Windrush*, the ship carrying these people, was owned by the New Zealand Shipping Company, which was in fact owned by the Jewish Isaacs family, one of the twenty Anglo-Jewish oligarch families.[392] Unsurprisingly, the Board of Deputies of British Jews, a centuries-old NGO, supports the erecting of a monument to

---

[389] Gonzalez, "Restrictionism's Last Stand." 26.6 percent of Californians were born outside the US as of 2020.
[390] Joyce, "The SS Empire Windrush."
[391] Ibid.
[392] Ibid.

the *Empire Windrush*, calling it a piece of "little known Jewish history."[393] Let's take their word for it.

We know that Jews know this immigration agenda is to the detriment of Whites and White nation-states, as the international Jewish community is among the most xenophobic communities on the planet, being the last ethnic group of the developed world to maintain a proper apartheid ethnostate in Israel. While Jews in the West are largely left-wing radicals (and even these supposedly liberal Western Jews utilize racialist dating apps and mingling groups so that their marital options are not polluted with gentiles), the Jews in their homeland of Israel are among the most reactionary people on Earth, with right-wing nationalist parties consistently holding a large plurality in the Knesset.[394] The inhabitants of the Jewish ethnostate are perfectly content with open racial warfare against their Palestinian neighbors, committing war crimes in Lebanon, illegally conquering land in the West Bank, sterilizing Ethiopian migrants, refusing refugees, and treating their Arab adversaries as animals.[395] In contrast, even the most right-wing groups in America would find similar acts in America to be far beyond the pale.

As has been shown, it would be highly foolhardy to assume that the Israeli Jews are much different from their Diaspora counterparts, who exert power in more implicit or subversive ways, as they are a small minority in a sea of adversaries. The Israelis are able to exert force as they have explicit control of the Jewish state, and have secured a blank check of international backing. Jews across the globe view other ethnicities as subhuman while they have the *chutzpah* to believe themselves to be "God's chosen people."[396]

---

[393] Board of Deputies of British Jews (@BoardofDeputies): "We were honoured to speak with @ppvernon @davidlmearn and learn about the exciting @anchor-windrushproject. We are deeply touched by the care they are taking to recognise the little known Jewish history of the HMT Empire Windrush and support their vision for a Windrush monument."

[394] Sachs, "Israel's Right-Wing Majority."; Lederman, "Knesset Elections 2021."; "Israel's Ultra-Right to Join Forces."

[395] Baroud, "Israel's Legacy of Terror and Ethnic Cleansing."; Basma, "Israel's Treatment of Ethiopian."; "Israel: 50 Years of Occupation Abuses."

[396] Peretz, "'Goyim Were Born Only to Serve Us.'"; Abu Naser, "Extreme Quotes From."

Maria Farmer's (a victim of the Jewish elite child traffickers Jeffery Epstein and Ghislaine Maxwell) testimony of the treatment of her and her fellow gentile underage girls, passed around by this cabal of evil elites, is chilling, but succinctly shows that the elites that Epstein and Maxwell socialize with are not simply "the elite," as more daring media outlets might go so far as acknowledging, but truly an ethnic clan, a mafia, of deranged, power hungry lunatics:

When I asked Ghislaine why I couldn't get food she said "It's a Jewish country club. You're not Jewish. They're not going to serve you." This is how this woman spoke to me. This is how these people [Jews] think! They honest to God think their DNA is better than everybody else's! I swear to you. It was a scene all the time with them. With [Eileen] Guggenheim, with Jeffery Epstein, with Ghislaine. . . . She was raping just as many people. And they could cut you down and it was so morally devastating. You just felt useless as a human being when you were told you were nothing because you're not Jewish, you're stupid, a useless white girl, poor little peasant, the things I was called, I believed it! Because it was a cult. . . . You wouldn't believe the way Jeffery spoke about African Americans. It just made my skin crawl. Anyone who was not Jewish. It was really horrifying. It showed me a great deal about how these people truly believe. And it was every one of them, the way they spoke. [Eileen Guggenheim's daughter once asked her,] "Mommy, why do you call Maria a nobody?" [And she said] "Honey, Maria is not a Jew, she is a nobody."[397]

In spite of the chauvinist worldview of the Jewish race, especially in Israel where their will can be carried out through hard power and violent action, the Diaspora Jews are incredibly supportive of immigration, but really only non-White immigration, into their host nations.[398] Whether one refers to the Jewish-controlled left wing or the similarly controlled establishment conservative bloc in the US

---

[397] Red Ice TV, "Epstein & Ghislaine Maxwell Victim."
[398] Washington Watcher II, "U.S. Ruling Class Reluctant to Accept Ukrainian Refugees."

matters not, as the near-universal view among them across political lines is that immigration, specifically of non-Whites, into the US and Europe is a positive occurrence.[399]

One well-documented case of Jews salivating at the mouth over White genocide, seen clear as day, is the case of the Jewish SPLC "hate expert" Mark Potok. While watching Potok being interviewed for a documentary on the alt-right, many pointed out two interesting images on the wall in his office in the form of a couple of charts. Some dared to look closer, finding that the charts were indeed charts of the decline of the White majority in the US and Europe.[400] Why would a Jewish activist at a thoroughly Jewish "anti-racist" NGO keep count of such numbers? Aren't Jews White? Evidently not. Indeed, these leftist Jews believe all Whites to be racist and hide behind a thinly veiled mask of "anti-racist" which, of course, is an easy-to-decipher code that necessarily means "anti-White." Being a member of the SPLC, a state entrenched NGO which operates largely as a government institution without any of the liability, Potok has testified before the Senate and the UN High Commission.[401] Complete control by anti-White Jews is an institutional problem aided by cross pollination and inter-institutional legitimization of the most evil characters and organizations imaginable, like the ADL, SPLC, Hope Not Hate, National The Lawyers Guild, The Bail Project, and Pro Publica.

Or take Barbara Lerner Spectre, an American Jew who founded a major Jewish studies NGO in Sweden. According to her:

> I think there's a resurgence of anti-Semitism because at this point in time, Europe has not yet learned how to be multicultural, and I think we [Jews] are going to be part of the

---

[399] Take for example how the late Sheldon Adelson was a Jew who leaned Republican but was still pro-immigration. Miller, "Bill Gates, Warren Buffett, Sheldon Adelson."

[400] Rotten Tomatoes Indie, "Alt-Right: Age of Rage." It can be seen at the 1:00 minute mark.

[401] Hamilton, "30 To Watch, They Say." "The SPLC works with, instructs, and sets racial and ideological agendas for local, state, and federal police agencies, including the FBI and Department of Homeland Security, supplying data on private citizens and groups that it is illegal for the government to collect." See also how this DHS report cites the SPLC:
Chermak et al., "The Organizational Dynamics."

throes of that transformation which must take place. Europe is not going to be the monolithic societies they once were in the last century. Jews are going to be at the center of that. It's a huge transformation for Europe to make. They are now going into a multicultural mode, and Jews are going to be resented because of our leading role. But without that leading role and without that transformation, Europe will not survive.[402]

Again, let's take her word for it. As pointed out by Scott Howard in *The Open Society Playbook*, American Jews subverting White countries, including America, is hardly anything new. Unsurprisingly, Spectre was educated at the State Department's and the globalist NGOs' favorite university, none other than Columbia. Of course, Spectre is well-aware of the benefits of a cohesive and homogenous society, having lived the majority of her adult life in the Jewish ethnostate of Israel before moving to the Whitest country she could find to encourage "diversity." Barbara Spectre is hardly an anomaly. Indeed, the specter of Spectres haunts all Western nations. For example, the Jewish sociologist Ronit Lentin plays a strikingly similar role in Ireland.[403]

Of course, there is the oft-repeated argument that immigration is actually saving Europe instead of destroying it, due to an aging population and low birth rates, similar to the situation in the US. Of course, if one ever promotes the idea of increasing native birthrates as the solution, it is attacked as "racist" or bad for the environment. Coincidentally however, increased immigration invariably leads to a lower standard of living for the native-born due to economic competition. And if the cost of saving the economy is turning London into an unrecognizable Londonistan, it is no victory at all, but an invasion and conquest by other means.

We must also not forget the reaction to the Kyle Rittenhouse self-defense case. Rittenhouse, a White teenager, defended himself from multiple Antifa attackers, at least two of whom were Jewish. The Jewish Joshua Ziminski fired a shot in the air, causing Rittenhouse

---

[402] Ivn 1977, "Barbara Lerner Spectre."
[403] Lentin was born in Israel and "has advocated an open-door immigration policy for Ireland and opposes all deportations," according to his Wikipedia page.

to stand his ground, which led him to shoot the Jewish Joseph Rosenbaum as he lunged at Rittenhouse. Kyle went on to defend himself from two other attackers, Anthony Huber who was also likely a Jew, and Gaige Grosskreutz.[404] Liberal Jews who deceive themselves and others into believing they are individualists who don't see race immediately outed themselves. While the case was clear self-defense and Kyle was acquitted with prejudice, the government still targeted him to make an example out of him. One might be forgiven if they infer a motivation of Jewish entitlement. "How dare this gentile peasant kill two of our own! Who does he think he is?" After months of the Jewish media lying about the situation, a Black career criminal, Darrell Brooks, let out on a frivolously minuscule bail by the Jewish judge David Feiss, drove his car into a crowd of White families at a Christmas parade in Waukesha, killing six. For the left, this was mission accomplished.[405]

Immediately afterward, many Jews went on to signal their approval for this anti-White terrorist attack on social media. For example, Democratic Party operative Mary Lemanski called the attack "karma," while "journalist" Robert Silverman went after journalists who reported on the perpetrator's identity, as opposed to the *genteel* thing to do, which is, of course, to show sympathy to victims no matter what group they come from.[406] All the ADL had to say about the situation was that the attacker once posted an anti-Semitic meme six years prior to the incident but "does not appear to actively subscribe to an extremist ideology."[407] To leftist Jews, Darrel Brooks' call to violence against White children and elderly before the attack doesn't count as extremism; it is expected and applauded.[408]

After being held on a five million dollar bail, a far cry from the attacker's thousand dollar bail he paid before the incident, The Bail Project, an NGO founded by the Jewish Robin Steinberg which works

---

[404] NJP, "Statement on the Kyle Rittenhouse Verdict": "The violent Antifa he killed and wounded that night when he was attacked included two Jews, a domestic abuser, and a convicted pedophile."

[405] Pajeet, "Judge Who Freed Darrell Brooks."; NJP, "Terror in Waukesha."

[406] Pajeet, "Activism Alert: Flood These Inboxes."; Andy Ngô (@MrAndyNfgo), "I don't want to speak to you & I stand by my reporting."

[407] "Alleged Waukesha Attacker."

[408] NJP, "Statement on the Anti-White Terror."

to free dangerous criminals, especially BLM and Antifa rioters, by paying their bail, started a GoFundMe page for the terrorist.[409] The fundraiser was specifically started by the Jewish Holly Zoller under the name "Bail fund for Darrell Brooks Jr." before it was taken down in response to public outcry.[410] It must be understood that the backgrounds of all of these characters are not only Jewish per se but *extremely* liberal, "anti-racist," and supposedly radical egalitarian leftists, a far cry from the Likud-esque racial hatred that they display when the chips are down.

The examples of open Jewish disdain for Whites and Christians go on and on. We need not list every example. From those already listed to other occurrences—such as Israeli spies celebrating 9/11 as it happened, Israel attacking the defenseless USS *Liberty* during the Six-Day War, lying about WMDs in Iraq, promoting mass non-White migration, subverting academia and now training pedophilic teachers to groom children (queer theory) and teaching non-White students to hate Whites at a young age (critical race theory), Israel refusing to fight in the so-called global war on terror despite having a massive American-paid-for military and actually being located in the most active region, cynically encouraging anti-Muslim hatred and subsequently framing blame for the Iraq War on suburban and rural Whites rather than the Jewish neocons who actually orchestrated it, and the list goes on—Jews have proven time and time again that they are an adversary to the majority population, and these are only some of the heinous actions they have taken in living memory alone.[411]

This type of behavior has been recorded since as early as the writings of Cicero in the Roman Republic.[412] They are a diaspora people and the only way for them to succeed as a cohesive and distinct group, on a sociobiological level, is as a parasite opposed to the host body politic. As the rulers and organizers of their hated host societies, they use their power and wrath, culminating in actively

---

[409] Go, "Who Is Holly McGlawn-Zoller."
[410] Ibid.
[411] Titor, "The Dancing Israelis."; WVradioman, "The USS Liberty Navy Ship."; Mac-Donald, "Understanding Jewish Influence III."; Howard, *The Transgender–Industrial Complex*; Connelly, "Critical Race."
[412] See Cicero's famous oration, *Pro Flacco*.

and gleefully harming their ruled-over people and using the working-class gentiles, and especially Whites, toward their own ends in the Middle East, while imported minorities (which are often their adversaries in the Middle East) are used to divide and conquer their host on sectarian lines.

V

Let us wrap up on the subject of the elite. We can now make a more educated estimate as to how power works under the current system. For much of our search on the nature of power, whether power is located in the Cathedral, moneyed interests, etc., one must ask the question of how much it actually matters where power truly lies as a "heart." Still, the thesis holds that power does reside in money, because international finance predominates over the Cathedral. Furthermore, power can be measured as a function of the will to power and capital together. The smaller the entity, the greater power that it can exert with a smaller amount of capital, meaning that the equation can be expressed as $(W + C) / N = P$ (N being a factor of personnel count). At the larger end of the spectrum would be a country which, due to its size, has competing interests, in the form of political parties and NGOs, that inhibit its will to power. The smallest N would of course be 1, the individual. As a result, individuals with massive amounts of wealth who have no need to squabble with other personalities can target funds more directly.

George Soros, Paul Singer, or Larry Fink, for example, are individuals who can direct world events through the utilization of billions of dollars. While this is a large sum of fluid capital to be wielded in terms of the individual level, on the global level it is a relatively small portion of pocket change. Still, this small amount of money is able to accomplish great feats. The danger of Jewish power when functioning in this way is that Jews operate as an organization with large portions of the world's wealth, and control of the world financial system. As individual actors working together, the best of both worlds is achieved as Jews are clearly generally on the same wavelength as pertains to certain existential issues, such as support for mass migration, the sexual revolution, racial integration, and the lessened influence of Christianity in the West, but can avoid many squabbles as their group seems to have a level of unspoken *a priori* understanding internally, thereby transcending the N of the equation and having an inherent advantage in wielding power against atomized adversaries.[413]

Of the first of the six frames discussed, that the current regime is simply a result of bureaucratic incompetence, we can flat out reject as an overarching cause for the behavior of the regime as a whole because we are overall more tyrannized by the bureaucracy when it is competent rather than incompetent. While the bureaucracy is incompetent, this in fact is a benefit to those who live under the regime. The ruling class would undoubtedly be willing to replace every incompetent low-level manager with a computer program if it meant that carrying out the will of the greater organization would be fulfilled. What incompetence can explain, however, is when the regime blunders. While Trump was a disappointment and far from the aristocratic warrior lion that he portrayed himself as, it is undeniable that Trump's first election was a complete accident of history caused by the regime's incompetence, especially in the media. We can see that this was a mistake not to be repeated, as the entire establishment (the FBI, Big Tech, the oligarch class, the poll workers and other bureaucratic level operatives, the media, federal courts, both party establishments, paramilitaries, etc.) united and marched in lock step over the course of the lame duck period and especially after the January 6th protest, culminating in one of the most blatant coups in the history of the developed Western world. While incompetence is a real factor, the truth is that it is less of a factor in the direction of the regime, but rather an explanation for when the regime's overarching plan is detoured. The Trump phenomenon of elite failure was short lived. We are not quite Brazil *yet*.[414]

---

[413] This is precisely why libertarianism is so caustic for Whites. Europe was able to conquer the world when their nations were united and their leadership was in detente. The Iron Law of Oligarchy of Michels predicts that, divided, every group will eventually fall to a well-organized minority.

[414] This was in part proven by the fact that Trump was only able to enter office for a second administration due to division within the elite, especially the tech elite, who saw usefulness in the mythos of Trump.

The second and third frames are inherently contradictory, and yet they work in tandem. The question is whether the elite work as an organized global conspiracy, like a pyramid, or whether there is a *zeitgeist* mainly portrayed within the Cathedral institutions which guides elite thought: essentially, convergent behavior. It would clearly *appear* that there is a conspiracy afoot, a true plan which "goes all the way to the top." And yet, no one is able to point out where this "top" truly lies. The closest thing that we could point to as a top are the various elite institutions whose memberships include the most powerful and influential people in the world: organizations such as the International Monetary Fund, the Trilateral Commission, the Council on Foreign Relations, the World Economic Forum, the Bilderberg Group, Bohemian Grove, etc. However, there is no true permanent leader of these groups outside of Klaus Schwab, who serves as the founder and main thought leader of the WEF. These are simply forums where elites meet, similar to how elites have always met together throughout history, the difference being that the elites of our age are deranged and entirely separate from the people over whom they presume to rule. Furthermore, while these groups certainly share rosters, there is no single master that also has control of all of them. There simply is no top of the pyramid, at least that we know of.

And yet they operate as if they are a cabal of conspirators all working toward the same end. And indeed they are, though largely by convergent thought and behavior and not always direct collaboration. The elite are largely Jewish, and Jews generally have similar beliefs and a racial spirit that is distinct from other peoples, meaning that they appear to conspire (and admittedly, they often do) when in reality they have a similar lived experience and thus behave similarly when viewed by an out-group, and especially one that has been indoctrinated to ignore racial patterns.[415] Undoubtedly, Jews likely believe themselves to be creative and original thinkers; we have all heard the proverbs about Jewish families arguing among each other. And it is true that Jews are a

---

[415] MacDonald, *Culture of Critique.*; For a discussion of what happens when Whites are color blind while everyone else is competing see Steuben, "Hate Game Theory" or Secor, "Game Theory and the Transactional Nature of Violence."

debating people and have developed much of the political theory of the past two centuries due to a leftist subculture which grew out of a general enjoyment of debate, which can easily be seen not only in modern intellectual culture, but potentially even in the Jewish barter culture common among Semitic peoples (and it is out of this debate culture that what Kevin MacDonald dubbed the "culture of critique" emerged).

This relatively united Jewish nucleus of elites allows for a complete change in the culture of an institution, elite or otherwise, as seen with the potentially "accidental" Judaization of the elite American institutions and social sciences in the early twentieth century. If one group is subliminally working together through ethnic solidarity while the competitors are atomized, an elite subculture is quickly created by a sort of interracial gravity pull of "compatible" individuals to the Jewish nucleus, as seen most notably with the token Whites in psychoanalysis (such as Carl Jung, until he became at odds with the Jewish nucleus), Boasian anthropology (as with Margaret Mead), and critical theory (as with Jürgen Habermas).[416] While in-group preference is generally prevalent in all races (modern Whites being an unusual exception outside of the most right-wing, in part due to White in-group preference being demonized by the establishment, which just so happens to be predominantly Jewish), Jews excel at out-competing other races through nepotism due to their unique historical experience as a diaspora.

This elite group is certainly gifted in business, as Jews have for centuries been a merchant people, and as we discussed, money is an important function of potential power exertion (at least after the end of the "noble ages" dominated by the priest and warrior castes, eras of higher spiritual quality, where money as we think of it today was much less relevant). Profit motive, which is our fourth power frame, has surprisingly low predicting capability. It is true that it is necessary for money to be raised to obtain large amounts of power. But when much of the capital of the world is already centralized by a moneyed elite made up largely of Jews and philo-Semites, and said individuals who make up the international oligarch class already

---

[416] Ibid.

have more money than what is possible to reasonably spend, further profits become less of an incentive, and any incentive toward more profits is toward the aims of power or, as they like to brand it, "philanthropy."[417] Of course, the oligarchs do utilize certain societal mechanisms, such as ESG ratings and other carrot-and-stick tactics, to goad high-level business bureaucrats such as CEOs in the right direction. While not entirely beholden to profits, board members would rather improve than destroy the company they have been given responsibility for. Nevertheless, the organizations who are most heavily invested in shadowy groups who provide such incentives are often much larger and often represent *trillions* of dollars in assets, such as the Jewish-owned BlackRock; or Vanguard, which has a large stake in MorningStar, the company that doles out ESG or "woke" scores to companies that abide by "stakeholder capitalism."[418] Stakeholder capitalism is an idea formulated by the WEF, another organization that dwarfs any normal corporation. Thus, while a large corporation such as Nike or GameStop might be simply bribed into going along with such counterproductive ideologies, in the end the money can be traced back to shadowy groups and banks that either own or control unimaginable amounts of capital (for example, the three largest owners of GameStop are the Jewish investor Ryan Cohen, as well as Vanguard and BlackRock, while the top Nike investors are BlackRock, Vanguard, State Street Global Advisors, and Alliance Bernstein, an asset management firm started by the Jews Zalman Bernstein, Paul Bernstein, Roger Hertog, and Lewis Sanders).[419] These groups and banks and the individuals who own large stakes in them can afford to take a small loss when their power is basically limitless. Chasing profits explains some of the elite phenomena, but not nearly enough for a satisfactory answer to the nature of power in the modern globalist world order.

Frankly, it would appear as though the Jewish race operates as a kin-based mafia or clan with little difference from the Sicilian or

---

[417] Gallindoss, "Jews Make-up 19%."
[418] Taranto, "How Woke Capital Politicized Your Retirement Account."; Doescher, "Destroying the Altar of 'Woke.'"
[419] These two examples were not cherry-picked but picked randomly. Pick corporations out of a hat and you will find similar phenomena taking place across the board.

Irish mafias that were dominant during the same era as the Jewish mass migration to the US. The mafia had large sway in the government, controlled the unions, the night clubs, gambling venues, and protected and produced the smut and vice. In fact, much of the reason that the mafia is incapacitated in the modern context, outside of Mexican and Black gangs taking over the drug trade, may be that the Jews have been instrumental in simply legalizing much of what was once illegal, or at least not tolerated in polite society.[420] The Jews, having a long history of legalism and studying fine print in their scriptures, and being more intelligent than other ethnic groups, were able to create an environment hospitable to their kind where other groups that could operate in an illicit environment, outside the purview of the law and therefore the prying eyes of say the IRS, could no longer compete.[421] Furthermore, the Italians and Irish largely assimilated into American White society while the Jews still have not, aiding them in continued in-group solidarity. It must be noted that "assimilate" should be taken to mean assimilated into the predominate cultural values and not just attaining high socio-economic status, for while Jewish success might be argued to be a form of assimilation, it is actually a form of subversion, as they use their positions to undermine America's White Christian culture. Today, certain addictive drugs are still largely illegal in the US but, where they have been legalized, it is not a criminal underworld that dominates the market, but relatively high-IQ enterprising merchants that are able to survive in a new environment more complicated than simply buying wholesale, reselling, and making profit.[422]

This has been the case in riotous community organizing, borderline illegal monopolism in the unions, the pornography industry, the casinos, lawfare, and the degenerate media, all of which were illegal or at least highly discouraged before Jewish

---

[420]See Hamilton, "The SPLC."
[421] See Wexler, "Jewish Word." And Sacks, "A Word of Torah."
[422] Take for example the Jewish Sackler family, which runs Purdue Pharma. It was the Sacklers who are in large part responsible for the opioid epidemic which decimated White rural America, and were able to realize their immoral venture through a complex scheme of lobbying Congress, incentivizing doctors, sophisticated marketing, influencing regulatory agencies, and manipulating studies. See van de Camp, "Work to Be Such a Man." See also Mulvihill and Peltz, "After Years of Pain."

capture of the US and, like in Weimar Germany, all largely in the hands of this subversive and antagonistic ethnic group.[423] It would be unsurprising if similar phenomena were not in action across the country and indeed across the globe; and of vices other than drugs, such as human trafficking, the scandal involving Jeffery Epstein, a Jewish oligarch with connections to the Mossad, has likely only given a sneak peek into the Jewish underground economy.[424]

This is not to say that Jews control the US through some grand Protocols of Zion-esque centralized conspiracy. Indeed, this small group would have much difficulty achieving their group goals alone. It cannot be denied that the interests of Jews often align with other groups, such as women (who have always been a potential force in society), and White ethnics such as Italians, Poles, and the Irish, who have played a large part in left-wing causes, such as in pro-immigrant legislation.[425] However, if one were to pin down a single community as the major power center of post-Hoover and especially post-1968 American society, it would be quite difficult to pin it down on any other group than a Jewish elite caste. Each of the previously discussed theories of power was, at least in part, correct but incomplete and therefore not wholly correct. What each of the previously discussed theories of power have in common that ties them all together is Jewish influence. Kennedy may have been Irish-American and the Poles may have once held large control over mid-Atlantic Democratic Party metapolitics, but there simply was no intellectual, capital, or bureaucratic mass movement by or led by White ethnics. Often it was these White ethnics, no different from Blacks, who were manipulated toward blatantly left-wing ends and then discarded. This can be seen in how the neighborhoods of the Catholic White ethnics have mostly been wiped out against their own interests by other groups, such as Blacks and Hispanics, which ultimately served the purpose of Jewish interests, not the interests of the White working class, as was promised. Beginning in the 1930s, and then rapidly accelerating in the aftermath of the Second World War, and finally being consolidated in the campus Vietnam

---

[423] Stuyvesant, "The German-Jewish Kulturkampf."
[424] "Jeffrey Epstein Was Blackmailing Politicians."
[425] Meagher, "Revisiting the History of Irish American Progressives."

protest movement of the late 1960s, Jewish power has been an undeniable matter of simple fact.

PART THREE

THE HOUR OF DECISION

7

The American Regime

"The pandemic represents a rare but narrow window of opportunity to reflect, reimagine, and reset our world."
— *Klaus Schwab,*
"Now Is the Time for a 'Great Reset'"

It has now finally become somewhat clearer who is in control, despite how the subject of power is highly complicated and thus difficult to grasp simply. The ancient Jewish race, which has seen the coming and going of empires over the course of thousands of years, knows well what environment is most suitable for its people. In this way, Jews can be characterized as similar to the beaver, gopher, or hamster: species which are not perfectly adapted to an environment as it is in its current state, but subconsciously aim to and are adapted to actively change their environment, whether that be the dam of the beaver, the cave systems of gophers and hamsters, or the decaying society of the Jew.

Jews are completely incapable of thriving in a society at its metaphysical apex, but flourish in a society at its material zenith, such as nineteenth- and twentieth-century Europe on the whole and the once rising star of the United States. When society is being built from the ground up, when Gothic cathedrals are being built, or great aqueducts, when seminal works of art are being made, when the hinterland is conquered, one would be amazed to find few if any

224 | THE AMERICAN REGIME

Jews.[426] They are not a people well-known for building, labor, or any sort of virtue that is indispensable for the founding of a great people, as they are a *fellah* people whose own empire was destroyed thousands of years ago, similar to Armenians, Chaldeans, and other ancient groups that still chug along.[427] As a people fallen from greatness some thousands of years ago, the role of building a great civilization has long since passed them after their rise and fall.

They are also well-adapted to an economically variable society, having good instincts in the world of material wealth. For hundreds of years in Europe and over a hundred years in the United States, the concerted, though often unconscious, movement of the Jews has been the creation of a global environment in which they are naturally capable of consistently rising to the top even without nepotism. For no longer is merit determined by martial ability, leadership, connection to a higher ideal, or transcendent value. No, by supposed mere coincidence, our society has been terraformed into one which values thievery, quantity, money, lawfare, deception, and propaganda: all the strengths of this ethnic clan. Largely through the control of world capital, and then through the hearts and minds in the Cathedral institutions, spreading and poisoning every last institution not yet already fallen, they now have a complete control that is so intact and anti-fragile that most attacks against it make them only stronger—at least for now. By controlling public discourse since the childhood of our oldest generations, it is impossible even to publicly criticize the regime of darkness cast upon us. Yes, they all want to know who rules, but God help you if you tell them. Under this globalist one-world economy and perhaps even one-world government, neoliberalism, degeneracy, and the mixing of all peoples into one easily-controlled mush will be sought

---

[426] Sarna and Golden, "The American Jewish Experience." Before 1900, when the Wild West was being conquered, Jews were less than 1% of the population. After 1900 their number grew to 3%. About half lived in urban New York City, far from the frontier.

[427] *Fellah*, or plural *Fellaheen*, usually means an Egyptian farmer, however, Spengler used it in a particular sense to convey the state of a culture when it has passed into its winter and has burnt out, and the people are content to be ruled over by others and no longer act as a historical force. One would imagine that the conquering Franks encountered a similar population that indifferently accepted them as their new overlords in Gaul during the collapse of Western Rome, just as the *fellah* were content to accept the conquering Arabs as their new overlords.

out as policy, and techno-hedonism will rule. The spine of all peoples will be broken under the yoke of a small but intelligent and well-organized unit of bloodthirsty moneychangers and the spiritual Jews: those who are born as vulture capitalists and other fallen merchants, and psychopathic sell-outs who cynically intermix with this alien people for power and undeserved prestige.

I

Rule by Jews will result in—and indeed already has in many ways— the extermination of White nations. The Jewish elite have consistently, since their first interactions with the peoples of Europe, allied themselves with other races and religions, or encouraged infighting to destroy Christendom and Europe. This was their *modus operandi* during the initial Islamic conquests, the revolutions of the nineteenth and twentieth centuries, and it continues in an even more out-in-the-open way today.

By encouraging particularly violent races, such as Blacks and Central Americans in the US and Africans and Arabs in Europe, to come into greater contact with the largely peaceful native Whites, the globalist empire actively encourages the murder, looting, and rape of millions of Whites.[428] As a result, White environments have been oversaturated with predators, preventing White population growth and accelerating the decline in White numbers within their homelands.[429] Intermixing of these populations also contributes to the decline in White numbers.[430] Meanwhile, the places in which these people are being produced, the entirety of the Asian and African continents, are reproducing themselves full-throttle, ever sure to keep up with demand.[431] They trick their gullible White hosts into foolish behavior, showing them *Coming of Age in Samoa* or climate change metrics stating that the world population must go down and therefore Whites must self-exterminate, always

---

[428] Coulter, *¡Adios, America!*
[429] Johnson, "White Extinction."
[430] Ibid.
[431] Roberts, "Islam Won't Conquer the World—but Africa Might." Note that Hispanic birthrates are falling precipitously.

neglecting to mention that humanity could go extinct tomorrow and the environment would still eventually be thrashed beyond our wildest dreams, assuming their own predictions are correct.

When asking if there is a narrative with a barely-hidden agenda, we need only ask what result is *always* the true end goal. Are mass immigration, depopulation, the Great Reset, and climate hysteria truly ends in themselves, and not merely the means toward a more insidious end? No matter what their supposed goal, the destruction of their historic enemy never ceases to *coincidentally* play a central role in the solution. Even when the cause and solution do not logically follow, such as in the idea that the White population must seriously decline, despite how the White birth rate has already been plummeting for decades while those of Asia and Africa sharply increase, the solution is always the same.[432] At the same time, one will find little grief from them on the higher birthrates of the impoverished migrants allowed to wash up on our shores to replace the productive members of Western civilization through Great Society-era welfare, designed to transfer resources from the productive to the unproductive. No, you will be amazed to find the environmentalist inviting these harbingers of the end with open arms, future comrades for Jewish-led "progress." The Great Reset is nothing but the handmaid of the Great Replacement.

"Oh, but the economy will suffer," they will say. To your amazement, the Marxist professor suddenly becomes an Austrian economist as soon as the precious immigrants are threatened from not being able to exercise their God-given right to access White countries. Of course, Whites are supposedly evil and racist according to these same Jewish intellectuals, so perhaps the nationalist movements are in actuality saving these poor defenseless souls![433] No, the Jew is animated by hatred for his gracious host more than he is by any consistent, logical aim.[434] To him, consistency is but a tool, part of a methodical cost-benefit analysis. It is no wonder that his intellectual endeavors over the past

---

[432] Ibid.; Ingram, "Seeds Unsown."
[433]Take Neol Ignatiev, a Jewish Harvard professor whose views are well received in academia. According to him, "Whiteness is . . . simply an oppressive social category." Per Eliasson, "Noel Ignatiev calls for the end of whiteness."
[434] Ibid.

hundred years have amounted to little more than animating the perpetual slop against natural order.[435] Furthermore, the same leftists who for the last sixty years have poorly pretended to represent the working class now have the gall to tell them that immigrants do the jobs we are supposedly unwilling to do, and indeed work harder! As to the counter argument that many Whites are purposefully unemployed or underemployed as evidenced by the proliferation of "help wanted" signs at almost every business over the past two years, one should keep in mind that pay has not kept up with inflation, and that immigration directly represses wages. It is difficult to disparage certain Whites for being work-shy when the juice is increasingly not worth the squeeze, and when previous generations took an honest day's pay for an honest day's work for granted. Not only is this a testament to the impotence of the Jewish-infiltrated union system—largely dismantled since its zenith—toward helping those who actually work with their hands; it is also a betrayal of their true feelings toward these wretches who find their way onto our shores. The globalists see Jamal, Parag, Juan, and Mohammed not with any of the compassion or empathy that they always harp on about when guilt-tripping Whites, but as nothing more than hardware to be utilized toward the inflation of their stock market holdings or, at best, a consistent voter base to acquiesce to whatever they wish to inflict on the population through sham democracy.

Diversity is another ploy, implicitly admitting they wish to extinguish both the White race and European-derived culture, precisely as was done to Haman in the Book of Esther.[436] The Jewish postwar left has been instrumental in undermining the cultural confidence of all European peoples, especially that of America. "America doesn't have a culture," "What even is 'white' anyway?," "Diversity is our strength," and all the rest are thinly-veiled jabs into the heart of White society by the antinomian intellectual class toward this end. Subversive memetic catch phrases such as these,

---

[435] MacDonald, "Understanding Jewish Influence III." Jews push for immigration via the neocon movement. See also Mercer, "The Great Replacement," for the Jewish litany of replacement. See also Peinovich, "Jewish Media Figures Celebrate White Decline in Latest Census."
[436] American Renaissance, "Diversity Means Fewer White People."

intended to slowly chip away the moral fortitude of a nation, and indeed a civilization, cause mass destruction to the greater whole, just as the waves erode the beach cliff over time, though one wouldn't notice after only a single day.

They wish for a world after Whites, a world after Europe and America; this is as clear as day. They have an unhealthy obsession with this apocalyptic future which their pets are too stupid to fully grasp. Indeed, I would need to change little of this chapter, beyond perhaps adding some explanation as to why their game is actually a good thing and frame it in a positive light, to have it published in *Haaretz* or *The New York Times.* Despite what they say, the question is not whether their aim is the destruction of our society, but whether they truly believe in their screed and if they are actively malicious. Historical and current behavior would certainly support both propositions.

II

We can already see the fruits of this Jewish globalist takeover, despite White minority status in the United States still being about twenty years away, and longer than that in Europe, which has largely been under the boot of the American empire since 1945 and has been succumbing to Judeo-New England NGO control in the East since 1989.[437] With the complete coalescence of the elite right and elite left under a Jewish consensus, the elite in America and most of the developed nations as well have instituted the beginnings of a one-world police state enforced by the state, their participant NGOs, and the international finance class, working hand-in-hand to back the masses into a corner, using emerging crises as a front for their "Great Reset" agenda.

Control of the education system, combined with the old age in which Whites and people who live in the West in general have children, is a recipe for the erasure of Western culture without even a single shot being fired. This is highly reminiscent of the Native American forced assimilation through state schools. As Native

---

[437] Gest, "What Happens When White People."

American culture was oral and the children were taught by those with a radically different worldview, their culture quickly died out. In America, this is already occurring with the erasure of "dead white men" from the curriculum and the complete disappearance of the classics in pedagogy.[438] Young Whites are sacrificed at the altar of "education," taught to hate themselves, to question their sexuality, and shun their heritage and religion. This is only exacerbated by the psychological warfare techniques passed as "philosophy," that we know as critical theory, critical pedagogy, critical race theory, and queer theory, all devised largely by Jewish academics and their token pets. The elite want an atomized and deracinated populace, starting with the Whites and then moving on to the next races until only two are left: the slaves and the masters.

The worst elements of society, once the butt of jokes and only found in hiding on obscure corners of the internet or in seedy alleyway-ridden parts of the inner city, were groomed and educated to rule the normal healthy world. Our governing elite class has been filled to the brim with the mentally ill, the degenerates, and most especially those with dark triad traits.[439] As for the lower bureaucracy, it is staffed with the dregs of society through worker programs for those who are too incompetent, stupid, or unlikeable for the private world.

These bureaucrats are not the true rulers, of course, but the strength of the bureaucratic theory of power is that, for the common man, for all intents and purposes, *indeed they are*. This is by design, no different from the Soviets utilizing the Jewish population to man the ranks of the secret police, knowing their disdain for the rural Ukrainians, or using the worst criminals to staff the gulags.[440] The American secret police come from the big cities, thousands of miles away from where they will carry out the will of the Jewish power elite. They are recruited from homosexuals, basket cases, already powerful families, and the over-ambitious who take themselves too

---

[438] For example: Hoyt, "Notre Dame Students Demand."
[439] Łobaczewski, *Political Ponerology*. For example, Rachel Levine, the assistant Secretary of Health is Jewish and transgender.
[440] Solzhenitsyn, *The Gulag Archipelago*; Devlin, "Solzhenitsyn on the Jews & Soviet Russia."

seriously.[441] This is also all by design. The system would not work as well if the security agencies were not staffed by those who have no connection to their own family, let alone the historical American people. These are the enforcers of the police state.

Is it any surprise then that already the globalist first line of defense has been gleefully enforcing international tyranny, when only months before serving as the flank guard of the state-sanctioned anarchists who tore down the traditional economy, paving the way for complete domination of the top multinational corporations? And is it any wonder why the top corporations and international finance supported, and even funded, these open terrorist organizations?[442] With the state monopoly of the legitimate use of force being centralized in the hands of the freaks and low-status dregs—and thus the criminals becoming the policemen—it is only inevitable that the lawful White populace will become the "criminals." The brutality that awaits us under this state of affairs is already occurring globally. Whether it be the parents spied on by the FBI and arrested for protesting the mind rape of their children, the Australian police pepper spraying protesters for having the audacity to leave their homes, or a Catholic father being raided by the FBI for *actually peacefully* protesting outside of an abortion clinic, tyranny is here, and here to stay.[443]

The controlled opposition, the center right, is always ready to come to the defense of the globalist world government as well, serving as the sword and shield of corporate interests. They rant and rave about the evils of big government, knowing full well that the government is hardly the only factor in this tyranny. They may make grandiose statements for audio clips to be used by the pretend right-wing news agencies and the cameras, but in the end, they know full well who really pays for their campaign. The private sector under our modern police state can't arrest us, this is true, but they can use their immense power to press the boot onto the neck

---

[441] Federale, "The FBI Question."
[442] Goldenberg, "Here Are the Companies."
[443] Emmons, "BREAKING: Biden Admin Mobilizes FBI."; HealthImpactNews, "Australian Police Attack Children."; Evans, "FBI Whistleblowers Claim Agents Investigated Parents."; Mullen, "New Information Raises Questions about FBI Raid."

of the American people and the people of the world through other means.

The government, at least in the US, does not yet have enough uncontested legitimacy to completely overthrow the Constitution and the First Amendment with it. If polls of non-White immigrants and the younger generations are any indication though, this won't last forever.[444] However, in the meantime the regime happily makes do by outsourcing censorship to the private sector. Under our current regime, a culture opposing the lockdowns, vaccine mandates, and the deep state coup is discussed in similar fashion as dissent in the totalitarian states of the last century. The punishment is not yet arrest, only de-platforming of speech, the seizure of bank accounts, and being fired from one's job.[445] Most major corporations were for months able to fire on a whim anyone who refuses their forced vaccination. Meanwhile, our supposed representatives screeched "It's a private corporation!"

Much violence is also outsourced from the government to other organizations.[446] The right to peacefully assemble is *de facto* abolished as the unofficial provocateurs of the government swoop in to break up any meaningful demonstration.[447] These agent provocateurs of the regime are heavily funded by the government with funds washed through NGOs, and their organization and communication is astroturfed by social media conglomerates facilitating communication.[448] They are able to run amok with impunity as the true counter-partisan enforcement arm of the state, attacking and intimidating protesters and bystanders through violence and harassment. Any violence short of murder is permitted by the legal system, already hollowed and bought out by elite financiers such as Soros.[449] Charges are simply dropped and crimes

---

[444] Poushter, "40% Of Millennials OK with Limiting Speech." See Ekins, "The State of Free Speech and Tolerance in America." Racial minorities support government banning public hate speech, including 56 percent of African Americans and 58 percent of Latinos. Conversely, a majority of white Americans (66 percent) oppose banning hate speech.

[445] Porter, "Alt-Right."; "Major U.S. Bank Shuts Down 'Alt-Right' Accounts."

[446] Malkin, "One Nation under Anarcho-Tyranny."

[447] Dickson, "Sam Dickson's Statement to Charlottesville Inquiry."; Dickson, "Sam Dickson on Deep State Attack."

[448] Athey, "The Mob That Doxxed Tucker Carlson."

[449] Alexander, "George Soros-Backed Groups."

so unforgivably heinous are lowered to an extent that the perpetrator is able to plead guilty and walk free with probation.[450]

Other forms of non-violent coercion are also outsourced to non-state actors.[451] Antifa, whose elite membership today is predominantly Jewish, just as it was in Weimar Germany, frequently uses infiltration and doxing to stifle free speech by Whites, and the right in general.[452] For example, by infiltrating Identity Evropa (a pro-White activist organization, whose members were revealed to mostly be upstanding members of their community, such as college students, businessmen, lawyers, and former military and police) and then collecting, organizing, and publishing their messages, Antifa was able to identify and then subsequently dox a significant number of their members. Evidence of this collaboration in my own life is that many of my political dissident compatriots who have never committed a crime are harassed every time they board a flight, presumed to be potential domestic terrorists. Beyond its effects on Identity Evropa and its successor, the American Identity Movement, this infiltration had a chilling effect on pro-White organizing in the US in general, as was intended. That this was all perfectly legal is highly indicative of the state of the legal system. However, the state is becoming increasingly brazen in doing such things themselves which they had formerly outsourced for the most part, as demonstrated by the FBI infiltrating a Bible study group with the intent to entrap good patriotic Christians.[453]

Even launching a protest in "our democracy," as the regime likes to call itself, is practically impossible now for any true dissident voice. Through collusion between local government and insurance agencies, protest can even be *de jure* illegal. Due to the state-sponsored private paramilitary groups causing damage around any protest they are unleashed upon, cities have begun requiring

[450] Of a single case in San Diego: Riggins, "Grand Jury Indicts Anti-Fascists."
[451] Brothers, "Heroes or Victims."; "National Justice Party Statement on the Kyle Rittenhouse Verdict." "The violent Antifa he [Rittenhouse] killed and wounded that night when he was attacked included two Jews, a domestic abuser and a convicted pedophile.
[452] Hampton, "Antifa Terror Is Here to Stay." "Antifa attracts plenty of mentally ill people who need little encouragement to rampage, and they know journalists and politicians defend their assaults and doxing."; Kessler, "Doxing the Doxers."
[453] Striker, "Jewish FBI Agent."

protestor insurance.[454] From there, all the "private" insurance companies have to do is deny coverage. This amounts to a brazen circumvention of the legal doctrine of the "hecklers veto." If the Supreme Court ever takes action on this issue it will probably be too little and certainly too late, as irreplaceable months of missed opportunities for free expression will have passed before a case challenging this practice is even placed on the SCOTUS docket.

III

The society provided to us by our overlords is worse than a tyranny. We inhabit an *anarcho*-tyranny. Not only are normal people repressed under this regime, but the lowest elements, the criminals, the psychopaths, the mentally ill, and the underworld are all given priority, and the draconian laws cease to be enforced on those they were originally written to check. Far from Marx's "dictatorship of the proletariat," our democracy is a dictatorship by Jewish moneyed interests and for the dregs.

With bipartisan support, we were tricked into "prison reform."[455] Oh, how naive the American people were! How could we have been duped, actually believing their lies of the poor "urban youths," these future astronauts and doctors who were unfairly persecuted by this White supremacist system? What a lie this was indeed. After all, the US has by far the highest incarceration rate. How much could it hurt to allow these fellows back on the street? Alas, White society—foolishly believing that this would result in less traffic tickets, police harassment, and arbitrary enforcement of draconian laws against victimless crimes—was amazed to find the entire country turned upside-down.

Within a year, police departments were defunded and handicapped under pressure of globalist institutional NGOs, police

---

[454] See *Cameron Padgett v. Board of Trustees Of Michigan State University*. MSU tried to demand that a right-wing student pay for unreasonable police protection and insurance for a campus speaking event, in an attempt to silence alternative view points. See also *New Century Foundation v. Michael Robertson*.

[455] Grawert and Lau, "How the First Step Act."; "Bipartisan Support for Criminal Justice Reform Still Strong."

began to walk off the job *en masse*, and criminals flooded onto the street and were unleashed onto civilized society.[456] More and more brazen, knowing the government would do nothing to quash their rampage, billions of dollars of property damage were incurred in the not-so-peaceful protests of the so-called "Summer of Love" by the Jewish officer corps of the career organizer class.[457] And it is this that ties in with the fall of White areas. The left cries foul—"White flight!"—knowing full well the release of the underworld, first in the cities and then upon the suburbs, will result in the destruction of the area in which Whites live. City after city, suburb after suburb, town after town, the Whites will either accept their fate or flee once more, like a troop of rare monkeys fleeing the destruction of their abode in the rainforest. Tree by tree, sector by sector, province by province, the tamarin is driven closer and closer to destruction, like the native Europeans.

All the while, the police are utilized in much greater proportion than they once were, all but declaring open war on the White and adjacent population, those who the left considers to be suffering from "Whiteness."[458] Whites, conservatives, red staters, and rural people all live in fear under this regime which has written the laws in such a way that normal people break "serious" laws daily without knowing it. These are not enforced on the dregs of humanity, but on the middle class, rounding up family men, sons, daughters, fathers, and mothers, for unconstitutional firearm laws, for supposed tax evasion, and for peacefully protesting.[459] All the while rapists, murderers, burglars, and other violent menaces to society roam free to continue their reign of terror, knowing their bail will be

---

[456] Houck, "Anarcho-Tyranny 2020." The other articles in this series are well worth reading, too. See also Johnson, *The Year America Died*. See also Gullick, "Fund the Police, Defund Blacks."

[457] Hampton, "A Mostly Peaceful Nobel Prize."; Spencer J. Quinn, "Black Lives Matter Is Black Supremacy." "Of course, there is more to this picture. Many Jews play a role, either in funding BLM, demonstrating along with them, or cheering them on from their perches in the mainstream media. Jews, by and large, have always shared the same anti-white agenda as blacks, and so this alliance is as strong as ever—despite the spate of black-on-Jewish violence from earlier in the year."

[458] See Taylor, "Want Equity? Punish White People."

[459] That the IRS originally required that its legions of new tax collectors be able to use deadly force is ominous to say the least. Mordowanec, "IRS Deletes Require-ment."; Albrecht, "Remembering Sam Francis."; Ertelt, "FBI Raids Home."; Mary Margaret Olohan, "FBI Arrests 11."

affordable or even free. Anarcho-tyranny terrorizes the population through a one-two punch of the underworld and the state apparatus. Thus, the productive members of society live in a by-design state of terror.

While the blatant acts of state terror go willfully unnoticed by those in power, the last vestiges of the good police are resigning, opening the door for an affirmative action hire or psychopathic careerist to take his place.[460] Precisely the same is occurring in the military, where the potentially quality personnel are not even enlisting in the first place. This litmus test of separating the wheat from the chaff, or in this case vice versa, is expounded by the vaccine mandates in the bureaucracy, including the government's outlets for violence.[461] Those who are willing to take the mystery injection, which any man of good instinct knows to be suspect, will be willing to follow the orders of the state, even if he disagrees with them. With some exceptions he has made his choice as to what he values more: his job or his honor, or even health. An army of these pushovers is an army of docile followers who will either begrudgingly, or often actually happily, fire on his fellow countryman or arrest him. "I don't write the law, I just enforce it" is the tacit acknowledgment of a man who has resigned his humanity for servitude: a well-broken horse who will jump on command.

As the country degenerates further into chaos, order will need to be restored. Out of the ashes of the old local police system, already highly corrupt and suspect, will arise the federal police force, already in the works, which will dissolve and supplant the old system, making the populace daydream with nostalgia of the "good old days," just as we do today of 2019. With the federal police will come a tyranny unimaginable for the naive and innocent American people. Under this totalitarian state, the regime will no longer need to utilize loopholes through the private sector. They will have true control. This is what must be stopped if we wish to live an existence worth living.

---

[460] Balsamini, "Nearly 2,000 NYPD Cops."; Bates, "Small-Town Cops."
[461] Ellis, "Biden: Fire Police Officers."; Rinckey, "U.S. Military Covid-19 Vaccine Requirement."; "Philadelphia Police Vaccine Mandate."

IV

The global elite seem to understand the cycles of history as laid out in Part 1, at least to an extent. They are an ancient people and know what happens to a soft-handed elite class after the collapse of civilization. Unless they are successful, they are in deep trouble. Their skills in manipulating markets, in sweet talking the masses, and in hoarding the wealth will mean nothing in the face of a barbarian horde with the will to take it from them. In the Dark Ages, possession of gold was, far from a virtue, a death sentence. This is the future which they wish to avoid, but which is necessary. It is better for a tree to die and leave seeds for something virile, rather than pridefully carry on forever in a geriatric state.

It is no secret that the global elite wish to institute a "managed decline." Beyond animus toward their host population, they probably understand at some level that overly complex societies, such as the current global order, tend to have diminishing returns as discussed by Joseph A. Tainter, and therefore that decline is inevitable. This is no different from the "Great Reset" of Schwab. They are describing precisely the same ideal, which is a downsizing of the world in a way in which the elite will not be overthrown, as is typical throughout history. Essentially, they intend to "end history," another of their ideals (in this case of the prolific neoconservative Francis Fukuyama).[462] To accomplish this, the elite are attempting to get ahead of the ball already rolling off the cliff. They wish to have all contingencies planned and slowly decline the world rather than crash it, thereby being ready at the bottom to catch the ball. They would rather rule over ashes than nothing at all.

This Great Reset is the true purpose of the COVID scare and the lockdowns of yesterday, which could potentially return in the future since the precedent was set, and which still continue at the time of writing in China.[463] To take away rights and freedoms is to turn them into tools to be used, carrots and sticks. Far from Bohemians, they are already using the freedom to travel, or rather the privilege, as something that can easily be taken away for improper behavior.

---

[462] Fukuyama, *End of History.*
[463] Magramo, "Anger at China's Zero-Covid Policy."

Those who will not comply with their whim are being made second-class citizens. The vaccine mandate, if nothing else, is the perfect friend-enemy distinction flare. Those with the vaccine will surely go along with anything and those who continue to receive boosters are guaranteed "good citizens."

By locking down the world economy, the oligarchs have been able to completely revamp the economy, and destroy a great swath of businesses not already absorbed into the big club.[464] The shutting down of in-person relations quickly created an asocial economy where workers no longer even need to interact with each other anymore. More and more, work is done at home and abroad behind a screen, artificially stunting the already largely anonymous bugmen of the hive cities. Masks, which are admitted to not prevent the spread of the virus, are used to even further intensify an asocial anonymous environment of dehumanized insectoid people.[465] By an artificial mass psychosis administered by the media and group psychology, those who step out of line are immediately identified by the hive and destroyed, solidifying the lockstep current, like a school of herring. Of course, while this specific hysteria has died down, the friend/enemy distinction continues elsewhere such as with support for "current things" like Black Lives Matter before COVID, and the Ukrainian/anti-Russia hysteria in the US afterward.

Despite the cohesive hive mind, humanity has become more and more atomized. The extended family has been dead for decades. The nuclear family is all but dead as well. Despite working from home seeming like something that could increase living standards, this won't matter, as many cannot afford a family anyway. With no family, most will live for work in loneliness. Perhaps we will see a resurgence in corporate housing. The "pod" living option is a rising trend in the cities already.[466]

The moneyed interests are already making a grab for the housing, especially family housing, making it even more difficult for normal people to live a dignified existence.[467] Klaus Schwab's

---

[464] Fiscal Policy Center, "Unequal Opportunities." "The number of small businesses in Colorado declined by over 40% from pre-pandemic levels by June 2021."
[465] Anderson, "Do Masks Work?"
[466] Mueller, "Pod Living."; Tangermann, "People Love Living in Pods."
[467] Houck, "The Fading Memory of American Homeownership."

famous proposal that "You will own nothing and you will be happy" goes further than this, however. Under their ideal, not only will owning real property be impossible, but it will also be encouraged to rent appliances and everything else we today traditionally own. Houses are already leased, as are cars. This encouragement will only increase. Rather than owning things, the rental companies will own the people, and make a fortune off of it, not to mention the complete control which seems to largely be an end in and of itself with these egomaniacal psychopaths. And it goes without saying that these control freaks who wish us to own nothing will themselves, not only own the means of production toward wealth, but the means of life itself. It is they from whom we will be leasing.

The final great leap will likely be instituted through a climate agenda, already in the works.[468] The elite are intelligent enough to know that nothing we do to conserve energy will prevent the destruction of the environment. If the climatology data is correct, net zero emissions as of today would do little to curb what is coming.[469] However, most are not as intelligent as the milieu found at the WEF or Bilderberg. Knowing that nothing can stop this inevitable environmental catastrophe, but also being aware that the average person believes that if they just try hard enough and recycle enough cans the world will be saved, they will use the climate issue to squeeze every last drop out of the people of the developed world. This can already be seen with the "renewable energy" grift, which has made Elon Musk the richest man in the world by selling electric cars, gaining his profits largely by fleecing off of US government subsidies.[470]

In comparison to a relatively banal sickness that has a low mortality rate even in the oldest demographic groups and is highly partisan, climate change is accepted by practically everyone.[471] It's just a matter of how much human activity is the culprit that is

---

[468] "Resolution Adopted by the General Assembly on 25 September 2015."
[469] "Is It Too Late?" NASA.; "If Emissions of Greenhouse."
[470] Hirsch, "Elon Musk's Growing Empire." By 2015 Musk's businesses had already gotten $4.9 billion in government subsidies.
[471] Strozewski, "10 Percent of Americans."; Roy, "Estimating the Risk of Death from COVID-19." "Under our assumptions, for example, school-aged children between 5 and 14 have a 1 in 200,000 chance of dying of influenza, but a 1 in 1.1 million chance of dying of COVID-19."

debated. Furthermore, climate change affects everyone and has wider implications for individual responsibility. This will be exacerbated as the results of climate catastrophe reach a head. India and China, two nuclear-armed countries, are already squabbling over the water supply on their border.[472] In Africa, climate change is currently being used as a justification for mass migration into Europe and the creation of a "EurAfrica" economic zone.[473]

As previously discussed, the end of a civilization will likely feature the degradation of the environment to a point at which it is impossible to rekindle human organization in the same way over the same geographic area for some time.[474] For our technologically advanced modern civilization, this could be even longer than usual: perhaps hundreds or even thousands of years, due to the fact that past civilizations lacked industrial technology, were not global, and were unable to utilize highly caustic energy resources, unlike our own civilization. The elite are well aware of this, but the laymen are not. If they are told that they must heavily reduce their standard of living, they will begrudgingly accept this fate. Many will even happily go along with it, as we have seen in the past few decades of anti-natal propaganda, often invoking the climate.[475] The end goal of this, of course, is a managed decline in which the world economy sinks at a constant rate rather than a complete collapse into chaos in which law and order breaks down. A merchant/bureaucratic elite cannot maintain order without having the military under their control. If order collapses and anarchy ensues, the eternal law of the jungle will become the only constitution in effect. This is the tubby piggy capitalist's worst nightmare. They see it on the horizon and are doing everything in their power to avoid the tide of history and their inevitable King Louis XVI moment, in which their indecisive nature will lead to them being deposed.

---

[472] Wuthnow et al., "Brahmaputra."
[473] "Climate Migration in Africa."; Ehui and Rigaud, "Climate Migration."
[474] Tainter, *Collapse of Complex Societies*, 44–51.
[475] Chittilapally, "Antinatalism."; Austin, "Could Not Having Kids Save the Planet?"

V

To avoid this doom as this age winds to a close, the elite have become highly invested in transhumanism, which seems to be one of their ultimate endgames. Virtual reality has been a pet project of powerful people since the 1960s, and is rapidly being introduced and popularized among the masses as technological advances make it more viable on the civilian market. The world they wish to create through late-stage capitalism, neo-feudalism, degeneracy, and deracination is a world in which the soul is destroyed; in which one would be better dead than among the living. Transhumanism will be used as the opiate of the masses. Like a good tactician, the oligarchs must at least maintain a facade that there is an escape from the situation. A cornered animal is most dangerous, but a foe attempting to escape through a tunnel of death is easily vanquished. This escape will be virtual reality, and if VR continues to be more lifelike, this will become a more enticing option for the already demoralized masses.

Augmented reality is another option. Elites like Elon Musk hold the "artificial intelligence" impossibility above our heads as a dangerous alternative that will destroy us if we don't merge with technology and embrace the transhuman future.[476] One solution to this problem is to put a chip in our head and become one with artificial intelligence. Elon Musk is currently working on his Neuralink device which does precisely this.[477] There was also the failed Google Glass project.[478] Today we have mRNA therapy in the form of vaccines, which are normalizing the idea of tweaking the genetic code of the individual, in however small of a way.[479] Media such as *Cyberpunk 2077*, a video game in which players can augment their bodies, may also be normalizing this dystopian possibility. And even before this, technology has been continually making life more comfortable, thereby making the people more and more flabby and

---

[476] Thacker, "Why Elon Musk's Transhumanist Dreams."; Weaver, "Elon Musk's Disturbing Dalliance."
[477] Hamilton, "The Story of Neuralink."
[478] Gvora, "Google Glass."
[479] "What Are MRNA Vaccines and How Do They Work?" While the official line is that these vaccines do not directly affect DNA, they do affect how DNA acts.

complacent. Smartphones are transforming our brains already, creating reliance, addiction, and ultimately the beginnings of a true symbiosis of man and machine.[480] While using technology can be helpful for the disabled to live a more normal life by replacing missing body parts, the ensuing singularity with technology is molding our brains toward a need for artificial "organs" we don't have, similar to how the sword becomes an "extension of the body" of the professional swordsman.

This dependence on social technology which has already been centralized under the thumb of this nefarious oligarchic class is not something that should be embraced by those who wish to retain their freedom and their humanity. They have already abolished Man in the West long ago. Now his carcass is a burning husk. The result of such a symbiosis is beyond dystopian. Imagine a world in which the elite—who have made it abundantly clear that they are perfectly comfortable with mind control (as proven in MKUltra), and have controlled the most expansive and expensive organizations of the age in the pursuit of useful information (as in the cases of Big Tech monopoly data collection schemes)—will have direct access to the brain. After decades, these companies have produced enough intelligence that they are able to largely control hundreds of millions of people simply through algorithms.[481] If the masses chip themselves and allow Google or Facebook into their brain physically, one cannot imagine a resulting scenario other than the true end of the world: the end of history under a literally inhuman, indeed anti-human, existence.

This transhuman ideal also ties into the transgender craze enabled by the elite. The transgender ideology relies on a hyper-dualistic view on the spirit, but also on a sort of spiritual anarchism, the rejection of the ultimate Truth, the transcendent, and what always was and always will be, the Logos, in favor of subjectivism, relativism, and the idea of "my truth" or "your truth." Those who mutilate themselves in a vain attempt to match their body to their sick mental state, rather than pursuing self-reflection and

---

[480] Honma et al., "Reading on a Smartphone."
[481] Ball, "The Secret Bipartisan Campaign." "They successfully pressured social media companies to take a harder line against disinformation and used *data-driven strategies* to fight viral smears" (Emphasis added).

understanding, are, rather than being treated by a benevolent and fatherly government, indeed *encouraged* to carry out "their" whims. But this is only a step toward further mutilation of the mind and body under a transhuman existence. The elite see laws and God as a hindrance to their ideal of true sovereignty, which only God can ever have. Thus, they aim for anarchy and total sovereignty for themselves and tyranny for the rest: one world controlled by them and only them, but also a tyranny in which those below them have only so much freedom as to keep them idle. Transhumanism is simply the most debased devolution of this Titanic-Luciferian grasping for what C. S. Lewis described as that "hideous strength" which is born from that most dangerous of sins: pride. Anarcho-tyranny is the ideal of the cosmopolitan elite who wishes to defeat God. In this way, he truly is an Antichrist.[482]

But he is also Kronos, he who destroyed his own children but was yet vanquished by them. This is part of the Greek story of creation. But if history has taught us anything, it is that the degeneration will be complete only at the bottom of Tartarus. We sit at home, believing the ancients to be so inferior, so unenlightened, so foolish in comparison to ourselves who have discovered the banal and profane "truth" of this world through "science" and "reason." Yet look around you. Where has this supposed truth and reason led, but to the exact same dead end as it always has? Will we really be so different from the Aztecs, the Carthaginians, and the Canaanites who sacrificed their own children to an evil, ancient, and perennial force which resides in the universe and soul or, for the secularists, in the psyche of man as an organic collective body? By using the lie of materialism, we have explained away the soul and thus, through "science," embraced child sacrifice of the unborn, have we not?

---

[482] Of course, this obsession with technology was not always in the extreme, de-monic form that we find it in today. The West, being Faustian in nature as described by Spengler, was always interested in technology, and especially technology that resonated with the drive to conquer space and time such as sailing, the telegraph, electricity, and railroads, etc. This reached its height in the Industrial Revolution, during which something went terribly wrong. This Faustian impulse became tainted with a drive toward profit, and next toward control. The Faustian technological im-pulse has burnt its original creativity out into a warped parody, if not satanic inver-sion, of its former self. The freedom and enjoyment of nature offered by sailing has been replaced by a technocratic tyranny and hatred of nature.

Rapidly, it has further degenerated from a cool, composed quantitative into an anti-quality where this neo-child sacrifice is indeed *celebrated*. And what of those who actively encourage the mutilation and castration of their own children? This grooming too has taken a quasi-religious form. That a sacrifice be willing is of importance in several religions and esoteric traditions. How far will it go? What depravity is man capable of at the end of our own civilization—the Faustian West?

8

Reign of the Counter-Tradition and From the Ashes

"Woe to you that call evil good, and good evil: that put darkness for light, and light for darkness: that put bitter for sweet, and sweet for bitter."

– Isaiah 5:20

The elite operate within a context of cyclical history. For all their immediate temporal power, they do not have ultimate power. There are still perennial rules and forces above them. Rather, the elite serve the role of guiding the first step of world events, but have minimal control thereafter. Imagine a man on the beach with a small boat. He can push the boat whichever way he wants, but he cannot guide it to the exact point that he wishes. This is the nature of elite action on a large stage.

It is clear that we live in the age of the proletariat, the rule of the slave ideology, the metaphysical dark age of our civilization. And yet, one may be surprised to still find that, as has been clearly demonstrated, the US, and in large part the Western world, is under the dominion of an oligarchy of largely moneyed elites, not bureaucrats. Money continues to be the main battery for the exertion of force in politics so the question remains how we can in good conscience reject the claim that the age of the merchant continues in Faustian civilization.

It should be stressed that man is a product of his own time and this time's spirit. It is difficult to imagine that the idealized past of two hundred or even twice as many years ago, which the most traditionally-minded people of the current age hold as a utopia, was in fact a degeneration, largely under the tutelage, either in the literal sense or in *zeitgeist*, of a profane and ignoble mercantile elite. One who recognizes the current oligarchy around us often sees a rule by merchants. But this view itself is a sign of the times. The fact that we often neglect the *zeitgeist* in favor of the material in our analysis on these subjects makes it evident enough that all idealism, all transcendent viewpoints, and all immaterial perspectives are absent, not just from society, but even from those of us who critique society from the right.

It is also clear enough that the age that we currently inhabit, which emerged out of the ashes of the two World Wars, is indeed a true paradigm shift. It was out of this era that Bolshevism and the other Jewish slumming ventures of subversive ideology finally took root in a distinctly fourth estate manner. Money still largely serves as the grease which facilitates the turning of the wheels, but the movement of those gears is guided by merchants whose true spirit is in the *shtetl* or in the *kibbutz*: a peasant (or worse, an outsider) spirit in its essence.

Indeed, when putting the new Bolshevism that took form in the revolutionary ideology that arose out of the postwar era (which is also a sign of the times) into context, it is difficult to find the bourgeoisie, outside of the mere fact that it was the social class that its proponents inhabited. This seems to be the pattern over and over again: bourgeois proponents, but with a spirit among the dregs. Spengler proposed that these radicals were either the *shudras* who felt disdain for the social class they felt superior toward, and yet could not escape from, or *vaishyas* who were not up to snuff in their social class, and thus were forced to slum with the dregs in a vain attempt to flip the chessboard and revolt against their own, leading their army of subhuman followers.[483] If one is to inspect the social movements of today, it is difficult to find the flaw in this analysis. Indeed, this was largely the profile of yesteryear's revolutionaries, and it continues today, exacerbated by the "surplus elite" phenomenon of the modern city.

---

[483] Spengler, *Hour of Decision*.

I

The "philosophy" of the postwar era is hardly philosophy at all, but an "anti-philosophy." Metaphysics and transcendent values are wholly dismissed. Right and wrong, good and evil, and their conclusions are all abandoned as well. What is left is the pure cynicism of Jewish pathological utilitarianism that only the most naive, shallow, or malicious characters latch onto. But when viewed in this lens, leftism has hardly changed since the nineteenth century. Since Marx, revolutionary strategy has largely focused on how to destroy civilization, but hardly any real effort has been put into thinking of what to build in the ashes of our great civilization after they destroy it. It has always been in the realm of Becoming, but never Being. Can it not be stated that Bolshevism is the rational conclusion of the Jewish revolutionary spirit, then? After all, they are, as MacDonald says, the *culture of critique*.[484]

In the social sciences, Jewish intellectuals seem to only be capable of tearing down and nitpicking, inducing death by a thousand peer-reviewed articles. And in the sciences, though their track record here is much more impressive, their achievements largely amount to nothing radically new. The *true* savants of the Jews are few and far between. Their main claim to fame in the sciences, Einstein, is highly overrated. History has given him credit for the Theory of Relativity, $E = MC^2$, when in fact this theory had already been introduced in the nineteenth century by European physicists like Poincaré and Poynting.[485] In fact, Jewish tenure over these studies has led to the complete destruction of savants as a group in mainstream society, relegating anyone who attempts to truly think outside the box to destruction, as in the case of academics like E. O. Wilson and Charles Murray. For such an antinomian group, the current intellectual elite are highly authoritarian and even totalitarian in their policing and gatekeeping of the mass feeling, and indeed of reality itself. Of course, as is so often the case, the Machiavellian realpolitik ethic of the elite stipulates that anything is permitted as a means to an end; "do what

---

[484] MacDonald, *Culture of Critique*.
[485] Rothman, "Was Einstein the First."

thou wilt," as the occultist Crowley famously remarked. The result is that developments in philosophy, social sciences, and hard science have come to a standstill as fresh, new theories cannot be explored. Scientist-priests of today, like the priests of yesteryear, are managers trusted to uphold stale dogma, pure and simple, from climate change to COVID, to the anti-White racial religion. Most forget that at first Galileo did not "prove" his theory of the heliocentric model of the solar system—hardly a mascot for the feat of science, but rather a feat of the Faustian soul's reach into darkness. It is leaps of faith like Galileo's that create progress, and it is leaps of faith like this that are stifled in all fields of study today. Most today further forget that the greatest scientists of all have been amateurs, not the hoity-toity politically correct nerds of today.[486]

What passes for philosophy in the modern academic world is nothing but profane tactics, a reflection of its leftist destructive origin. It is base and contains no true attempt at truth, and indeed usually denies epistemology outright. Critical theory, which is the basis for much of modern philosophy in the West, can be summed up as Jewish evolutionary strategy writ large, a system which oh-so-conveniently promotes Jewish upward mobility while targeting the White majority population at every possible angle, weaponizing their pets in the form of ethnic minorities, sexual freaks, and outcasts. The other prong is postmodernism, which works in sync with the Frankfurt ideology and toward the same ends. The postmodernists raise the question of what is truth, and they propose that there is no truth, yet the only target of their ireful gaze is the White, Christian norms of the West, while ignoring the enemies of our civilization. The proponents of critical theory do the same, picking apart transcendental, supra-rational cornerstones of our society, but again ignore our enemies and indeed themselves.

These ideologies cannot exist in a vacuum. Rather, they require fertile soil to be allowed to thrive. As the US sinks deeper into a psychotic frenzy, it seems clear that this malaise is not of a material nature. It is in this spiritually corrupt environment that the seeds of

---

[486] Tesla, for example, was an eccentric genius ahead of his time, and also died penniless and mostly unrecognized until later. Milojković, "17 Weird Facts about Nikola Tesla."

chaos are able to be sown. Former KGB agent Yuri Bezmenov spoke of "demoralization," a process in which his spy agency would subvert other nations and create this type of environment where communism would become approved by the masses.[487] In the West, we see precisely this phenomenon, though it is clearly not the long-dead Soviet Union which is carrying this mission out. The people have been thoroughly demoralized, and pathological behavior is completely normalized. Whether it be cynical sociopaths who rise to the top of the hierarchy and use these malicious pseudo-sciences for personal gain, psychopaths who simply wish to inflict damage on others, neurotic Jews whose aim seems to boil down to a humiliation ritual of their ethnic rivals, or the brainwashed zombie who is functionally mentally ill and has lost all control of the brain via mental and spiritual manipulation, it is largely deranged people who accept ideology that cannot pass a simple test of logic that children learn in elementary school. What is infinitely more dangerous than a stupid violent lunatic is an intelligent religious zealot who can control his or her wrath for a potentially more fruitful opportunity to strike.

What we are beholding in the up-and-coming *zeitgeist* is not the cold, calculating, and secular bourgeois spirit which exalted logic and reason to a fault and expressed itself in the scientific nationalism and eugenics elite ideal of the pre-1945 era, but something wholly new: an inversion of quantity into something darker, more base, and quite obviously what the ancients warned of when they spoke of *Iblis*, the Devil, Lucifer, the left hand, and evil itself. The plebeian impulse, when left to its own devices, inevitably corrupts. This inversion is what was originally meant by the word *satanic*, and Satan has always been known as the "father of lies," of that which is wrong, the opposite, the inversion. In symbology, it is for this reason that the upside-down cross and upside-down pentagram, among other symbols, are associated with evil. What has been awoken is of far greater significance than the Mammon of the last few centuries.

---

[487] Porlando, "Bezmenov's Steps (Ideological Subversion)."; Persian Atheist, "KGB defector Yuri Bezmenov's warning to America."

As the age continues, this will all become more and more clear. The current oligarchs will not maintain their power forever. However, this is not necessarily a case to be celebrated. What is coming after may make the current regime seem like a utopia, just as the degenerated eighteenth century seems to many of us today. When modern society reaches its low point, the human race, so interconnected today, may see its greatest trial yet.

II

There are two most potential options for the future of Western civilization, the first of which I will talk about in this section and the second in the next. The first, which I very much doubt will actually come to fruition, is the rise of the Caesar or Napoleon figure. In this scenario, the downtrodden and oppressed will conduct a populist revolt against the oligarchy but paradoxically be led by an elite, usually from the oligarchy itself, who will institute an imperial state. Historians remember these "Bonapartist" leaders as centrists who simply carry out the general will in an authoritarian top-down manner.[488] If this occurred today, however, the leader would likely be seen as a reactionary leading the people against an out-of-touch aristocracy.

This was an option in the US and it is still potentially an option in other Western nations. However, as a trend, Bonapartism is unlikely to characterize the greater Western world, which will likely not even exist as it is currently understood within the next few decades. The US could have possibly accomplished a Bonapartist regime had Trump's populist uprising been more energetic, had there been more disaffected elites, had the masses represented been younger, rather than the aging White demographic of comfortable cattle, and had Trump actually been the lion he portrayed himself as. However, this was not the case. Trump was a merchant unwilling to cross the Rubicon, unlike Julius Caesar or Napoleon before him—they who shouldn't even be compared to what ended up being a pathetic, washed-up opportunist.

---

[488] Spengler, *Decline of the West*.

However, even if this were the case, I suspect that an American Caesar would be sorely disappointing to true men of the right, but also beyond the wildest dreams of the American White working class. Of the two true supporters of the Trumpism phenomenon, the "alt-right" and what was eventually transformed into the "Q" movement—which can be best described as a schizophrenic cult of personality and whose explanations and predictions read like a parody of a Tom Clancy novel—the QAnon supporters are by far in the majority, even on alternative social media platforms, and in spite of how Trump has been not only defeated, but completely emasculated. While the more sophisticated alt right reactionaries latched onto Trump, as they saw in him the potential for a mass White awakening toward the traditionalism and White identity of earlier decades, the Q crowd easily turned from a benevolent parasite into a malevolent one able to command the entire body, just like the zombie-ant fungus.[489] That the entry barrier was simply so low for them, combined with how there is such a large surplus of alienated but unintelligent White proletarians in the US and other Anglosphere nations, meant that the growth of this tide was inevitable.

It is the interests of this particular type that would have been represented under a Caesarist takeover of the US. While the Caesar worship of the Q movement goes beyond any reasonable level of sanity (although it is still vastly preferable to the neo-Baphometism of the alternative), it is still far from a glorious revival of the classic Faustian order which reactionary visionaries hope for. However, due to the demoralization and lack of fortitude of the already *fellah*-fied American suburban and rural classes, they were incapable of even accomplishing a sad parody of Bonapartism. In spite of how the elite is unified against the interests of the White working and middle class, this class could hardly hold its own even if there was a serious segment of rogue elites willing to aid them. Perhaps there are potential rogue elites who would be willing to aid this lost class if they saw even *any* potential in them. However, they clearly have little or no political, let alone *revolutionary*, potential. This is despite

---

[489] *Ophiocordyceps unilateralis* is a tropical fungus that infects ant brains and then reproduces in a bizarre manner that leads to the ant's death.

a market in politics for their issues, and how, if it weren't for media homogeneity, the Trumpian issues of 2016 would likely have supermajority support.

But few ask *why* the elites (that is, middle and lower-level, non-Jewish elites who are capable of empathizing with the masses) should go rogue. There are few motivating factors for such a move and, as has become painfully obvious, it is base human nature to act as an automaton in pursuit of benefit, the path of least resistance, via a trivial cost-benefit analysis that motivates men, even highly prescient men such as the type that inhabit the elite echelons. The cost of backing a peasant revolt, even a peaceful one through the voting booth, is a great cost, *while the benefit is quite little as chances are that the rogue elite will likely have a greater sense of patrimony and idealism toward their followers than even these populist followers feel toward themselves.* The latter phenomenon is due to how the peasants on the ground are also partaking in an active cost-benefit analysis. The vast majority are all talk and no bite. They masquerade as revolutionaries when the reality is that their ideal is a world where they can live a decadent, lazy life like they or their parents did in the 1950s and 1960s. They have spent their entire lives in denial, watching their country slowly fade, and have thus far done nothing meaningful to hamper it.[490]

It is no wonder that the communists see the Blacks rather than the White working class as having revolutionary potential.[491] Blacks have for over a hundred years rioted when it suited them, even under segregation, while Whites, even in the 1990s militia movement, other than Timothy McVeigh (assuming he was even a grassroots actor) in retaliation for Waco, did nothing. It was only after the mass murder of dozens of innocent Christian sectarians at Waco who threatened the system by showing that it was possible to escape it, that retaliation was had. And even then, it was only one case. If the police today murdered seventy-six blacks, including

---

[490] For example, consider how the various trucker convoys were derailed. Steuben, "Woodstock on Wheels."

[491] Berland, "The Emergence of the Communist Perspective." The American Communist Party generally ignored Blacks for about a decade until in 1928, when the 6th Congress of the Comintern identified the "black belt" as a subject nation and thus having revolutionary potential. The Negro question was then given high priority.

twenty-five children, on their property for minding their own business, as was the case with the mostly White Branch Davidians at Waco, the greatest civil conflict of the last hundred years would spark overnight, leading to the deaths of tens of millions in America, and possibly across the Western world. The fact that no real civil unrest occurred then, nor in Europe throughout the waves of ISIS terror, nor in the aftermath of the reign of Black terror in 2020, or after the Black nationalist Darrel Brooks rammed through a White Christmas parade killing six, is a testament to how White conservatives in America lack any revolutionary potential and would rather die lying down than put up even a modicum of fight, fearing that they may be dubbed "racist." Far from the cornered animal that fights to its dying breath, the conservative White population is an old man paralyzed by fear, in denial of his fate.

The reactionary right has latched on to these types, not necessarily because they are fellow travelers in any way, but out of necessity in a last-ditch effort. Unfortunately for them, there is no revolutionary potential here. The revolutionary right is motivated by a higher aristocratic creed in most cases, or as we must admit in some cases, by sheer insanity and an inability to cope with greater society. As they are "right-wing," and the "yokels" and "well to do" are also right-wing, they have become seemingly inseparable partners. And yet, the revolutionary right has actual goals, while the normal peasant and middle classes simply want to hold on to what little power it still has. There is no push to go back with the conservatives, as there is with the reactionaries. Indeed, it often appears, and rightly so, that the reactionaries are more emotionally invested in the quality of life of these classes, than they are *even with themselves*. The revolutionary right latches on to the establishment right out of want for numbers while the establishment right tolerates the revolutionary right, albeit barely, as long as the votes are there. However, these two factions are in fact quite different. Usually, it is the normal right-of-center types who understand this fully, while the reactionaries in their idealism do not. The reactionaries wish to bring the mainstream "up to their level," which is very reminiscent to the communists of the last century, who wished to instill a revolutionary ethos in the proletariat. On the other hand, the normal folks usually want nothing to do with the radicals who they see as "racist," "sexist," "homophobic," or even, God forbid, "anti-Semitic," and wanting to squander what little that they still have left, rocking the boat and thus spoiling the party. In many ways, the mainstream right resembles a drowning swimmer, who in a confused panic lashes out at the reactionary lifeguard trying to save him, thus endangering them both. The reactionary faction is a general without an army. The mainstream faction is an army without a general, or at least a competent or trustworthy one. The refusal of the masses to compromise and revolt against the modern world is to the destruction of all. They will always fall to grifters and controlled opposition swamp creatures, bedazzled by their cheap parlor tricks and mediocre political knowledge.

Even if a Caesar was somehow able to seize power, this would hardly be what the idealists had hoped for. Until Trump, the American public was lulled to sleep. It was only by this jolt that a large amount of people began seeing through the smoke and mirrors of the regime. This process is now occurring faster through the antagonism of the regime and its hordes of violent dregs. By targeting children and parents directly, many more are seeing that something is deeply wrong. Even so, it is clear that the major organizers of right-wing dissent simply cannot cope with the deeper truths of the matter, or are content to tell the people what they want to hear for the sake of income. Nevertheless, the little revolutionary potential still left in the White well-to-do class is wholly a cause born out of necessity and antagonism. If law and order were restored, they would return to their old ways, as there would no longer be any necessity, in contrast to the American South or in South Africa, where the Whites maintain group cohesion, not necessarily out of any hatred, but simply out of safety concerns.

Even today, most Whites refuse to speak out on issues of race and Jewish power. These two issues are the most taboo topics in our society, not due to any particular rudeness, but by design, as they are the most important hurdles to cross. Even today, with Jews abandoning any semblance of subtlety in their hatred, Blacks ramping up violence against Whites, and the government explicitly targeting their children, most continue to see the world not as it is, but how they want to see it: through a 1990s Hollywood kabuki theater lens. The average right-thinking person would rather live through the consequences of their foolish beliefs than abandon them, and that is not hyperbole.

The situational worldview of the citizenry would be even worse under a populist dictatorship of a Trump type. Rather than the potential for radicalization on the margins, the people would once again be lulled back to sleep. An ever-so-slight decline in quality of the surrounding world would not arouse much suspicion, and any suspicion would be written off as exaggeration or conspiracy mongering. The frog would be further boiled. Thus, potential Caesarism is not the golden opportunity to return to a past greatness that it may seem, even if it was once likely not that long ago.[492] At best, Caesarism is but a lost opportunity to turn the clock back *maybe* a few decades.

III

No, our fate appears to be much darker than this. Make no mistake: the Jewish spiritually proletarian but materially bourgeois order is at its height today. It will not likely last. Just as the Anglo-Saxon Protestant order was usurped by their pet Jews, the Jewish order will eventually be usurped by their rabid pets as well. After decades of marination, the ethno-elite are now succumbing to their own subversion. They have summoned forth the left-swimming Cthulhu, but they cannot put him down. Slowly but surely, just as all great empires and civilizations are already declining before their zenith, and just as acceleration by the laws of physics always decreases to its lowest point at the apex, so too has the current Jewish order *already begun to pass* the torch as it has reached its height of power.[493]

The Jews are a mercantile people and it is only natural that they would be the conquerors of this age in Europe and the transition

---

[492] Jeelvy has argued that we are long past the age of a Caesar, and that the best we can hope for is an "Ataturk" who can create a new, smaller nation out of the dying US, much as modern Turkey was born from the collapse of the Ottoman Empire. Jeelvy, "For the Coming American Atatürk."

[493] This is not to say that the Jewish ethno-elite caste, who we have exhaustively analyzed, is somehow a phenomenon of the past, but rather that we can expect a circulation of elites in the near future.

period in America. Thus, we can expect a proletarian race, or even perhaps casteless, deracinated anti-race to transition into masterdom as the true height of the last age of our civilization approaches. But what will the height be? Communism fails due to the iron law of oligarchy.[494] *Leadership* in the factory and in all places is a necessity. Egalitarianism is a contemporary myth and anarchy is a pipe dream. It can be inferred that the true last era will be itself characterized not just as anarchy but, in reality, as brief chaos.

But anarchy is like an artificial isotope; it is only possible for a fraction of a second. Nearly immediately, the power vacuum will be filled, though by who or what only fate can determine. To this, perhaps a Napoleon or Caesar figure will indeed emerge. Was it not the chaos of the apocalyptic French Revolution and the Roman Civil War, respectively, which brought Napoleon, Caesar, and his successor Augustus to power? To this, some credence can potentially be merited toward the Spenglerian predictions on the inevitability of Caesarism, though in a somewhat distant future. Whatever the case may be, it seems clear that a "collapse" is in store for the West, as it has been for all empires and civilizations, no matter how hard the intellectual lightweights of the neoliberal/neoconservative political class may complain.

Who will take the reins of Western civilization as the Jewish elite are slowly cycled out? We can already see the beginnings of this process, though those in power likely view the "far-left" side as little more than a sideshow to be used toward their own ends. And yet it is unlikely that the Anglo-Saxon world order of Europe and the US foresaw the immigrants from the *shtetls* of the Russian Pale as any more of a threat to their dominance than they did toward the other poor immigrants of Ireland, Southern Europe, and the Slavic areas. And yet, within fifty years, they controlled the intellectual space in America and the Anglosphere just as they did on the Continent before.[495]

---

[494] For the Iron Law of Oligarchies, see Robert Michels, *Political Parties*.
[495] In reference to the urban Jews of Western Europe, as opposed to the more rural, rustic Jews of Easter Europe who did not rise to prominence until immigrating to the US.

Thus, we may be able to infer that the groups which will inherit the ashes of Western civilization are those who are currently seen as benign pets today. A large portion of the Jewish community, who have little shame and have succumbed to their own cynical propaganda, is converting from the racist quasi-White supremacist international Ashkenazi-Jewish culture into a truly assimilated degenerate anti-culture which their forefathers wished to avoid for themselves but pushed onto the host population. Today we see an incredible amount of miscegenation, homosexuality, and transsexuality among the Diaspora Jews and even in Israel, phenomena that were once largely on the fringe.[496] The loss of religion in the early and mid-twentieth century among many Jews was a clear precursor to this.[497]

As often happens in these situations, the revolution will eat its own creator. This is what happened during the French Revolution when Robespierre was destroyed by his own, and when the legacy of Lenin and Trotsky was captured by Stalin. The same will happen in our own case, though the current elites are clearly trying their hardest to maintain their contingency plans to maintain control indefinitely. It is in this final phase, in which our civilization is in full decline, that the frames of Cathedral control, managerial power theory, and incompetency will likely have more accuracy as true predictive factors of the way of the world.

We are already seeing the institutions transition into these frames. The seemingly paradoxical decline in competency coupled with the increase in the regime's willingness to use hard power is in fact predictable. Soft power requires finesse, sophistication, and ultimately, intelligence. Indeed, it is necessary that the regime use a hard-handed approach when that is the final card in its hand. It would be preferable to continue the slow boil but, due to a generational dysgenic effect apparent in all declining "dynasties," which is further exacerbated by nepotism (as most notably seen in the constant rise and fall of Ottoman dynasties, for example), the elite have become far less competent in comparison to their

---

[496] For example, approximately 25 percent of Tel Aviv identifies as homosexual. See "Why Tel Aviv Is the Ultimate LGBTQ Travel Destination."
[497] Socolovsky, "American Jews Worry."

predecessors, which can be clearly seen in the inability of the mass media to properly veil their propagandistic intentions through nuance and subliminal messaging, preferring to go full throttle, thus counterproductively providing ammunition to dissent.

This is visible in the new media narrative that is now increasingly critical of Israel. Once a taboo subject, it is now perfectly fine, as long as the criticism is coming from the comical extremist, far-left, anti-colonial frame. For decades, the Jewish intellectual class was able to co-opt the Israel issue as a White colonial versus brown Muslim indigenous narrative. The result was that, knowing that the relationship between Israel and the US would never be broken and that this frame posed no real threat to the "special relationship," the issue of Jews behaving as they do everywhere was used *against Whites* rather than the Jews themselves, displaying another masterful demonstration of their mastery of the frame game as they did in Iraq, pinning the war on the powerless Christian working class Whites of the heartland, as opposed to powerful Jewish neoconservative interests in DC and New York.[498] Not so anymore, however. The anti-White frame has caught up to them as the rabid mob of anti-White lunatics, who have bought into the Jewish elite's cynical propaganda, has increased exponentially over the past few decades. Rapidly, the internalized propaganda is forming a mind of its own, a meme, which cannot be destroyed. The current elite will be able to co-opt it for the time being, but sooner or later, the new bureaucratic elites which are flooding into every industry will obtain more influence than their predecessor.

We can slowly see this also in the university system, where Jewish leftist Eric Weinstein, a professor at Evergreen State College, was harangued for not being far left enough by a mob of Black students and their "allies."[499] The Jewish leftist power structure is faced with two options: either allow themselves to be subsumed into the plebeian, or be overthrown by their own pets. Either way, the reign of a distinct class is coming to an end.

---

[498] Vaa, "Project for the New American Century."
[499] Spegman, "Evergreen Professor at Center of Protests."

IV

So, who will be the new and final elite of Faustian civilization, if we can even call it that? As we have seen, the march of history continues to degrade society. Gothic civilization has its roots in the late Roman Empire, the formative period in which the Germanic and Roman worlds clashed, leading to Charlemagne, with the Germanic world prevailing but influenced by Rome and Christianity, then mercantilism and industrialism, and finally the low-class age of today, post-nobility in any sense but figurative. However, it should be stressed that, despite the fact that we are entering the final stage *of* the final stage of our civilization, this does not mean that the proletariat will rule in the literal sense.

The iron law of oligarchy stipulates that there will always be an elite minority of some sort; any other model of political organization is impossible. History and basic human psychology confirm this to be true. Therefore, the "dictatorship of the proletariat," like that of the Soviet Union, will hardly resemble the democratic workers' paradise which the idealists dream of. Increasingly the regime will resemble more and more a bureaucratic nightmare that we are already somewhat accustomed to. This is in fact a micro-stage within each stage. Whether it may be the managerial McNamaraism of the death knells of the Old Left WASP regime that was usurped between 1945 and 1968, or the gradual move toward court adviser- and janissary-centered power during the final stages of a monarchical dynasty, we see a similar occurrence.

And so, the future power center will be made up of spiritual bureaucrats turned elite managers such as Schwab, Gates, and other internationalist quasi-governmental figures. In contrast to the old neoconservative Jewish Zionist elite who are actively destroying their host societies for the greater good of their race as a whole, the new elite truly rejects race altogether. The old ideal was little more than an international nationalism. The new ideal is simply globalism. The old elite will largely be assimilated into the new elite, but in the future, analysis of the elite as essentially Jewish will cause problems in analyzing power if viewed from this Jewish essentialist lens. As a consequence, the Jewish community's issues will only be relevant insofar as they align with internationalism, which they do to a large extent. However, when there is a conflict of interests, the new globalist elite will likely be able to easily sidestep their Jewish forefathers.

This can already be seen in the very recent and stark rebranding of the ADL from a Jewish ethno-nationalist organization which was consequentially anti-white European, to an all-but-solely anti-White organization which just so happens to be run by Jews, little different from the SPLC or Hope Not Hate in the U.K. This is all unsurprising, as the same phenomenon occurred when the mercantile WASP elite were overthrown by the managerial Jewish elite in the 1930s–1960s:

The Progressive Movement and the New Deal represent the emergence of a managerial elite that holds power through its expertise in the technical and administrative skills that enable it to operate and control overgrown organizations in the state, economy, and culture and which makes use of what has come to be known as liberalism to justify its challenge to an older bourgeois elite that seized national power in the Civil War and its aftermath.[500]

The left-wing Anglo elite certainly continued to exist after 1968, but largely only insofar as they kowtowed to the ADL, AJC, AIPAC, etc.[501] The same phenomenon applies to Anglo institutions which continue to serve a world order long having succeeded their own, such as the Ford Foundation, Chatham House, and Harvard.[502]

To conclude, it should be noted that as the elite become even more cosmopolitan and rootless than their Jewish predecessors, an incredible feat indeed, the nature of power transitions further from the domestic to the international, which is out of the scope for this work. The United States is but one node in this system, in which the only borders that matter are those at which the power of the unified

---

[500] Francis, *Beautiful Losers*, "The Secret of the 20th Century," 202–203.
[501] Across the pond in the United Kingdom, Prince Charles awarded the Jewish banker Jacob Rothschild an award (see "Prince Charles Honours."). This is despite how Rothschild has condescendingly poked Prince Charles in the chest (see "Prince Charles, Heir to the British Throne.").
[502] Chatham House awarded its Diversity Champion Award to BLM: "Undercurrents: Black Lives Matter, and Chatham House's Edi Working Group."

oligarch class cannot quite reach yet. Whether there is anywhere that they have not reached yet is a debate in and of itself, though again not within the scope of this work.

V

There is something in the air that many more perceptive minds can sense, though it is difficult to identify after decades, if not centuries, of secularization. After a long era of opulence following the Second World War, it became easy to accept that we were "beyond good and evil," as Nietzsche said—notwithstanding, of course, the long dead bogeymen prescribed by the truth regime of the foundation myths. And yet the air is thick enough to cut with an indescribable sense, a return to instinct, the feline raising of the hair on the neck, that a metaphysical, existential, and ancient danger is upon us. What we sense is the return of evil.

Perhaps some elites even at the very top of the food chain, such as those who meet at the WEF, Bilderberg, the World Jewish Congress, etc., are not familiar with the true nature of what is happening today, of what Guénon referred to as the *counter tradition*.[503] While the Jewish elite seem to be genuinely filled with malice and open hatred for the people of the world, with Whites at the top of their hit list, the globalist elites at least seemingly want to perfect the world. However, this is an illusion. Let us not forget that the nefarious interests of world Jewry largely agree with the globalist international view, and that spiritually the globalists are "hyper-Jews" in the same way that Jews are "hyper-merchants."

While the Jewish elite, which is now being eclipsed, at least had somewhat relatable and understandable goals, however pathological they might be, the new elite's ideals are wholly post-human, trans-human, and in the end *anti-human*: among these being artificial intelligence, virtual reality, augmented reality, DNA manipulation, and transhumanism generally. The old Jewish elite had the excuse of a twisted and extreme, though still ultimately natural, ethnocentrism and in-group preference, but it is difficult to

---

[503] Guénon, *The Reign of Quantity & the Signs of the Times.*

find a purely material excuse for the behavior of the new elites. Though it has become abundantly clear that the atheism and nihilism of our age are little more than a sign of the times, and need not even necessarily have a "supernatural" explanation, those of the psychological school of thought are ultimately mistaken in their description and, therefore, prescriptions.

The "woke" phenomenon, clearly a worship of evil, is another sign of the times. One needs little justification, when staring into the soulless eyes of demon-possessed rabble in the streets, shells of what were perhaps once people, in seeing that a historically evil time is upon us. The people have no guidance from any truly higher, transcendent belief system, and have been easily swayed toward the cliffs by the Adversary himself. Crowds of "people," if we can even refer to them as such, are without reason, and have no discernible humanity to differentiate themselves from the animals, and are spiritually, mentally, and even physically inverted.

This new religion is none other than satanism, the inversion of all. The deconstruction of all our supposed "assumptions" pushed by this force conveniently never questions itself. It is curious that they have never deconstructed their degeneracy, libertinism, abomination-worship, or even their deconstruction. It is wholly cynical through and through, preying on fools, the mentally ill, and socially manipulable toward their own pathological ends. Their philosophy is little more than tactics, coded in long unused and utterly obtuse forms of prose, or even outright writing in code through made-up words.[504] At least since Marx, the writings of this current have been weak on improving actual people's lives and strong on simply overthrowing the system. And as we can now see as the system has indeed been overthrown, a *Revenge of the Nerds* scenario except with Humvees and tear gas, they have been caught essentially winging it.

From the beginning, the revenge of the inferior subhuman dregs of society has been only for the overthrow of the good, of *nomos*, of all order, spawned from a malicious rage, all obscured by half-baked

---

[504] Has "diversity" ever meant anything other than fewer straight White males? Has "equity" meant anything other than forced redistribution? Has "political correctness" meant anything other than obeying the party line? And of course, "gender affirming care" means genital mutilation.

childish idealism, and barely hiding its predilection for pedophilic fantasy. But the inferior are now on top. Oh, what greater calamity could be faced than a ruling elite which still feels persecuted? One need only look at the atrocities of the twentieth century, from Ukraine to Rwanda, to see the result.[505] And make no mistake, the inferior will always fear and hate the strong, until the strong are eliminated from the equation once and for all. Nietzsche was right that "Nothing on earth consumes a man more quickly than the passion of resentment."[506] The only thing that remains to be seen is how much damage these resentful subhumans, these spiteful mutants, can inflict on the rest of humanity before they inevitably destroy themselves.

In the era after the New Atheism that spelled the precise moment of inflection, from the total death of all things metaphysical, at least in this country, to the slow and then rapid transition to this darker force, we can observe this process in which seemingly benign secularism becomes far darker than anticipated, as was also arguably the case in the French Revolution. For immediately after New Atheism came the obvious satanism in public life that may very well have been lurking in certain elite circles for some time. To what extent the rumors of depravity are true we may never know. However, with connections with elites across the world, Jeffrey Epstein's life and death shines a great light on the behavior of the elites and their operations.

Once seemingly normal people have clearly gone completely insane; they unwittingly sacrifice their unborn children, or even conduct genital sacrifice of their living children. One cannot be mistaken in seeing the resemblance to the genital mutilation sacrifices of the ancient Mesoamericans, or the frenzied, ritualized castration practiced by the cult of Magna Mater.[507] And let us also remember that the child sacrifices of Carthage were by the rich elite caste of the city who could afford to sacrifice a child, no different from the upper-middle class demographic which conducts the

---

[505] "The Number of Holodomor."; "Aftermath," Encyclopædia Britannica.
[506] Nietzsche, *Ecce Homo.*
[507] For Magna Mater: Ferguson, *Religions of the Roman Empire*, 27. For the Maya: Munson et al., "Classic Maya Bloodletting."; Masterson, "Mayans Self-Mutilated to Appease the Gods."

modern equivalent of this rite today. Indeed, it has been noted that this religion they piously subscribe to is largely made up of "luxury beliefs" which only the privileged classes can afford to exercise.[508] It is not the poor today who mutilate their children's genitals in a display of transgender virtue signaling. This can be no coincidence, nor can the fact that this widespread phenomenon only truly became easily recognizable immediately after the ultimate secularization of the West in the early 2000s, paving the way for something new and sinister to emerge.

VI

The West as we know it can be saved no more than the United States' war in Afghanistan can still be won. And the cycle of history cannot be stopped any more than the waves of the ocean. As Spengler wrote about women—that the moment they question childrearing, as opposed to accepting it as no less a given than breathing, that civilization is already on a trajectory downward—so is any civilization unsalvageable the moment the idea of questioning eternal truths is injected into the zeitgeist.[509] This may seem disturbing to some but, in reality, this is the light at the end of the tunnel for the people of the West, and indeed the world. The satanic impulse of the perennial counter-tradition sees the march of history as one step after another until the ultimate defeat of God by Lucifer and his fallen angels. In contrast, the impulse of the Tao, the Logos, the true tradition, the eternal truth which we cannot as mere humans fully understand, is the cycle and new beginning of the Phoenix, of Christ triumphantly risen again, of Ragnarök in which

---

[508] Noor Beckwith et al., "Factors Associated with Gender-Affirming Surgery." See table 1. Out of a sample size of 145 adults who were transgender, while 41.3 percent were at or below the poverty line, it then dipped to 13.1 percent at 100 to 200 percent of the poverty line, but then rose to 19 percent for 200 to 300 percent of the poverty line and then 24.8 percent for 300 percent and above the poverty line. This suggests transgenderism is mostly a phenomenon among the very poor or very rich.
[509] "When the ordinary thought of a highly cultivated people begins to regard 'having children' as a question of pros and cons, the great turning-point has come. . . . When reasons have to be put forward at all in a question of life, life itself has become questionable." Spengler, Decline of the West, 104–106.

the heroes of old defeat this eternal undying evil, even if they themselves must heroically perish to do so, as Vishnu incarnated as Kalki to herald the end of the dark age, and of the vanquishing of Lucifer at the end of the age.

The enemies of humanity are at war with the universe and order itself. They are the antinomian, anarchic, entropic, inverted force which always existed and always in the end is vanquished, perhaps by self-inflicted wounds. This unnaturalness cannot exist for an extended period of time without a host and thus will eventually fail, creating the fertilizer for something wholly new to appear.

However, not only are we approaching the end of the American empire, and not even just Western civilization either, but potentially an entire cycle of the whole world. The globe is connected in a way that it has never been in known human history. As a result, the globalized world, which may for a time be assimilated into a true one-world government, as opposed to the current in-all-but-name global government, has become a global civilization reliant on other sub-civilizations, whether that be reliance on the West for military stability and cheap foodstuffs, reliance on the Oriental civilizations for cheap labor, technological improvement, and rare earth minerals, or exotic cuisine and oil from Latin America and the Islamic world. The obsession with economics and scientific efficiency in the reign of quantity has created international economies of scale in all aspects, meaning that the collapse of one domino will spiral out of control, leaving none standing. The sober mind of Joseph A. Tainter has also raised these concerns.[510] And this interlocking system will give in. Supply chains are breaking down while at the same time becoming ever more complex, and supplied increasingly by a labor pool incapable of meeting demands in either quantity or intelligence.

The postmodern religion is, further than "post-truth," rather anti-truth. Its entire *modus operandi* from the beginning has been the twisting of the real and, for what other reason than to institute the anti-world which has been its result within only a few decades of its adoption? "It would not be difficult to collect from various passages [of their writings] what their ideal is," as C. S. Lewis

---

[510] Tainter, *Collapse of Complex Societies.*

remarked; and eighty years later we can see out in the open what their ugly and evil minds truly intended, even if subliminally.[511] It is no surprise, then, that preventing the mental illness that is now known as "transgenderism" is considered genocide, while the actual gradual genocide of Whites and Western culture is simply taken for granted as a good thing, a steppingstone toward eliminating "Whiteness." As with most things in the demonic politics of our time, all righteous authority is questioned while all totalitarian and evil authority is worshiped under the cult of the state; all libertine and evil freedoms are allowed while true liberty and self-reliance are restricted.

The first death pangs of this global catastrophe can already be seen. The elites are degenerating, not evolving. The managerial state of affairs that we are once again entering is based off the mechanical post-human ideal of robotic perfection, the elimination of all variables. In Asimov's *Foundation* we can see this ideal in literary form, of a world of materialism in which, with an effective enough calculator, even the future can be predicted scientifically.[512] Of course, our world is not a wholly material one, and this elite nihilistic future will thus inevitably fail. As variables are eliminated, innovation will become impossible, meaning the inability to keep up the velocity, much less the acceleration, which had already been declining far before Faustian man's crowning achievement of Apollo 11. If the elites are aware of this destiny, it may be a fueling factor of their insecurity and obsession with artificial intelligence and the "singularity."[513] However, I suspect that even this science fiction race against time between the physical nihilist counter-tradition and the metaphysical tradition is a false dichotomy which assumes that artificial "intelligence," in the true sense, is even possible as an adversary, *ipso facto* presupposing materialism. It is no fluke that the materialists and scientists continue to push back the timeline of when this supposed artificial intelligence will be possible; though

---

[511] Lewis, *Abolition of Man.*
[512] Asimov, *Foundation.*
[513] The WEF says AI is vital for achieving its SDGs (Sustainable Development Goals): Gast, "Why Artificial Intelligence Is Vital." See the following for the elites' interest in the singularity, etc: Ward, "The Price of Silicon Valley's Obsession."; Rushkoff, "Survival of the Richest."

this is not to downplay the very real threat of proto-artificial intelligence in the form of manipulating the mass feeling through algorithms.

No, our true adversary is not the distraction of a hyper-technology let loose (though it still poses a threat), but metaphysical evil. It is less likely that we will be persecuted by death robots, so much as it is that we will simply be burned at the stake or sacrificed at the altar by a Baphometian transvestite priest atop a bloodstained pyramid. The history of dying civilizations is full of satanic blood sacrifices; as for androids from Hell, not so much.[514] The demonic, antinomian *zeitgeist* which has always lurked, watching and waiting, like the serpent in Eden, even at the very beginning constantly evolving, is not yet done with its plans. It is not the material fruits of the modern, elite, scientistic philosophy that we must be vigilant of specifically, but the post-human and *post-*postmodernist philosophy itself to which the transhuman and artificial intelligence ideals are but microcosms of the greater macrocosm.

And whether its kingdom will see its fall tomorrow or in a hundred years is yet to be seen, though the good-willed people of this world must prepare for the disturbing possibility that we will not see the end of this cycle before the end of our lifetime. The evil that a dying beast is capable of inflicting before its final destruction must not be underestimated. I do not lie when I say that many good people will fall before all is said and done. To say otherwise would simply be to delude the reader with yet another one of the many "cowardly optimisms" that the masses use to cope with reality.

While the demonic elite will eventually be defeated, perhaps being crushed under the weight of their own utopian system, it remains necessary to combat these forces, if not just to know in your heart that you contributed to a battle greater than yourself, while most others sluggishly crawl through a meager existence in this fallen world, then to hopefully cause a knock-on effect for the next *cycle of civilization—perhaps even the inheritor of Western*

---

[514] The Aztecs practiced extensive human sacrifice. "Human Sacrifices: How Many Were Killed in Aztec Culture?" See Smith, "Canaanite Child Sacrifice," for Carthaginian and Canaanite child sacrifice. As for modern times, *The New York Times* recently published a disturbing article about cannibalism: Beggs, "A Taste for Cannibalism?"

civilization. Most importantly, we must, God willing, defeat this satanic system before an unnecessary amount of damage is incurred on the world. The forces of chaos will fail, let us pray, but will they take Europe and the greater West with them, as is surely their intention? Will the environment be destroyed, so that recovery takes hundreds or even thousands of years, before they are stopped? Will all remnants of high civilization be leveled, with not one brick atop another, by the time the catastrophe is over? These possibilities must motivate the righteous warrior in his quest against evil, even if evil will inevitably fall. Humanity must unite against this final foe if the new world we bequeath to our posterity will be one worth living in.

Death to the New World Order.

Originally published on Counter-Currents, May 1st, 2024

What is America? What does it mean to be an American? Today it seems as though there are as many answers to these questions as there are people to provide them. This is especially pertinent for nationalists. One answer to this is it simply means possessing United States citizenship. Even more extreme is the idea that everyone is a potential American; or that illegal aliens, who are being used by rival civilizations to colonize the US, are no less American than the descendants of the *Mayflower.* These are the most popular definitions of the limits of Americanness propagated by the bi-marionette political system. The true Right, however, offers older, more primal definitions: that Americans are in fact unhyphenated Americans, synonymous with white/European-descended Americans, or that those with no American ancestry from before 1965 are not "ethnic Americans."

All of these definitions are lacking in some way, which cuts to the heart of the issue: There is no objective definition of what an American is. Its meaning has been in flux since the founding, making America a sort of "nation of Theseus" in which the question of a definition becomes a paradox. The Ship of Theseus was the vessel in which the hero Theseus returned to Athens after slaying the Minotaur in his labyrinth. The Athenians preserved his ship for generations, until eventually not a single part of was original—leading to the famous paradox of whether it remained the same ship. In the same way, while the descendants of those who founded America remain, Anglo-Americans are a now small minority. Thus, this can only be solved by looking forward, rather than solely back to the past.

America's unique history as a settler-colonialist nation makes its ethnos more difficult to determine than, say, that of Norway or the Czech Republic. We know that Norwegians are the Nordic, Norwegian-speaking people of western Scandinavia, descendants of the Norsemen. The Czechs are the Czech-speaking peoples of the former kingdoms of Bohemia and Moravia. This issue is thornier in America, which was founded by many men who were technically foreigners, such as Alexander Hamilton. And while the founders were almost all either Anglo-Saxon, the first immigration act opened the country to all "free whites of good character." Thomas Jefferson even toyed with the idea of allowing "Mohammedans" into America. This laid the seeds of the identity crisis that America is in today.

America welcomed millions of white immigrants from all over Europe. After the Civil War, not only were the former slaves made citizens, but immigration was soon opened to foreign-born blacks and Chinese guest workers, as well as Europeans from other parts of the Continent, especially Italians and Eastern Europeans (and to whom most Americans can trace their ancestry today), including Jews. This was eventually stopped, although Native Americans were soon also inducted into the brotherhood of citizenship. There were enough Japanese living in America by the start of the Second World War that it was seen as a national security issue.

Despite initial white resistance to the beginnings of a racial transformation in America which peaked during Reconstruction and the Great Depression, it had completely fizzled by the time of the 1965 Immigration Act. In fact, many of the nativists themselves were descended from non-Anglo-Saxons who would have been seen as less than entirely American by some of the Founding Fathers, such as Benjamin Franklin, who famously argued against German immigration. Thus, an ethnic basis for American nationalism is complicated by the fact that the US has been continually expanding its definition of who can become an American since its earliest days.

America has long been called an "experiment" and the flux of its identity has been at least in part due to this unique experimental nature, which has in turn been adopted by the rest of European civ-

ilization as well. This has developed into the idea of civic nationalism and America as a "propositional nation." Both sides of the political mainstream accept some variation of this view. Thus, the mainstream "Right" position is that an Indian immigrant or an urban
black—both of whom have their own ethnos, complete with its own
symbols, aesthetics, and heroes, as well as disdain for America's European heritage—are no less American than a "Boston Brahmin" or
a Wyoming rancher descended from *Mayflower* colonists. The globalist Left would go even further: If everyone can be American, then
America is at best a way of being, and at worst completely meaning-
less. Why not just get over the concept of the nation and become a
"post-national nation," as Canada is attempting to do—where symbols and identity are simply garnishes from a half-remembered
past, whose only purpose is to unite us as diverse free spirits seeking individual pleasure?

There has always been a dichotomy in America between urban
and rural spirits, the urban being a more imperial vision and the
rural a *Völkisch* one. It could be seen already in the political battles
between Federalists and Anti-Federalists, typified in Alexander
Hamilton and Thomas Jefferson. Later, it spilled over into the War
of Secession. At first the rural element tended to win out, but since
the Civil War, the imperial-urban element has won just about every
battle. For a short time, it seemed as though there could be a real
synthesis in the philosophy of the journalist and progressive
political theorist Herbert Croly, who influenced Theodore
Roosevelt. But the Great Depression, the cultural baggage attached
to the Second World War, and mass elite Jewish migration into the
US ruined first the progressive and then the conservative political
platforms. By the end of the twentieth century, neither Jeffersonian
classical liberalism (conservatism), Hamiltonian imperialism, or a
synthesis of the two (Rooseveltian progressivism) provided a viable
platform for real American nationalism.

The urban-rural divide today is between visions of America as a
homeland versus America as "Airstrip One"—nationalism versus
globalism. This divide is still between the *Völkisch* and imperialistic
aspects of the American collective spirit. Globalists—not just
Americans, but also the "culturally Americanized" elites—see
America as the world's preeminent economic zone, a place to climb

the ladder of the global oligarchy, and a military base that secures Pax Americana and the safety of the liberal world order. In contrast, those who are *Völkisch* would say that America is a homeland for "Americans"—once again bringing us back to the original issue.

White Americans today don't generally see themselves as a distinct people, nor can you artificially force them to. Ask an American what ethnic group—and therefore, what nation—they are a part of, and they will invariably reply with something about their highly mixed ancestry. I've even witnessed a few instances of white people claiming they aren't white because "my mom is Mexican" (it turned out she is 100% Spanish) or "I'm half Italian" and so on. These people were genuinely embarrassed to be of European stock. Thus, as a whole white Americans lack a distinct ethic consciousness.

Real nationalism is felt instinctually, not simply justified by facts. It is something a priori. It can only grow and survive out of one a specific type of soil: that of struggle, the greatest glue of all. What unites a German-American frontiersman who is fighting Indians, an Irish-American Yankee soldier, and an Italian-American GI storming the beach at Peleliu? They are all in a common struggle for their new team: those Americans who came before them. This explains the patriotism and white-adjacency of many non-white combat veterans.

The closest thing to a real struggle in the modern age that had the potential to bind Americans into a distinct people once again were the events of September 11, 2001. For a brief period, patriotism, American chauvinism, and the idea of the West being in a clash of civilizations was normalized even in the liberal cities. But the Twenty Years' War in the Middle East was no genuine civilizational struggle. Not enough people were involved either on the front lines or on the home front, and thus this patriotic effect was fleeting. Although the brief period from 2001 to 2003 nevertheless showed the effect that a civilizational struggle can have on national unity.

If America is to once again become a real nation in the classical sense of *natio*, there must be another defining struggle in which everyone has real skin in the game. This could be something along racial/cultural lines as race relations in the US deteriorate and racial schisms become more evident. Blacks and "Chicanos"— descendants of Latin American colonists who have developed an ethnic identity as mestizo north of the Rio Grande—have already developed racial consciousness not just in terms of blood, but also of soil . . . our soil. In this scenario, whites would be forced to identify as a legitimate nation—Americans—or simply be subsumed by rival groups.

Another possibility is that the US may enter a real clash of civilizations, perhaps with China, Iran, Russia, or all of the above. This would have the potential to unite America as a multiracial nation in which all biological races see themselves as ethnic Americans due to fighting for a common cause. This outcome is disturbing, as it would spell the end of White America, solidify federal control, and of course in the case of a world war destroy much of the world and many millions of lives in the process.

The bad news is that if the elites believe this is the best way to cool off the boiling frog of race relations in the US, then they are more likely to be hawkish on foreign policy. The good news is that this is probably not on their minds, as unifying an artificial empire through common struggle is easier said than done. A Third World War would bring too much risk of their conservative troops and citizens identifying with Russia, for example, and their liberals identifying with Iran. For the first time in decades, the US appears to be gradually retreating in the Middle East rather than jumping on any excuse for intervention. Besides which, ethnonationalism was heightened, not dampened, in the former European empires after the Great War. In other words, white ethnonationalism in America in the sense of becoming "ethnic Americans" is probably inevitable over the long term. To what extent these ethnic Americans will even be relevant, however, is a matter of how many there are by the time this racial consciousness is awakened.

Though ethnonationalism, unlike liberalism, is based in biology and human nature, the future has yet to be written. Furthermore, the past is mixed in terms of who has the right idea about what America is. While white American nationalists can rightly claim that America was an explicitly white super-majoritarian nation until 1965, the diversity crowd are also right when they claim that America is a "nation of immigrants," white or otherwise, and that the Constitution is a "living document." But from the First National Bank to Sherman's March to the Sea, America has constantly betrayed its own ideals for political expediency. Even our revered religious scripture, the Constitution, isn't even our original constitution! Jefferson himself flippantly suggested that every generation might need another revolution. Thus, neither side has a monopoly on historical precedence.

While most of us on the true Right have gone through a "conservative" phase, and many of us still consider ourselves to be conservative or perhaps reactionary, the truth is that not only is historical precedence overrated; it's beta. Yes, I understand that it's a necessary propaganda tool to win over the center-Right masses who instinctually legitimize nostalgia, but we still need to do better.

Just look at the "Chicanos" in America or the Muslims in Europe. Despite the fact that Chicanos are descended from indigenous peoples south of the Rio Grande as well as Spaniards (though Chicanos seem to repudiate any trace of Europeanness), they have no moral or philosophical qualms about colonizing the southwestern United States. The relationship between Europe and the Muslims is likewise one of perpetual enmity, yet the same is true there. You might not like it, but this is what peak performance looks like. Not so long ago, I'm told white men did the same thing—though at this point this claim might as well be an ancient legend of original sin. The point is that a vital people doesn't need a moral argument. They do not ask for permission. They have a will to survive, and indeed, a will to power. If America is going to once again become a real nation, it's going to take a lot more than smart arguments and policy conferences to get there.

BIBLIOGRAPHY

Books

Asimov, Isaac. *Foundation*. New York, NY: Bantam Books, 2004.

Ayers, Bill. *Fugitive Days*. Boston, MA: Beacon Press, 2001.

Buchanan, Patrick J. *Where the Right Went Wrong: How Neoconservatives Subverted the Reagan Revolution and Hijacked the Bush Presidency*. New York, NY: Thomas Dunne Books, 2005.

Burnham, James. *The Managerial Revolution: What Is Happening in the World*. Lume Books, 2021.

Caldwell, Christopher. *The Age of Entitlement: America since the Sixties*. New York, NY: Simon & Schuster Paperbacks, 2021.

Coulter, Ann. *¡Adios, America!: The Left's Plan to Turn Our Country into a Third World Hellhole*. Washington, DC: Regnery Publishing, 2016.

Dalrymple, Theodore. *Life at the Bottom: The Worldview That Makes the Underclass*. Chicago: Ivan R. Dee, 2006.

Davis, Jefferson. *The Rise and Fall of the Confederate Government*. New York, NY: D. Appleton, 1881.

Degrelle, Léon. *The Burning Souls*. Antelope Hill Publishing, 2020.

Dutton, Edward. *Spiteful Mutants: Evolution, Sexuality, Religion, and Politics in the 21st Century*. Radix, 2022.

Evola, Julius. *The Hermetic Tradition*. Inner Traditions, 1995.

Evola, Julius. *Revolt against the Modern World*. Rochester, VA: Inner Traditions International, 1995.

Evola, Julius. *Ride the Tiger*. Rochester, VA: Inner Traditions International, 2018.

Ferguson, John. *Religions of the Roman Empire*. Ithaca, NY: Cornell University Press, 1976.

Fisher, Sydney George. *The True History of the American Revolution*. Kessinger Pub., 2006.

Francis, Samuel T. *Beautiful Losers: Essays on the Failure of American Conservatism*. Columbia, MO: University of Missouri Press, 1994.

Fukuyama, Francis. *The End of History and the Last Man*. Penguin Books Ltd, 2020.

Glubb, Sir John. *The Fate of Empires and Search for Survival*. Edinburgh: William Blackwood & Sons Ltd, 1977.

Goldwater, Barry. *Conscience of a Conservative*. Victor Publishing Company, 1960.

Greer, Germaine. *Daddy, We Hardly Knew You*. New York, NY: Fawcett Columbine, 1991.

Greer, John Michael. *Dark Age America: Climate Change, Cultural Collapse, and the Hard Future Ahead*. Gabriola, BC: New Society Publishers, 2016.

Guénon René. *The Crisis of the Modern World*. Hillsdale, NY: Sophia Perennis, 2004.

Guénon René. *The Reign of Quantity & the Signs of the Times*. Hillsdale, NY: Sophia Perennis, 2001.

Haidt, Jonathan. *The Righteous Mind: Why Good People Are Divided by Politics and Religion*. Vancouver, B.C,: Langara College, 2020.

Herrnstein, Richard J., and Charles A. Murray. *The Bell Curve: Intelligence and Class Structure in American Life*. New York, NY: Free Press, 1997.

Howard, Dylan, Melissa Cronin, and James Robertson. *Epstein: Dead Men Tell No Tales: Spies, Lies & Blackmail*. New York, NY: Skyhorse Publishing, 2021.

Howard, Scott. *The Open Society Playbook*. Antelope Hill Publishing, 2021.

Howard, Scott. *The Transgender-Industrial Complex*. Antelope Hill Publishing, 2020.

Johnson, Greg. *The Year America Died*. San Francisco, CA: *Counter-Currents*, 2021.

de Jouvenel, Bertrand. *On Power*. Boston, MA: Beacon Press. 1967.

Jünger, Ernst, and David C. Durst. *On Pain*. Ingram, 2008.

Kirchheimer, Otto, Herbert Marcuse, and Franz Neumann. *Secret Reports on Nazi Germany: The Frankfurt School Contribution to the War Effort*. Princeton, NJ: Princeton University Press, 2013.

Klein, Aaron, and Brenda J Elliott. *The Manchurian President: Barack Obama's Ties to Communists, Socialists and Other Anti-American Extremists*. WND Books, 2010.

Kroc, Ray, and Robert Anderson. *Grinding It Out: The Making of McDonald's*. New York, NY: St. Martin's Press, 2016.

Lewis, C. S. *The Abolition of Man*. HarperCollins, 2009.

Lichter, S. Robert, Stanley Rothman, and Linda S. Lichter. *The Media Elite: America's New Power Brokers*. Hastings House, 1990.

Lobaczewski, Andrew M. *Political Ponerology: The Science of Evil, Psychopathy, and Totalitarianism*. RED PILL PRESS, 2022.

Lynn, Richard. *Dysgenics: Genetic Deterioration in Modern Populations*. Praeger Publishing Group, 1996.

MacDonald, Kevin B. *The Culture of Critique: An Evolutionary Analysis of Jewish Involvement in Twentieth-Century Intellectual and Political Movements*. Westport, CT: Praeger, 1998.

Mead, Margaret. *Coming of Age in Samoa*. William Morrow and Co., 1928.

Mearsheimer, John J., and Stephen M. Walt. *The Israel Lobby and U.S. Foreign Policy*. New York, NY: Farrar, Straus and Giroux, 2007.

Michels, Robert. *Political Parties: A Sociological Study of the Oligarchial Tendencies of Modern Democracy*. Martino Fine Books, 2016.

Miller Harris, Sarah. *The CIA and the Congress for Cultural Freedom in the Early Cold War: The Limits of Making Common Cause*. London: Routledge, Taylor & Francis Group, 2018.

Moldbug, Mencius. *Technology, Communism, and the Brown Scare*. Unqualified Reservations, 2016.

Neal, Josh. *American Extremist*. Imperium Press, 2021.

Nietzsche, Friedrich Wilhelm. *Ecce Homo: How One Becomes What One Is*. London: Penguin Books, 2004.

Plato. *Republic VIII* in *Plato Complete Works*. Hacket Publishing Inc., 1997.

Quinn, Spencer J. *Solzhenitsyn and the Right*. Antelope Hill Publishing, 2021.

Salatin, Joel. *Everything I Want to Do Is Illegal: War Stories from the Local Food Front*. Swoope, VA: Polyface, Inc., 2007.

Samuel, Maurice. *You Gentiles*. Antelope Hill Publishing, 2022.

Schwab, Klaus, and Peter Vanham. *Stakeholder Capitalism: A Global Economy That Works for Progress, People and Planet*. Hoboken, NJ: Wiley, 2021.

Sealey, Raphael. *A History of the Greek City States ca. 700–338 B.C.* University of California Press, 1976.

Shankman, Paul. *Trashing of Margaret Mead: Anatomy of an Anthropological Controversy*. Madison, WI: University of Wisconsin Press, 2009.

Solzhenitsyn, Aleksandr. *The Gulag Archipelago: An Experiment in Literary Investigation*. Harper Perennial Modern Classics, 2007.

Spengler, Oswald. *The Hour of Decision*. Rogue Scholar Press, 2020.

Spengler, Oswald, and Helmut Werner. *The Decline of the West*. Oxford: Oxford University Press, 1932.

Tainter, Joseph. *The Collapse of Complex Societies*. Cambridge: Cambridge University Press, 2017.

Videos

Central Intelligence Agency. "Humans of CIA." March 25, 2021. YouTube, 2:26. https://www.youtube.com/watch?v=X55JPbAMc9g.

Conte, Greg. "Abolish The FBI!" *National Justice Party*. Speech, September 3, 2022. https://nationaljusticeparty.com/2022/09/09/abolish-the-fbi/.

Hamilton, Hattie and Jenny Ky. "Jeffrey Epstein Was a Mossad Spy, Says Investigative Journalist Dylan Howard." *The Morning Show*. 7News, December 8, 2019. https://tinyurl.com/bjpdwhej.

HealthImpactNews. "Australian Police Attack Children for not Wearing Masks: Pepper-Spray 12-Year-Old." August 17, 2021. Bitchute video, 9:39. https://www.bitchute.com/video/Gooq0cYwlYdw/.

Ivn1977. "Barbara Lerner Spectre calls for destruction of Christian European ethnic societies." September 9, 2015. YouTube video, 1:17. https://www.youtube.com/watch?v=G45WthPTo24&t=26s.

Krogan, American. "*Counter-Currents* Radio Podcast No. 389 Greg Johnson & Thomas Steuben Talk to *BioShock* Documentary Producer American Krogan." Interview with Greg Johnson and Thomas Steuben. *Counter-Currents*. Podcast audio, November 16, 2021. https://tinyurl.com/58apnmuy.

Misesmedia. "Hans-Hermann Hoppe: Why Democracy Fails." March 11, 2016. YouTube video, 11:29. https://www.youtube.com/watch?v=hUzkZaD1xDs.

National Justice Party and Media2Rise. "Terror in Waukesha." February 8, 2022. Odysee video, 33:58. https://tinyurl.com/bd28j44b.

Nicholas Marshall. "FULL INTERVIEW with Yuri Bezmenov: The Four Stages of Ideological Subversion (1984)." August 22, 2020. YouTube video, 1:21:28. https://www.youtube.com/watch?v=yErKTVdETpw.

Offensive Freedom. "KGB defector Yuri Bezmenov's warning to America (1984)." June 27, 2020. YouTube video, 6:49. https://tinyurl.com/3r55nhfb.

Per-Inge Eliasson. "Noel Ignatiev calls for the end of whiteness." April 26, 2022. Odysee video, 1:45. https://tinyurl.com/mrxtwdzy.

Persian Atheist. "KGB defector Yuri Bezmenov's warning to America." February 1, 2013. YouTube, 13:36. https://www.youtube.com/watch?v=bX3EZCVj2XA.

Red Ice TV. "Epstein & Ghislaine Maxwell Victim Maria Farmer Speaks About The Belief They Are Superior & Chosen." December 9, 2021. Odysee video, 4:29. https://tinyurl.com/2s49ea6n.

Rotten Tomatoes Indie. "Alt-Right: Age of Rage Movie Clip - Threats (2018) | Movieclips Indie." November 13, 2018. YouTube, 1:55. https://www.youtube.com/watch?v=_wtqPCdi9M.

VDARE TV. "Why Michelle Malkin Is Banned from Airbnb." February 2, 2022. VDARE Video, 1:39. https://tinyurl.com/bdhhhkya.

WVradioman. "The USS Liberty Navy Ship - Who Attempted to Sink It..?!?!" March 9, 2019. Bitchute video, 52:15. https://tinyurl.com/mr2z6zam.

Articles and Other Resources

"20. If Emissions of Greenhouse Gases Were Stopped, Would the Climate Return to the Conditions of 200 Years Ago?" The Royal Society, Accessed December 14, 2022. https://tinyurl.com/53prh9ju.

"8. U.S. Jews' Political Views." Pew Research Center, May 11, 2021. https://www.pewresearch.org/religion/2021/05/11/u-s-jews-political-views/.

Abdulrazaq, Tallha. "Iraq Lost Its Future the Day It Invaded Kuwait." *TRT World*, August 2, 2019. https://tinyurl.com/4dv4an2s.

Abu Naser, Zinaid. "Extreme Quotes From Judaism – Laws About Non Jews – The Talmud Exposed – Death To The Goyim Infidels – The Jewish God Jehovah Studies The Talmud?" Zinaid Abu Naser, August 10, 2012. https://zinaidabunaser.com/2012/08/10/extreme-quotes-from-judaism/.

Albrecht, Beau. "Remembering Sam Francis: The Rising Tide of Anarcho-Tyranny." *Counter-Currents*, April 28, 2021. https://tinyurl.com/4zakwzu9.

Albrecht, Beau. "Take Your Choice, Part II: Stop the Hate!" *Counter-Currents*, August 12, 2020. https://tinyurl.com/2t2nzma2.

Alexander, Harriet. "George Soros-Backed Groups Have Spent $40 Million to Elect 75 Progressive Prosecutors over the Last Decade - Meaning One in FIVE Americans Now Live in Areas Covered by His Criminal Justice Reformers." *Daily Mail Online*, June 8, 2022. https://tinyurl.com/55xbrpa6.

"Alleged Waukesha Attacker Shared Conspiratorial, Antisemitic Content in 2015." ADL, December 1, 2021. https://tinyurl.com/mr3f38k4.

Allen, Glen. "The Sines v. Kessler Lawfare Litigation: A National & Historic Disgrace." *Counter-Currents*, November 22, 2021. https://tinyurl.com/573err4k.

Alper, Becka A., and Alan Cooperman. "10 Key Findings about Jewish Americans." Pew Research Center, May 11, 2021. https://tinyurl.com/2p8mkbw9.

"American War and Military Operations Casualties: Lists and Statistics." Congressional Research Service, July 29, 2020. https://tinyurl.com/mvn3daf5.

Analysis, Shimmer. "Vietnam War: Yes, the Media Did Undermine the War Effort." Medium, June 9, 2021. https://tinyurl.com/4yxywe4y.

Anderson, Jeffrey H. "Do Masks Work?" *City Journal*, August 11, 2021. https://tinyurl.com/kfxekuae.

Anderson, Joel. "30 Most Powerful Unions in America." GOBankingRates, April 23, 2021. https://tinyurl.com/ywwdwwk4.

Andy Ngô (@MrAndyNgo). "I don't want to speak to you & I stand by my reporting." Twitter, November 22, 2021. https://tinyurl.com/brw6654k.

Appell, G.N. "Freeman's Refutation of Mead's Coming of Age in Samoa: The Implication for Anthropological Inquiry." *The Eastern Anthropologist* 37 (1984): 183–214. http://www.gnappell.org/articles/freeman.htm.

"Are Students Engaged?" YouthTruth, December 14, 2022. https://youthtruthsurvey.org/student-engagement/.

Athey, Amber. "The Mob That Doxxed Tucker Carlson Is Already Back on Twitter." *The Daily Caller*, November 14, 2018. https://tinyurl.com/bdh4bf68.

Aurélie, Campana. "'The Soviet Massive Deportations - A Chronology." *SciencesPo*, November 5, 2007. https://tinyurl.com/2reuuwt4.

Austermuhle, Martin. "Bowser Had 'Black Lives Matter' Painted on a D.C. Street. Now Other Groups Want a Turn." NPR, August 6, 2020. https://tinyurl.com/3ee28t4a.

Austin, Bethany. "Could Not Having Kids Save the Planet? Antinatalism and Why It's More Popular than Ever." *Wearth London*, April 13, 2022. https://www.wearthlondon.com/blog/could-not-having-kids-save-the-planet/.

Ausubel, Jacob. "Globally, Women Are Younger than Their Male Partners, More Likely to Age Alone." Pew Research Center, January 3, 2020. https://tinyurl.com/3fvw6r6u.

Baldor, Lolita C. "US Military's Elite Commando Forces Look to Expand Diversity." ABC10, June 16, 2021. https://tinyurl.com/42484a9v.

Ball, Molly. "The Secret Bipartisan Campaign That Saved the 2020 Election." *Time*, February 4, 2021. https://time.com/5936036/secret-2020-election-campaign/.

Balsamini, Dean. "Nearly 2,000 NYPD Cops Quitting before Getting Full Pensions - a 71% Jump from 2021." *New York Post*, August 6, 2022. https://tinyurl.com/2p9dn4yb.

Baroud, Ramzy. "Israel's Legacy of Terror and Ethnic Cleansing." *Gulf News*, January 10, 2018. https://tinyurl.com/ysxt77bz.

Barth, Brian. "Pro & Cons of Petrochemical Fertilizers." *SF Gate*, December 14, 2022. https://homeguides.sfgate.com/pro-cons-petrochemical-fertilizers-86254.html.

Basma, Victoria. "Israel's Treatment of Ethiopian Migrants Is Part of a Legacy of Violent Xenophobia." *Gal-Dem*, October 3, 2018. https://tinyurl.com/n6knfmnr.

Bates, Josiah. "Small-Town Cops Are Quitting En Masse as Police Come Under More Scrutiny." *Time*, July 28, 2022. https://tinyurl.com/ypw2jyv3.

Beckett, Jesse. "The Absurd Rules-of-Engagement GIs Had to Follow during the Vietnam War." War History Online, November 17, 2021. https://tinyurl.com/yb4tx6y9.

Beckett, Lois. "At Least 25 Americans Were Killed during Protests and Political Unrest in 2020." *The Guardian*, October 31, 2020. https://tinyurl.com/y3r84u55.

Beckwith, Noor, Sari L. Reisner, Shayne Zaslow, Kenneth H. Mayer, and Alex S. Keuroghlian. "Factors Associated with Gender-Affirming Surgery and Age of Hormone Therapy Initiation among Transgender Adults." *Transgender Health* 2, no. 1 (2017): 156–64. https://doi.org/10.1089/trgh.2017.0028.

Beggs, Alex. "A Taste for Cannibalism?" *The New York Times*, July 23, 2022. https://tinyurl.com/tw7wrrz4.

Ben Zion, Ilan, and AP. "Jewish Donors Prominent in Presidential Campaign Contributions." *The Times of Israel*, October 20, 2012. https://tinyurl.com/y328dkkr.

Bergman, Jerry. "Ratio of Liberal to Conservative Professors Has Profoundly Changed." *KPCNews*, October 10, 2019. https://tinyurl.com/5n842erb.

Berland, Oscar. "The Emergence of the Communist Perspective on the 'Negro Question' in America: 1919-1931: Part Two." *Science & Society* 64, no. 2 (2000): 194–217. https://www.jstor.org/stable/40403839.

Berman, Russell. "Trump's Border-Wall Blink." *The Atlantic*, April 25, 2017. https://tinyurl.com/2z4hzxp4.

Bernstein, Andrew. "The Vindication of Joseph McCarthy." *The Objective Standard*, November 20, 2016. https://tinyurl.com/3zjks225.

Bew, John. "Marxists and the Office of Strategic Services." *War on the Rocks*, September 5, 2013. https://tinyurl.com/bddfjt6r.

Bhagat, Sanjai. "Outsourcing Manufacturing to China Endangers U.S. Security and Public Health." *The Washington Times*, April 13, 2020. https://tinyurl.com/uprxbvx9.

Bier, David. "Matt Ridley: How Fossil Fuels Helped End Slavery." GlobalWarming.org, November 17, 2011. https://tinyurl.com/4upxmmuj.

"Bin Laden: Palestinian Cause Prompted 9/11." *CBS News*, May 16, 2008. https://tinyurl.com/42ew3hxn.

"Bipartisan Support for Criminal Justice Reform Still Strong." Equal Justice Initiative, December 20, 2018. https://tinyurl.com/ycy7rr6z.

Board of Deputies of British Jews (@BoardofDeputies). "We were honoured to speak with @ppvernon @davidlmearn and learn about the exciting @anchorwindrushproject. We are deeply touched by the care they are taking to recognise the little known Jewish history of the HMT Empire Windrush and support their vision for a Windrush monument." Twitter, December 8, 2021. https://twitter.com/BoardofDeputies/status/1468703884000571394

Board, Ibd Editorial. "Obama's Military Coup Purges 197 Officers in Five Years." *Investor's Business Daily*, October 29, 2013. https://tinyurl.com/4hukar59.

"Bourgeois Overproduction and the Problem of the Fake Elite." *New Discourses*, May 20, 2021. https://tinyurl.com/5n6dfsrs.

Bova, Alex. "J.P. Morgan Is Celebrating Pride." J.P. Morgan, June 30, 2022. https://tinyurl.com/3jzyzvme.

Bovard, Jim. "Teachers Unions Have Always Been Terrible." *The American Conservative*, February 15, 2021. https://tinyurl.com/2s46dxht.

Bowden, Jonathan. "Marxism & the Frankfurt School." *Counter-Currents*, May 9, 2012. https://tinyurl.com/yc2eswc9.

Brothers, Eric. "Heroes or Victims? The Role and Antifascist Culture of Jews in the German Democratic Republic." *European Judaism: A Journal for the New Europe* 25, no. 2 (1992): 21–27. https://www.jstor.org/stable/41432744.

Brown, Anna. "1. A Profile of Single Americans." Pew Research Center, August 20, 2020. https://tinyurl.com/mrx4vhfu.

Brown, Lee. "Woke Walmart Trains Staffers in Critical Race Theory: US A 'White-Supremacy System.'" *New York Post*, October 15, 2021. https://nypost.com/2021/10/15/walmart-trains-staff-in-critical-race-theory/.

Brown, Patrick T. "U.S. Marriage Rates Hit New Recorded Low." United States Congress Joint Economic Committee, April 29, 2020. https://tinyurl.com/t4dxjv6p.

Buchanan, Patrick J. "Behind the Sinking of the Lusitania." *VDARE*, September 1, 2014. https://vdare.com/articles/behind-the-sinking-of-the-lusitania.

Buchanan, Patrick J. "Court Clerk Kim Davis vs. Anti-Christian Judicial Tyranny." *VDARE*, September 10, 2015. https://tinyurl.com/ywf5vdtc.

Budiman, Abby. "Indians in the U.S. Fact Sheet," Pew Research Center, April 29, 2021. https://tinyurl.com/4mbjy7uv.

Burke, Lindsey M. "Unions Double down on Inserting Critical Race Theory into Education." The Heritage Foundation, July 6, 2021. https://tinyurl.com/3n84u5ks.

Burt, Andrew. "'These United States': How Obama's Vocal Tic Reveals a Polarized America." *The Atlantic*, May 13, 2013. https://tinyurl.com/24xyatat.

Cain, Áine, and Taylor Borden. "20 US Presidents Who Belonged to Secret Societies." *Business Insider*, August 21, 2020. https://tinyurl.com/yc6m9jjr.

Calhoun, S. Brady. "FBI Agent Who Investigated Sex Crimes against Children Charged with Sex Crimes against Children." WFLA, August 27, 2021. https://tinyurl.com/325e2r3j.

van de Camp, Morris. "Know Your Enemy: Antifa." *Counter-Currents*, December 14, 2020. https://counter-currents.com/2020/12/know-your-enemy-antifa/.

van de Camp, Morris. "Not Kinder, Not Gentler, but Ineffective." *Counter-Currents*, February 22, 2022. https://tinyurl.com/yc6wheuu.

van de Camp, Morris. "Work to Be Such a Man." *Counter-Currents*, May 17, 2022. https://counter-currents.com/2022/05/work-to-be-such-a-man.

Carpenter, Ted Galen. "How the National Security State Manipulates the News Media." Cato Institute, March 9, 2021. https://tinyurl.com/3zj9mur9.

Center, Fiscal Policy. "Unequal Opportunities, Unequal Outcomes: The Covid-19 Recession in Colorado." Independence Institute, November 1, 2021. https://tinyurl.com/yc89y5xn.

Chakra, Hayden. "The Brutal Military Tactics of the Mongols Make ISIS Look like Child's Play." About History, February 9, 2021. https://tinyurl.com/4ywua2nz.

Chantrill, Christopher. "US Government Spending History from 1900." USGovernmentSpending.com, December 14, 2022. https://www.usgovernmentspending.com/past_spending.

Chea, S.G. "Michel Foucault and Other Progressive Intellectual Heroes Were Pedophiles." *Evie Magazine*, April 5, 2021. https://tinyurl.com/48bybu9u.

Chermak, Steven M., Joshua D. Freilich, and Michael Suttmoeller. *The Organizational Dynamics of Far-Right Hate Groups in the United Sttates: Comparing Violent to Non-Violent Organizations*. National Consortium for the Study of Terrorism and Responses to Terrorism, December 2011. https://tinyurl.com/yan7fwkn.

Chibbaro, Lou. "CIA Hands out 'Gay' Recruitment Brochure at D.C. Pride Festival." *Washington Blade*, June 13, 2013. https://tinyurl.com/bddn2j9p.

Chittilapally, Joslyn. "Antinatalism, Why People Are Going Child-Free for the Environment." *LifeGate*, February 5, 2020. https://tinyurl.com/56ss49yr.

Chomsky, Noam. "Full Transcript: Noam Chomksy on the Anti-War Movement." *The Guardian*, February 4, 2003. https://tinyurl.com/yckkw6ax.

Chomsky, Noam. "Wars, Bailouts, and Elections." Interview by David Barsamian. *Z Magazine*, September 10, 2008. https://chomsky.info/20080910_2/.

Chulov, Martin, and Helen Pidd. "Defector Admits to WMD Lies That Triggered Iraq War." *The Guardian*, February 15, 2011. https://tinyurl.com/4sbxxm8c.

Clark, Cory. "Biased Science Makes Bad Policy." *Psychology Today*, June 29, 2021. https://tinyurl.com/5emhc38e.

"Climate Migration in Africa: How to Turn The Tide." The World Bank, January 5, 2022. https://tinyurl.com/mrm5jme7.

Cohen, Marsha B. "Israel's Stolen Nuclear Materials: Why It Still Matters." *Lobe Log*, April 28, 2014. https://tinyurl.com/2snekxf4.

Cohn, Jonathan. "Iraq War at 15: Who Voted for It, Who Didn't, and Where Are They Now?" Medium, March 20, 2018. https://tinyurl.com/8tntcen5.

"College Guide Search." Hillel International, December 14, 2022. https://hillel.org/college-guide/search#radius=10&select=top60.

Connelly, Edmund. "Christmas Special: More on the Jewish War on Christmas." *Counter-Currents*, December 22, 2010. https://tinyurl.com/2xhxn5vh.

Connelly, Edmund. "Critical Race Theory as a Jewish Intellectual Weapon." *The Occidental Observer*, June 21, 2021. https://tinyurl.com/2n2vn2vy.

Coulter, Ann. "Ann Coulter: Have a Historically Accurate Thanksgiving!: Articles," *VDARE*, November 25, 2020. https://tinyurl.com/2pdvefht.

Creitz, Charles. "Blackrock, Other Investment Firms 'Killing the Dream' of Home Ownership, Journalist Says." *Fox News*, June 12, 2021. https://tinyurl.com/y8yt9r4c.

Curry, Peter. "How Many People Died in the First World War?" History Hit, October 16, 2018. https://tinyurl.com/28h47jc2.

Daily Wire News. "Watch: CNN Claims Kenosha Protests Are 'Fiery but Mostly Peaceful' as City Burns Behind Reporter." *The Daily Wire*, August 27, 2020. https://tinyurl.com/asbydxfc.

Daley, Kevin, and Chuck Ross. "Meet the Progressive DA behind the Waukesha Bail Catastrophe." *The Washington Free Beacon*, November 22, 2021. https://tinyurl.com/5cukd2ss.

DaSilva, Steve. "Elon Musk Is Being Investigated like a Mob Boss." *MSN*, September 8, 2022. https://tinyurl.com/mczeucyf.

Davis, Daniel. "How 50 Years of No-Fault Divorce Gave Us a Throwaway Culture." *The Daily Signal*, September 3, 2019. https://tinyurl.com/45w9ac7k.

Debenedetti, Gabriel. "Ranking the Most Influential Democratic Donors in the 2020 Race," *Intelligencer*, August 22, 2019. https://tinyurl.com/5n6vrwhz.

Derbyshire, John. "Conquest's Laws." *National Review*, June 25, 2003. https://www.nationalreview.com/corner/conquests-laws-john-derbyshire/.

Devlin, F. Roger. "Solzhenitsyn on the Jews & Soviet Russia." *Counter-Currents*, July 9, 2015. https://tinyurl.com/5582t8t2.

Dickson, Sam. "Sam Dickson on Deep State Attack on Patriot Front's 1A Rights:" *VDARE*, June 14, 2022. https://tinyurl.com/2mvctk36.

Dickson, Sam. "Sam Dickson's Statement to Charlottesville Inquiry: Police Were Acting under Orders. Who Gave Those Orders?" *VDARE*, November 30, 2017. https://tinyurl.com/39ctm34j.

"Did the Menstrual Cycle of Officers Aboard the USS Fitzgerald Become a Contributing Factor in the June 2017 Collision That Claimed the Lives of Seven American Sailors?" Military Corruption, January 28, 2019. https://militarycorruption.com/fitzgerald-report/.

"Discrimination in College Admissions." Asian American Coalition for Education, December 14, 2022. https://tinyurl.com/27fc3efj.

Dixon, S. "U.S. Online Dating Website and App Usage Motivations 2021, by Gender." Statista, April 28, 2022. https://tinyurl.com/2pv25m58.

Doescher, Tim. "Destroying the Altar of 'Woke.'" The Heritage Foundation, May 24, 2022. https://tinyurl.com/4kwv668y.

Donovan, Jack. "Misrepresenting Masculinity: The Forty-Nine Percent Majority." *Counter-Currents*, November 10, 2011. https://tinyurl.com/2d3raar5.

Dreher, Rod. "Can You Normalize Queerness without Pedophilia?" *The American Conservative*, April 15, 2022. https://tinyurl.com/ycwr4pk2.

Durocher, Guillaume. "White Nationalism Explained with Charts, Part III: Jewish Privilege." *Counter-Currents*, December 3, 2015. https://tinyurl.com/4hubca4j.

Dwyer, Colin. "'Black Lives Matter Plaza,' across from White House, Is Christened by D.C. Leaders." NPR, June 5, 2020. https://tinyurl.com/2p9er88c.

Ehui, Simeon K., and Kanta Kumari Rigaud. "Climate Migration-Deepening Our Solutions." Brookings, March 17, 2022. https://tinyurl.com/yck6zztj.

Ekins, Emily. "The State of Free Speech and Tolerance in America." Cato Institute, October 31, 2017. https://tinyurl.com/yerfzb4m.

Ellis, Ralph. "Biden: Fire Police Officers Who Violate Vaccine Mandates." WebMD, October 22, 2021. https://tinyurl.com/5xxunya3.

Emmons, Libby. "BREAKING: Biden Admin Mobilizes FBI against Parents Opposing CRT and COVID Restrictions." *The Post Millennial*, October 5, 2021. https://thepostmillennial.com/biden-admin-doj-fbi-against-parents.

Emmons, William R. "Education and Wealth: Correlation Is Not Causation." Federal Reserve Bank of St. Louis, October 27, 2015. https://tinyurl.com/4fjebbz5.

Epstein, Robert. "How Google Could Rig the 2016 Election." *Politico*, August 19, 2015. https://tinyurl.com/58nd8p5n.

Ertelt, Steven. "FBI Raids Home of pro-Life Advocate Who Prayed and Sang Outside Abortion Biz." *Life News*, October 5, 2022. https://tinyurl.com/587ak2wk.

"Estate Taxes Are a Threat to Family Farms." American Farm Bureau Federation, October 19, 2020. https://tinyurl.com/4ydud2jm.

Evans, Zachary. "FBI Whistleblowers Claim Agents Investigated Parents Accused of Threatening School Boards over Mask Policies." *National Review*, May 11, 2022. https://tinyurl.com/2zu3mjyb.

Evola, Julius. "Judaism in the Ancient World." Translated by Das Gletscherkreuz. *Counter-Currents*, January 16, 2018. https://tinyurl.com/32h9tbt3.

"Fact Sheet: Cuban Support for Terrorism." Center for a Free Cuba, May 12, 2021. https://tinyurl.com/4jy57kbm.

Fairbanks, Cassandra. "Wife Suffers Miscarriage Day After FBI Raids Home Over Combat Veteran Husband's Presence at US Capitol." *Gateway Pundit*, March 22, 2021. https://tinyurl.com/2p92pp45.

Fang, Jenn. "Graduate Student Workers Still Struggle without Benefits and a Living Wage." *Prism*, August 19, 2021. https://tinyurl.com/ykzvrrh4.

Farberov, Snejana. "Two California Men Slapped with Hate Crime Charges 'after Drunkenly Vandalizing BLM Mural.'" *Daily Mail Online*, December 16, 2021. https://tinyurl.com/354x85tt.

Federale. "The FBI Question: Reassign, Reform, or Abolish?" *VDARE*, August 31, 2022. https://vdare.com/posts/the-fbi-question-reassign-reform-or-abolish.

Feldberg, Michael. "Anti-Semitism in the U.S.: Harvard's Jewish Problem." Jewish Virtual Library, December 14, 2022. https://tinyurl.com/2p8ufaxf.

Fleming, Thomas. "The Enigma of General Howe." *American Heritage* 15, no. 2. February 1964.

Flynn, Jack. "25+ Essential Average American Income Statistics [2022]: Household + Personal Income in the US." Zippia, October 26, 2022. https://www.zippia.com/advice/average-american-income/.

Frantzman, Seth J. "Was the Russian Revolution Jewish?" *The Jerusalem Post*, February 7, 2018. https://tinyurl.com/mkjfd526.

Frey, William H. "US White Population Declines and Generation 'Z-plus' Is Minority White, Census Shows." Brookings, June 22, 2018. https://tinyurl.com/scszdnj5.

Fulford, James. "Download Ketanji Brown Jackson's Harvard Law Review Article on Being Nicer to Sex Offenders: Blog Posts." *VDARE*, March 22, 2022. https://tinyurl.com/426my6b5.

Fulford, James. "Patriot Professor John Eastman out at Chapman University Because He Spoke at Trump Rally." *VDARE*, January 14, 2021. https://tinyurl.com/m2st7kvb.

"Full Text: Bin Laden's 'Letter to America'." *The Guardian*, November 24, 2002. https://www.theguardian.com/world/2002/nov/24/theobserver.

"Full Text: Bush's Speech." *The Guardian*, March 17, 2003. https://www.theguardian.com/world/2003/mar/18/usa.iraq.

Fung, Katherine. "Banks Have Begun Freezing Accounts Linked to Trucker Protest." *Newsweek*, February 18, 2022. https://tinyurl.com/35ew4a7t.

Gallindoss, Alan. "Jews Make-up 19% of Forbes 200 World's Richest List." *Jewish Business News*, March 7, 2018. https://tinyurl.com/59a64sv9.

Gangitano, Alex. "Biden Calls on Employers to Mandate Vaccines despite Supreme Court Ruling." *The Hill*, January 13, 2022. https://tinyurl.com/5n8384bu.

"Gangs in the Military." Gang Enforcement, December 14, 2022. https://www.gangenforcement.com/gangs-in-the-military.html.

Garrison, Trey, and Mike Peinovich. "On the Groomer Question." *National Justice Party*, April 10, 2022. https://tinyurl.com/3fvxu7yx.

Gaspard, Patrick. "Why Open Society Is Pledging $220 Million to Racial Justice." Open Society Foundations, July 13, 2020. https://tinyurl.com/bdmmkmfr.

Gast, Alice. "Why Artificial Intelligence Is Vital in the Race to Meet the SDGs." World Economic Forum, May 11, 2022. https://tinyurl.com/bdd8smzn.

Geraghty, Jim. "The Remarkable Apathy about Biden-Family Corruption." *National Review*, August 19, 2022. https://tinyurl.com/bdesn63m.

Gest, Justin. "What Happens When White People Become a Minority in America?" *Foreign Policy*, March 22, 2022. https://tinyurl.com/wfprrc7k.

Giraldi, Philip. "America's Jews Are Driving America's Wars." *The Unz Review*, September 19, 2017. https://tinyurl.com/bddds8hv.

Go, Jay. "Who Is Holly McGlawn-Zoller, the Spiritually(?) Jewish Self-Admitted Antifa 'Bail Disruptor' for the Bail Project?" *Hyphen Report*, November 28, 2021. https://tinyurl.com/53cdtpe4.

Goldenberg, Ashley Rae. "Here Are the Companies That Support Antifa, Black Lives Matter." *American Renaissance*, June 3, 2020. https://tinyurl.com/2j5ajm9e.

Goldsbie, Jonathan. "Coat of Many Mottos." *NOW Magazine*, November 27, 2014. https://nowtoronto.com/coat-of-many-mottos/.

Gonzalez, Pedro. "Restrictionism's Last Stand." *The American Conservative*, July 2, 2021. https://www.theamericanconservative.com/restrictionisms-last-stand/.

Goodman, Melissa, Catherine Crump, and Sara Corris. "Disavowed: The Government's Unchecked Retaliation Against National Security Whistleblowers." ACLU, 2007. https://www.aclu.org/sites/default/files/pdfs/safefree/disavowed_report.pdf.

Gordon, David. *America First: The Anti-War Movement, Charles Lindbergh and the Second World War, 1940-1941.* Presented at a joint meeting of the Historical Society and The New York Military Affairs Symposium, September 26, 2003. https://bobrowen.com/nymas/americafirst.html.

Graber, Richard. "Woke Foundations, Beneficiaries of Capitalism, Undermine Free Market." *The Daily Signal*, May 18, 2021. https://tinyurl.com/2tyzrbye.

Grawert, Ames, and Tim Lau. "How the First Step Act Became Law - and What Happens Next." Brennan Center for Justice, January 4, 2019. https://tinyurl.com/2aprfcr3.

"The Great Replacement." *American Renaissance*, October 5, 2015. https://www.amren.com/news/2015/10/the-great-replacement/.

Greenfield, Daniel. "A New Color of Censorship from the SPLC." *American Greatness*, September 9, 2018. https://tinyurl.com/35zh4us7.

Gross, Terry. "The CIA's Secret Quest for Mind Control: Torture, LSD and a 'Poisoner in Chief'." *Fresh Air*, NPR, November 20, 2020. https://tinyurl.com/thybv9je.

"GT Investigates: US Wages Global Color Revolutions to Topple Govts for the Sake of American Control." *Global Times*, December 2, 2021. https://www.globaltimes.cn/page/202112/1240540.shtml.

Gullick, Mark. "Fund the Police, Defund Blacks." *Counter-Currents*, November 10, 2021. https://counter-currents.com/2021/11/fund-the-police-defund-blacks/.

Guzeva, Alexandra. "How the Bolsheviks Tried to Destroy the Russian Orthodox Church." *Russia Beyond*, March 29, 2022. https://tinyurl.com/y5whmeb7.

Gvora, Joe. "Google Glass: What Happened To The Futuristic Smart Glasses?" *Screen Rant*, June 15, 2022. https://tinyurl.com/mr2rtfex.

Hamilton, Andrew. "30 To Watch, They Say." *Counter-Currents*, September 14, 2012. https://counter-currents.com/2012/09/30-to-watch-they-say/.

Hamilton, Andrew. "The SPLC, Pornography, & 'Hate Speech.'" *Counter-Currents*, February 28, 2014. https://tinyurl.com/ykyr9x3k.

Hamilton, Isobel Asher. "The Story of Neuralink: Elon Musk's Ai Brain Chip Company Where He Had Twins with a Top Executive." *Business Insider*, July 7, 2022. https://tinyurl.com/39u42rmw.

Hampton, Robert. "A Mostly Peaceful Nobel Prize." *American Renaissance*, February 3, 2021. https://tinyurl.com/bddjdxy9.

Hampton, Robert. "Antifa Terror Is Here to Stay." *Counter-Currents*, July 17, 2019. https://counter-currents.com/2019/07/antifa-terror-is-here-to-stay/.

Hankinson, Simon. "A U.S. Embassy Should Fly Only One Flag." The Heritage Foundation, June 8, 2022. https://tinyurl.com/ye9saw4a.

Hartney, Michael T. "Teacher Union Power in California: The More Things Change, the More They Stay the Same." Hoover Institution, June 24, 2021. https://tinyurl.com/mu9zerz3.

"Harvard Professor Says 25 Percent of Ivy League School Professors Are Jewish." *Jewish Telegraphic Agency*, April 22, 1971. https://tinyurl.com/3ezaztn2.

Hastings, Max. "The Hidden Atrocities of the Vietnam War." *The Wall Street Journal*. Dow Jones & Company, October 4, 2018. https://tinyurl.com/23yvh65f.

"He Kept Us out of War (until the Last Election That Is)." *LiveJournal*, April 6, 2012. https://potus-geeks.livejournal.com/211304.html.

Hengest, Duncan. "Diversity in the Army." *American Renaissance*, October 2, 2016. https://tinyurl.com/2s3wwp8b.

Hill, Christopher. "Cromwell and the English Middle Class Revolution." *The Labour Monthly* 19, no. 11 (November 1937): 707–9. https://www.marxists.org/archive/hill-christopher/1937/11/x01.htm.

Hirsch, Jerry. "Elon Musk's Growing Empire Is Fueled by $4.9 Billion in Government Subsidies." *Los Angeles Times*, May 30, 2015. https://tinyurl.com/2p8fu7hh.

von Hoffman, Nicholas. "Was McCarthy Right about the Left?" *The Washington Post*, April 14, 1996. https://tinyurl.com/4489uj4a.

Holland, Steve. "Trump Defends His Syria Pullout against Republican Criticism." *Reuters*, October 9, 2019. https://tinyurl.com/3f5uctbf.

Honma, Motoyasu, Yuri Masaoka, Natsuko Iizuka, Sayaka Wada, Sawa Kamimura, Akira Yoshikawa, Rika Moriya, Shotaro Kamijo, and Masahiko Izumizaki. "Reading on a Smartphone Affects Sigh Generation, Brain Activity, and Comprehension." *Scientific Reports* 12, no. 1 (January 31, 2022). https://doi.org/10.1038/s41598-022-05605-0.

Hood, Gregory. "Betrayal: American Conservatives and Capitalism." *American Renaissance*, January 28, 2019. https://tinyurl.com/4dbp3jr.

Hood, Gregory. "FBI Arrests White 'Serial Rioters,'" *American Renaissance*, October 8, 2018. https://tinyurl.com/5d5e4d8t.

Houck, Richard. "Anarcho-Tyranny 2020 & Beyond, Part I: The Age of Covid-19, BLM, & Apex Parasites." *Counter-Currents*, July 30, 2021. https://tinyurl.com/mr3ncvc3.

Houck, Richard. "Anarcho-Tyranny 2020 & Beyond, Part II: The Age of Covid-19, BLM, & Apex Parasites." *Counter-Currents*, August 3, 2021. https://tinyurl.com/bdfcvrm8.

Houck, Richard. "The Fading Memory of American Homeownership." *Counter-Currents*, August 16, 2022. https://tinyurl.com/2hw3xy9m.

Houck, Richard. "Open Borders Caused the Covid-19 Pandemic." *Counter-Currents*, March 19, 2020. https://tinyurl.com/yckep49t.

Hoyt, Gregory. "Notre Dame Students Demand All White Authors Be Removed from Curriculum." *Law Enforcement Today*, November 28, 2019. https://tinyurl.com/28enc2p3.

Human Rights Watch. *"Punished Peoples" of the Soviet Union: The Continuing Legacy of Stalin's Deportations*. 1991. https://tinyurl.com/bpac2v8j.

"Human Sacrifices: How Many Were Killed in Aztec Culture?" History on the Net, December 14, 2022. https://tinyurl.com/4x2wrhez.

"Immigration." American Federation of Teachers. https://tinyurl.com/yny9sbev.

Ingraham, Christopher. "The Share of Americans Not Having Sex Has Reached a Record High." *The Washington Post*, March 29, 2019. https://tinyurl.com/5tn8sw6k.

Ingram, John. "Seeds Unsown: Lamenting the Childless White Adults." *American Renaissance*, January 21, 2021. https://tinyurl.com/y762zdtv.

"Is It Too Late to Prevent Climate Change?" NASA, Accessed December 14, 2022. https://climate.nasa.gov/faq/16/is-it-too-late-to-prevent-climate-change/.

"Israel: 50 Years of Occupation Abuses." Human Rights Watch, June 4, 2017.
　　https://www.hrw.org/news/2017/06/04/israel-50-years-occupation-abuses.
"Israel's Ultra-Right to Join Forces in next Election." *Middle East Monitor*, August 4,
　　2022. https://tinyurl.com/4e4rcwe8.
"Italian Residents Hug Chinese People to Encourage Them in Coronavirus Fight."
　　CGTN, February 5, 2020. https://tinyurl.com/2ke4774z.
Jackson, Ashley. "Perspectives on Peace from Taliban Areas of Afghanistan." United
　　States Institute of Peace, May 29, 2019. https://tinyurl.com/2jurd5rj.
Jackson, Thomas. "The Animal in the Man." *American Renaissance*, September 2,
　　2018. https://tinyurl.com/3nzrbhud.
"Japan, China, the United States and the Road to Pearl Harbor, 1937–41." U.S.
　　Department of State Office of the Historian, Accessed December 19, 2022.
　　https://history.state.gov/milestones/1937-1945/pearl-harbor.
Jeelvy, Nicholas R. "For the Coming American Atatürk." *Counter-Currents*, December
　　23, 2021. https://tinyurl.com/4jpsndzw.
"Jeffrey Epstein Was Blackmailing Politicians for Israel's Mossad, New Book Claims."
　　Middle East Monitor, January 6, 2020. https://tinyurl.com/yc4y7nca.
Jeffries, Stuart. "The Frankfurt School: A Timeline." Verso, September 29, 2017.
　　https://www.versobooks.com/blogs/2844-the-frankfurt-school-a-timeline.
Jensen, Michael C., and Kevin J. Murphy. "CEO Incentives-It's Not How Much You
　　Pay, but How." *Harvard Business Review*, 1990. https://tinyurl.com/34rerbv6.
"Jewish Billionaire Seth Klarman's Fund Revealed as Secret Holder of $1 Billion in
　　Puerto Rico Debt." *Haaretz*, October 9, 2017. https://tinyurl.com/mtcctj2n.
Johnson, Greg. "White Extinction." *Counter-Currents*, June 15, 2017. https://counter-
　　currents.com/2017/06/white-extinction-2/.
Jones, Nicholas, et al. "2020 Census Illuminates Racial and Ethnic Composition of
　　the Country." Census.gov, August 12, 2021. https://tinyurl.com/y2e5dkhk.
Joyce, Andrew. "Jews in the Cathedral: A Response to Curtis Yarvin." *The Occidental
　　Observer*, October 17, 2020. https://tinyurl.com/2r7keshs.
Joyce, Andrew. "The SS Empire Windrush: The Jewish Origins of Multicultural
　　Britain." *The Occidental Observer*, July 12, 2015. https://tinyurl.com/yr8yrk85.
"The Julian Marriage Laws." UNRV Roman History, December 14, 2022.
　　https://www.unrv.com/government/julianmarriage.php.
Jusslm, Lee. "Political Biases in Academia." Psychology Today, May 29, 2020.
　　https://tinyurl.com/5brujd8j.
Kampeas, Ron. "Meet the Leading Jewish Political Donors in This US Election Cycle."
　　The Times of Israel, September 25, 2020. https://tinyurl.com/2vyxx97c.
Kampeas, Ron. "US Air Force Commander David Goldfein Retires." *The Times of
　　Israel*, August 8, 2020. https://tinyurl.com/mt67zswc.
Kassam, Raheem J., and K. Christopher Powell. "'We'll Steal Your Soul' – Biden's
　　Monkeypox Spox Has a Penchant for Pentagrams, Occultism, and Satanism." *The
　　National Pulse*, September 9, 2022. https://tinyurl.com/y7jf3ezh.
Keller, Jared. "The Top 5 Reasons Soldiers Really Join the Army, According to Junior
　　Enlisted." *Task & Purpose*, May 14, 2018. https://tinyurl.com/2x4cw4fu.
Kelly, Julie. "Surveillance Video Shows D.C. Police Beating Women on January 6."
　　American Greatness, December 28, 2021. https://tinyurl.com/56a8avzc.
Kennedy, Lesley. "How the Immigration Act of 1965 Changed the Face of America."
　　History.com, August 12, 2019. https://tinyurl.com/yrz2vyms.
Kessler, Jason. "Doxing the Doxers: Antifa's War against Regular Americans Is Run
　　by Spoiled Rich Kids." *VDARE*, March 13, 2021. https://tinyurl.com/44y8whmt.
Kilpatrick, William. "The Long March through American Institutions Continues." *The
　　Catholic World Report*, June 17, 2020. https://tinyurl.com/2p8xvwcn.

Kirkpatrick, James. "FBI Announces War on White Supremacist Terror, Actual Racial Terrorism against Whites Ignored." *VDARE*, June 15, 2021. https://tinyurl.com/2ahhmyra.

Krikorian, Mark. "How Labeling My Organization a Hate Group Shuts down Public Debate." *The Washington Post*, March 17, 2017. https://tinyurl.com/yckwyfbm.

Krinsky, Alan D. "Libertarianism, Jews, and the Future of the Two-Party System." Academic Studies Press, October 27, 2020. https://tinyurl.com/bdfkczjc.

Lambert, Josh. "'Dirty Jews' and the Christian Right." *Haaretz*, February 3, 2014, https://tinyurl.com/4na4b6se.

Landy, Benjamin. "A Tale of Two Recoveries: Wealth Inequality after the Great Recession." The Century Foundation, August 28, 2013. https://tinyurl.com/58ned47u.

"Lauren Witzke Says Capitol Hill Police Brutality Caused Trump Supporter Kevin Greeson's Death." *VDARE*, February 12, 2021. https://tinyurl.com/yuuascw7.

"Leaked Amazon Document Shows Why 'Diversity' Is an Advantage to Big Tech." *Katehon*, April 27, 2020. https://tinyurl.com/3ywcw39w.

Lederman, Alex. "Knesset Elections 2021: A Guide to Israel's Political Parties." *Israel Policy Forum*, March 10, 2021. https://tinyurl.com/yyw4cbmd.

Leiter, Brian. "Top Ten Law Faculty (by Area) in Scholarly Impact, 2009-2013." Brian Leiter's Law School Rankings, June 11, 2014. http://www.leiterrankings.com/faculty/2014_scholarlyimpact.shtml.

Liu, Angus. "Pfizer to Become $100B Behemoth next Year Thanks to Covid-19 Drug and Vaccine: Analyst." *Fierce Pharma*, November 23, 2021. https://tinyurl.com/yefkxwfe.

Lockwood, Nick. "How the Soviet Union Transformed Terrorism." *The Atlantic*, December 23, 2011. https://tinyurl.com/4ev23ap2.

Ludwig, Hayden. "Wokeism in Private Schools: Go Woke or Get Out." Capital Research Center, March 15, 2022. https://tinyurl.com/56pvussc.

Lupkin, Sydney. "A Look at How the Revolving Door Spins from FDA to Industry." NPR, September 28, 2016. https://tinyurl.com/2p9zpmv2.

Lutton, Wayne. "Immigration and Race in America." *American Renaissance*, July 13, 2019. https://tinyurl.com/mwmx5jn4.

M., Dave. "My McDonald's Restaurant Signs Support the Black Lives Matter Message to Represent Those without a Voice." Corporate McDonald's, June 26, 2020. https://archive.vn/anYom.

MacDonald, Kevin. "Are These Antifa/ BLM Riots a Jewish Coup?" *VDARE*, September 12, 2020. https://vdare.com/articles/are-these-antifa-blm-riots-a-jewish-coup.

MacDonald, Kevin. "Black History Month Special: Jews, Blacks, & Race." *Counter-Currents*, February 15, 2012. https://tinyurl.com/b5yk8577.

MacDonald, Kevin. "Understanding Jewish Influence III: Neoconservatism As A Jewish Movement." *The Occidental Quarterly* 4, no. 2 (2004): 7–74. https://www.toqonline.com/archives/v4n2/TOQv4n2MacDonald.pdf.

Magramo, Kathleen. "Anger at China's Zero-Covid Policy Is Rising, but Beijing Refuses to Change Course." *CNN*, October 13, 2022. https://tinyurl.com/2scuuhmw.

"Major U.S. Bank Shuts down 'Alt-Right' Accounts." *WND*, April 16, 2019. https://tinyurl.com/3cc5ykh7.

Malkin, Michelle. "Beware of the Flu Shot Bullies." *Blue Water Healthy Living*, October 6, 2020. https://tinyurl.com/2xkdjxmd.

Malkin, Michelle. "Covid-19, Catholics and Illegal Alien Charities." *American Renaissance*, July 28, 2021. https://tinyurl.com/32ezf7wd.

Malkin, Michelle. "GLSEN's Groomers in Plain Sight." *VDARE*, April 12, 2022. https://vdare.com/articles/michelle-malkin-glsen-s-groomers-in-plain-sight.

Malkin, Michelle. "Michelle Malkin: GLSEN's Groomers in Plain Sight." *VDARE*, April 12, 2022. https://tinyurl.com/2p84f99c.

Malkin, Michelle. "One Nation under Anarcho-Tyranny." *American Renaissance*, July 22, 2020. https://tinyurl.com/4jjsaaey.

Maltz, Judy. "U.S. Envoy Ranks Recognition of Jerusalem as Trump's 'Most Important Achievement' in Israel." *Haaretz*, January 11, 2021. https://tinyurl.com/ymxh23wb.

Maria Milojković. "17 Weird Facts about Nikola Tesla, the Man Who Invented the 20th Century." *Medium*, December 7, 2020. https://tinyurl.com/mtk22wrj.

"Masks Are Dehumanizing–Whether You Believe It or Not." *Teaching with an Edge*, January 3, 2022. https://tinyurl.com/3a9e2z2m.

Masterson, Andrew. "Mayans Self-Mutilated to Appease the Gods." *Cosmos*, May 9, 2019. https://tinyurl.com/7ecyencm.

McCool, Daniel. "China's White Skin Obsession Explained." *eChinacities*, March 26, 2018. https://tinyurl.com/2238tvx7.

McElroy, Ken. "A Nation of Workers: How Public Education Is Dummying down Our Labor Force." *Jetset Magazine*, August 15, 2016. https://tinyurl.com/2p4u58kh.

McGregor, Jena McGregor, and Tracy Jan. "Big Business Pledged Nearly $50 Billion for Racial Justice after George Floyd's Death. Where Did the Money Go?" *The Washington Post*, August 23, 2021. https://tinyurl.com/bde8p75p.

McGuigan, Brendan. "What Is the Prussian Education System?" CulturalWorld.org, October 12, 2022. https://tinyurl.com/ywjsxrw8.

McKay, Hollie. "Behind Susan Rosenberg and the Roots of Left-Wing Domestic Extremism." *Fox News*, November 17, 2020. https://tinyurl.com/5fdcv99p.

Meagher, Timothy. "Revisiting the History of Irish American Progressives." *Network Lobby*, March 16, 2018. https://networklobby.org/20180316justice/.

"Melvin Douglas Lastman." *Jewish Virtual Library*, December 14, 2022. https://www.jewishvirtuallibrary.org/lastman-melvin-douglas.

Members of the 117th Congress with Law Degrees. American Bar Association Governmental Affairs Office, January 21, 2021. https://tinyurl.com/vsfhjy2y.

Mercer, Douglas. "The Great Replacement." *Counter-Currents*, November 2, 2021. https://counter-currents.com/2021/11/the-great-replacement/.

Merriejayne. "Prince Charles, Heir to the British Throne, Getting Poked on the Chest by Evelyn De Rothschild." December 14, 2022. iFunny. https://tinyurl.com/5n6ffxuc.

Miessler, Daniel. "A Visual Breakdown of Intellectual Dark Web (IDW) Political Positions." *Daniel Miessler*, June 5, 2020. https://tinyurl.com/4tvumphk.

Miller, Jake. "Bill Gates, Warren Buffett, Sheldon Adelson Push Immigration Reform." *CBS News*, July 11, 2014. https://tinyurl.com/mr3etvnv.

Mitchell, David Fontaine. "The Monumental Plot: An Overview of the 1965 Conspiracy to Destroy the Statue of Liberty, Liberty Bell, and Washington Monument." *The Journal of Counterterrorism* 16, no. 4, 2010. https://tinyurl.com/2p9fue87.

Moldbug, Mencius. "Why I Am Not an Anti-Semite." *Unqualified Reservations*, June 23, 2007. https://tinyurl.com/5rpyhbns.

Mordowanec, Nick. "IRS Deletes Requirement That New Agents Be Willing to Use 'Deadly Force.'" *Newsweek*, August 12, 2022. https://tinyurl.com/736mdsea.

Morelock, Jeremiah. "Introduction: The Frankfurt School and Authoritarian Populism – A Historical Outline." *Critical Theory and Authoritarian Populism* 9 (2018): xiii-xxxviii. https://tinyurl.com/7xxjsr4j.

Morgan, A.W. "It's Time to Ban Chinese Students and Academics from Universities. They Are Spies and Possibly Sleeper Saboteurs for the Red Regime." *VDARE*, July 28, 2022. https://tinyurl.com/y4e7pf54.

Mott, Christopher. "Woke Imperium: The Coming Confluence between Social Justice and Neoconservatism." The Institute for Peace and Diplomacy, June 27, 2022. https://tinyurl.com/2p9968j5.

Mueller, Laura. "Pod Living: What It Is and Why It's Booming." Moving.com, July 28, 2020. https://tinyurl.com/3t5eh7yy.

Mullen, Shannon. "New Information Raises Questions about FBI Raid on Catholic Father of 7." Catholic News Agency, September 25, 2022. https://tinyurl.com/mr3bv5vv.

Mulvihill, Geoff, and Jennifer Peltz. "After Years of Pain, Opioid Crisis Victims Confront Sackler Family in Court." PBS, March 10, 2022. https://tinyurl.com/6aysdycb.

Munson, Jessica, Viviana Amati, Mark Collard, and Martha J. Macri. "Classic Maya Bloodletting and the Cultural Evolution of Religious Rituals: Quantifying Patterns of Variation in Hieroglyphic Texts." PLoS ONE 9, no. 9 (2014). https://doi.org/10.1371/journal.pone.0107982.

Murdock, Deroy. "Obama's Weathermen Pals Should Worry You." National Review, October 13, 2008. https://tinyurl.com/2nvud8vc.

"Nancy Pelosi Visits San Francisco's Chinatown amid Coronavirus Concerns." NBC Bay Area, February 25, 2020. https://tinyurl.com/tu3zhyja.

National Justice Party. "National Justice Party Statement on the Kyle Rittenhouse Verdict." National Justice Party, November 19, 2021. https://tinyurl.com/3ps4ajr5.

National Justice Party. "NJP Condemns the Travesty of Justice in the Charlottesville 'Unite the Right' Lawsuit." National Justice Party, October 26, 2021. https://tinyurl.com/y5syyh9w.

National Justice Party. "NJP Statement on the Anti-White Terror Attack in Waukesha, Wisconsin." National Justice Party, November 22, 2021. https://tinyurl.com/3w6888mf.

Neale, Spencer. "Chris Cuomo: 'Show Me Where It Says That Protests Are Supposed to Be Polite and Peaceful.'" Washington Examiner, June 3, 2020. https://tinyurl.com/yc839s2j.

Nelson, Steven, and Juliegrace Brufke. "AOC Slapped with Ethics Complaint for Accepting Free Met Gala Tickets." New York Post, September 14, 2021. https://tinyurl.com/msxv96ty.

Nevradakis, Michael. "'Brought to You by Pfizer': Pharma Giant Spends More on Ads, News Sponsorships, than Research." The Defender, November 2, 2021. https://tinyurl.com/3mjsdtj4.

Newman, Alex. "Frankfurt School Weaponized US Education Against Civilization." The Epoch Times, March 10, 2020. https://tinyurl.com/yuznahew.

"The Number of Holodomor-Genocide Victims in Ukraine Are Often Intentionally Diminished – Scientists." National Museum of the Holodomor-Genocide, September 13, 2018. https://tinyurl.com/yc68kbr9.

Obafemee80. "$100m F-35 Fighter Jet Crashed by U.S Female Pilot on Her First Flight Recovered from China Sea." AutoJosh, March 14, 2022. https://tinyurl.com/yzj8cyuc.

"Obama's Military Coup Purges 197 Officers in Five Years." Investor's Business Daily, October 29, 2013. https://tinyurl.com/4hukar59.

Olohan, Mary Margaret. "FBI Arrests 11 pro-Life Advocates, They Could Face Decade in Prison for Saving Babies." Life News, October 6, 2022. https://tinyurl.com/yscraj8w.

Parker, Tom. "PayPal Is Still Threatening to Fine Users $2,500 for Promoting 'Intolerance That Is Discriminatory.'" Reclaim the Net, October 12, 2022. https://reclaimthenet.org/paypal-fine-2500-intolerance-discriminatory/.

Pajeet, Hyphen. "Activism Alert: Flood These Inboxes with Your Concerns." *Hyphen Report*, November 22, 2021. https://tinyurl.com/2bnrakky.

Pajeet, Hyphen. "Judge Who Freed Darrell Brooks Is Extremist Jew Activist and Nazi Hunter." *Hyphen Report*, December 22, 2021. https://tinyurl.com/2fcmubew.

Peinovich, Mike. "Jewish Media Figures Celebrate White Decline in Latest Census." *National Justice Party*, August 26, 2021. https://tinyurl.com/h3d2fud6.

Peinovich, Mike. "Leader of Jewish-Zionist Group Calls for Massive Crackdown on Internet Free Speech." *National Justice Party*, January 3, 2021. https://tinyurl.com/yv3h4u48.

Perazzo, John. "Black Lives Matter: Marxist Hate Dressed up as Racial Justice." *Front Page Magazine*, September 1, 2020. https://tinyurl.com/yc428ejf.

Peretz, Martin. "'Goyim Were Born Only to Serve Us': The Moral Wisdom of Rabbi Ovadia Yosef." *The New Republic*, October 19, 2010. https://tinyurl.com/yhyu8jbd.

Peterson, Hayley. "Amazon-Owned Whole Foods Is Quietly Tracking Its Employees with a Heat Map Tool That Ranks Which Stores Are Most at Risk of Unionizing." *Business Insider*, April 20, 2020. https://tinyurl.com/2p8eaftz.

Peterson, Jordan B. "On the New York Times and 'Enforced Monogamy.'" Jordan Peterson, December 14, 2022. https://tinyurl.com/4u2bfwd6.

Pfeffer, Fabian T., Sheldon Danziger, and Robert F. Schoeni. "Wealth Disparities before and after the Great Recession." *The Annals of the American Academy of Political and Social Science* 650, no. 1 (November 2013): 98–123. https://doi.org/10.1177/0002716213497452.

"Philadelphia Police Vaccine Mandate Latest to Be Upheld despite Legal Challenge." Fisher Phillips, February 4, 2022. https://tinyurl.com/5xjvhxte.

Phillips, Alyce. "No Spouse, No Children: 'Solo' Seniors Entering Retirement on Their Own." *Wilmington Biz*, September 1, 2019. https://tinyurl.com/mv5msdra.

Phillips, Amber. "What We Know about Rep. Eric Swalwell's Ties to an Alleged Chinese Spy." *The Washington Post*, December 11, 2020. https://tinyurl.com/5n8pdy97.

Pierce, John. "The Reasons for Secession: A Documentary Study." *American Battlefield Trust*, December 14, 2022. https://tinyurl.com/397e6r5n.

Pinkard, Terry. "The Spirit of History." Edited by Sam Haselby. *Aeon*, January 13, 2019. https://tinyurl.com/2p8yzs2f.

Piper, Kelsey. "The Charitable Deduction Is Mostly for the Rich. A New Study Argues That's by Design." *Vox*, September 3, 2019. https://tinyurl.com/4r256jpp.

Piro, Graham. "Professor Injured, Students Sanctioned at Middlebury College in Vermont after Conservative Speaker Is Protested." The Free Speech Project, June 20, 2020. https://tinyurl.com/yk8yvj79.

"Ponerology: The Science of Evil." Systems Thinker, December 14, 2022. https://www.systemsthinker.com/interests/ponerology/.

Porlando. "Bezmenov's Steps (Ideological Subversion)." *Unintended Consequences*, July 14, 2020. https://unintendedconsequenc.es/bezmenovs-steps/.

Porter, Tom. "Alt-Right: Maryland Teacher Gregory Conte Fired After Double Life as White Nationalist Exposed." *Newsweek*, January 8, 2018. https://tinyurl.com/ye2aw66e.

Poushter, Jacob. "40% Of Millennials OK with Limiting Speech Offensive to Minorities." Pew Research Center, November 20, 2015, https://tinyurl.com/mrx6dysm.

del Prado Alanes, Matilde Nuñez. "What Is Factory Farming and Why Is It Bad?" *Sentient Media*, October 28, 2022. https://sentientmedia.org/factory-farms/.

Press, John. "Myths About Slavery and Lynching." *American Renaissance*, February 15, 2018. https://tinyurl.com/bdzj2a59.

Price, Greg. "Conservative YouTube Content Leads to 'De-Radicalization,' Study Finds." *The Daily Caller*, October 25, 2019. https://tinyurl.com/bdde58jp.
"Prince Charles Honours Lord Rothschild with Prestigious Interfaith Prize." *Jewish News*, December 16, 2019. https://tinyurl.com/ynf8pc79.
Quinn, Jimmy. "'The Department of Woke.'" *National Review*, July 29, 2022. https://www.nationalreview.com/corner/the-department-of-woke/.
Quinn., Spencer J. "Black Lives Matter Is Black Supremacy." *Counter-Currents*, June 23, 2020. https://tinyurl.com/ycxjz76r.
Quinn, Spencer J. "Suing the SPLC." *Counter-Currents*, March 8, 2019. https://counter-currents.com/2019/03/suing-the-splc/.
"Release Detail." Quinnipiac University Poll, June 3, 2009. https://tinyurl.com/yrnsrc5r.
Renatus, Flavius Vegetius. "The Military Institutions of the Romans (De Re Militari)." Translated by John Clarke. *Digital Attic*, December 14, 2022. http://digitalattic.org/home/war/vegetius/.
"Report: Israel Passes U.S. Military Technology to China." Military.com, December 24, 2013. https://tinyurl.com/743r2c2.
Resolution Adopted by the General Assembly on 25 September 2015. United Nations, October 21, 2015. https://tinyurl.com/3mfvfsd3.
Riga, Liliana. "The Ethnic Roots of Class Universalism: Rethinking the 'Russian' Revolutionary Elite." *American Journal of Sociology* 114, no. 3 (November 2008): 649–705. https://www.journals.uchicago.edu/doi/10.1086/592862.
Riggins, Alex. "Grand Jury Indicts Anti-Fascists Previously Charged in Pacific Beach Protest Violence." *The San Diego Union-Tribune*, June 7, 2022. https://tinyurl.com/mryrfw7d.
Rinckey, Tully. "U.S. Military Covid-19 Vaccine Requirement For Service Members." Tully Rinckey PLLC, November 14, 2022. https://tinyurl.com/y4d57yc8.
Roberts, Chris. "Islam Won't Conquer the World - but Africa Might." *American Renaissance*, December 19, 2021. https://tinyurl.com/ynd7jrbb.
Roberts, Paul Craig. "Surviving Sailors Break Their Silence 40 Years after Israeli Attack on US Navy Ship." *VDARE*, June 21, 2008. https://tinyurl.com/yeamsuzm.
Roberts, TJ. "McCarthy Was Right: There Were Communist Infiltrators in America!" *Liberty Hangout*, May 30, 2017. https://tinyurl.com/4vsbjekz.
Roertson, C.B. "What Did the Founders Mean By 'Liberty'?" *Counter-Currents*, July 11, 2018. https://tinyurl.com/2p8rmu4z.
Roesenau, William. "The Dark History of America's First Female Terrorist Group." *Politico*, May 3, 2020. https://tinyurl.com/ydnudce8.
Romm, Tony. "Amazon, Facebook, Other Tech Giants Spent Roughly $65 Million to Lobby Washington Last Year." *The Washington Post*, January 22, 2021. https://tinyurl.com/mshxefpj.
Root, Danielle, Jake Faleschini, and Grace Oyenubi. "Building a More Inclusive Federal Judiciary." Center for American Progress, October 3, 2019. https://tinyurl.com/3ubwsm9v.
Rothman, Tony. "Was Einstein the First to Invent E =MC2?" *Scientific American*, August 24, 2015. https://tinyurl.com/3kx83r66.
Roy, Avik. "Estimating the Risk of Death from COVID-19 vs. Influenza or Pneumonia by Age." Freopp.org, May 18, 2020. https://tinyurl.com/5em5k2j4.
Royal, Robert. "The Calvary of Romania." Catholic Education Resource Center, December 14, 2022. https://tinyurl.com/25jrtutm.
Rushdoony, R.J. "The Changed Meaning of Liberty." Chalcedon, December 29, 2011. https://tinyurl.com/mvhmk4y.
Rushkoff, Douglas. "Survival of the Richest." *Medium*, July 5, 2018. https://onezero.medium.com/survival-of-the-richest-9ef6cddd0cc1.

Sachs, Natan. "Israel's Right-Wing Majority." Brookings, April 11, 2019. https://tinyurl.com/mrxw8n6h.

Sacks, Jonathan. "A Word of Torah: Why Are There So Many Jewish Lawyers?" *The Detroit Jewish News*, July 16, 2021. https://tinyurl.com/4zd9cz7x.

Sailer, Steve. "White Sergeant Convicted by Black Female Judge of Defending Neighborhood Women from Brain-Damaged Black Baby-Snatcher." *VDARE*, August 25, 2021. https://tinyurl.com/2s3j65ad.

Sailer, Steve. "White U.S.S. Bonhomme Richard Arson Suspect Acquitted of Destroying Carrier during Racial Reckoning, Black Sailor Not Even Investigated." *VDARE*, October 1, 2022. https://tinyurl.com/2v29dzfc.

Sailer, Steve. "'You Have to Tell the Truth'-the Bell Curve after Ten Years." *VDARE*, October 10, 2004. https://tinyurl.com/ycr74p4m.

Sales, Ben. "5 Key Takeaways, Some Surprising, from New Survey of US Modern Orthodox Jews." *The Times of Israel*, September 30, 2017. https://tinyurl.com/294nxdhp.

Samuels, Ben. "Trump Pardons Charles Kushner, Father of Son-in-Law Jared Kushner." *Haaretz*, December 24, 2020. https://tinyurl.com/kc23ednj.

Sand, Larry. "Elite Private Schools Go Woke." The Heartland Institute, February 17, 2021. https://tinyurl.com/yc2k427p.

Sarna, Jonathan D., and Jonathan Golden. "The American Jewish Experience in the Twentieth Century: Antisemitism and Assimilation." TeacherServe. National Humanities Center, October 2000. https://tinyurl.com/jnm324md.

Sarnoff, Marisa. "Jeffrey Epstein Flight Logs, Showing Detailed Passenger Lists, Entered into Evidence at Ghislaine Maxwell Trial." *Law & Crime*, December 20, 2021. https://tinyurl.com/mvwbse2k.

Scholl, Natalie. "'The Bell Curve' 20 Years Later: A Q&A with Charles Murray." *American Renaissance*, October 16, 2014. https://tinyurl.com/43h6n3ht.

Schwab, Klaus. "Now Is the Time for a 'Great Reset.'" World Economic Forum, June 3, 2020. https://tinyurl.com/bdfvrhc8.

Seger, Karl A. *Left-wing Extremism: The Current Threat.* U.S. Department of Energy Office of Safeguards and Security, 2001. https://irp.fas.org/world/para/left.pdf.

Shankman, Paul. "The 'Fateful Hoaxing' of Margaret Mead." *Current Anthropology* 54, no. 1 (February 2013): 51–70. https://doi.org/10.1086/669033.

Shapira, Ian. "Before Asian Americans Sued Harvard, the School Once Tried Restricting the Number of Jews." *The Washington Post*, October 15, 2018, https://tinyurl.com/264x77bj.

Sharon, Jeremy. "US Jews Contribute Half of All Donations to the Democratic Party." *The Jerusalem Post*, January 14, 2018. https://tinyurl.com/c4tc8432.

Sharp, Rachel. "Parents of Kids at New England Private Schools Fight 'Indoctrination' of Students with 'Woke' Ideas." *Daily Mail*, July 12, 2021. https://tinyurl.com/388uumws.

Sheth, Sonam, and Eliza Relman. "Michael Flynn Said in a Secretly Recorded Call That He Thinks Qanon Is a 'Disinformation Campaign' and 'Total Nonsense.'" *Business Insider*, November 29, 2021. https://tinyurl.com/24c3jwra.

Shields, Jon A. "The Disappearing Conservative Professor." *National Affairs*, 2018. https://tinyurl.com/yr386vm8.

Sibarium, Aaron. "Insurance Companies, Reaping Benefits from Protests, Get in Line with Black Lives Matter." *The Washington Free Beacon*, March 23, 2021. https://tinyurl.com/ctnh4rtp.

Sibarium, Aaron. "Why Private Schools Have Gone Woke." *The Washington Free Beacon*, July 28, 2021. https://tinyurl.com/48mdtc8k.

Sigalos, MacKenzie. "You Can't Sue Pfizer or Moderna If You Have Severe Covid Vaccine Side Effects. the Government Likely Won't Compensate You for Damages Either." *CNBC*, December 23, 2020. https://tinyurl.com/26jrfma8.

Silver, Laura, and Moira Fagan. "2. American Views of Israel." Pew Research Center, July 11, 2022. https://tinyurl.com/2crhac7b.

Simmons, Dominique A. "Sex Offender Typologies." Office of Sex Offender Sentencing, Monitoring, Apprehending, Registering, and Tracking, December 14, 2022. https://tinyurl.com/4yd7xskh.

Simonson, Joseph. "How the CDC Coordinated with Big Tech to Censor Americans." *The Washington Free Beacon*, July 27, 2022. https://tinyurl.com/ycywmdnu.

Smith, Allan. "Parents Guilty of Murder and Raised by Radicals, Chesa Boudin Is San Francisco's Next District Attorney." *NBC News*, December 16, 2019. https://tinyurl.com/5n8yfavu.

Smith, Ben. "Obama Once Visited '60s Radicals." *Politico*, February 22, 2008. https://tinyurl.com/bdet7beh.

Smith, Henry B. "Canaanite Child Sacrifice, Abortion, and the Bible." *The Journal of Ministry and Theology* 7, no. 2 (May 24, 2019): 90–125. https://tinyurl.com/2p87n25d.

Smith, Zack, and Charles Stimson. "Meet Chesa Boudin, the Rogue Prosecutor Wreaking Havoc in San Francisco." The Heritage Foundation, August 11, 2021. https://tinyurl.com/38u2hsf4.

Smithee, Alan. "Pizzagate." *Counter-Currents*, December 2, 2016. https://counter-currents.com/2016/12/pizzagate/.

Socolovsky, Jerome. "American Jews Worry about Declining Religiosity among Young." *Voice of America News*, December 18, 2013. https://tinyurl.com/4zu6433p.

"Some 2022 Left-Wing Candidates Espouse Troubling Rhetoric on Israel." ADL, April 5, 2022. https://tinyurl.com/3sfjjd6m.

Spegman, Abby. "Evergreen Professor at Center of Protests Resigns; College Will Pay $500,000." *The Seattle Times*, November 17, 2021. https://tinyurl.com/yfhbbdfk.

Stephens, Bret. "The Secrets of Jewish Genius." *The New York Times*, December 27, 2019. https://tinyurl.com/mwcvbek5.

Steuben, Thomas. "Hate Game Theory, Not the Player, Part 1." *Counter-Currents*, December 3, 2021. https://tinyurl.com/muspzu5c.

Steuben, Thomas. "The Military's Culture of Careerism." *Counter-Currents*, September 2, 2021. https://tinyurl.com/yrbwjwc8.

Steuben, Thomas. "The Road to Kabul." *Counter-Currents*, August 24, 2021. https://counter-currents.com/2021/08/the-road-to-kabul/.

Steuben, Thomas. "Woodstock on Wheels." *Counter-Currents*, March 1, 2022. https://counter-currents.com/2022/03/woodstock-on-wheels/.

Steven. "A Historical Look at Attitudes to Homosexuality in the Islamic World." libcom.org, August 1, 2016. https://tinyurl.com/mryjpv7b.

Striker, Eric. "Jewish FBI Agent Infiltrates Bible Study Group; Then Tries to Entrap Its Members." *The Unz Review*, July 7, 2021. https://tinyurl.com/bdddk8ut.

Strozewski, Zoe. "10 Percent of Americans Don't Believe in Climate Change, 15 Percent Unsure: Poll." *Newsweek*, October 26, 2021. https://tinyurl.com/mv62n8vf.

Stuyvesant, Peter. "The German-Jewish Kulturkampf in the Weimar Republic." *The Occidental Observer*, January 23, 2012. https://tinyurl.com/2ddypbvy.

Talbott, Clint. "Sex, 'Lies' and Videotape." *Colorado Arts and Sciences Magazine*, December 1, 2009. https://tinyurl.com/yc6k67re.

Tangermann, Victor. "People Love Living in Pods so Much They're Getting Neck Tattoos about It." *Futurism*, April 25, 2019. https://tinyurl.com/yc6tpabk.

Taranto, James. "How Woke Capital Politicized Your Retirement Account." *The Wall Street Journal*. Dow Jones & Company, August 9, 2022. https://tinyurl.com/479m5hmp.

Taylor, Jared. "Diversity Means Fewer White People." *American Renaissance*, December 20, 2019. https://tinyurl.com/bdejt9a7.

Taylor, Jared. "Diversity or Standards: You Can't Have Both." *American Renaissance*, August 27, 2021. https://tinyurl.com/yeyryp5r.

Taylor, Jared. "Police Racism: A Manufactured Crisis." *American Renaissance*, June 5, 2020. https://tinyurl.com/h93k5dmr.

Taylor, Jared. "The Proud Boys and Antifa." *American Renaissance*, October 23, 2018. https://www.amren.com/commentary/2018/10/the-proud-boys-and-antifa/.

Taylor, Jared. "Want Equity? Punish White People." *American Renaissance*, April 1, 2022. https://tinyurl.com/2afmbr5f.

Taylor, Jared. "Would They Let Him Die?" *American Renaissance*, September 6, 2020. https://tinyurl.com/2725bp27.

"Teachers Unions." OpenSecrets, December 14, 2022. https://www.opensecrets.org/industries/indus.php?ind=L1300.

Telushkin, Shira. "The Vanishing Ivy League Jew." *Tablet Magazine*, October 15, 2018. https://tinyurl.com/5b9vpsda.

Thacker, Jason. "Why Elon Musk's Transhumanist Dreams Are Flawed." The Ethics and Religious Liberty Commission. The Southern Baptist Convention, September 7, 2020. https://tinyurl.com/mn5ahw4d.

Thulin, Lila. "In the 1980s, a Far-Left, Female-Led Domestic Terrorism Group Bombed the U.S. Capitol." *Smithsonian Magazine*, January 6, 2020. https://tinyurl.com/275enmzx.

Titor, John. "The Dancing Israelis: FBI Docs Shed Light on Apparent Mossad Foreknowledge of 9/11 Attacks." We Are Change, September 10, 2020. https://tinyurl.com/3z8urcd5.

TOI Staff. "At Israel's Request, Trump Pardons Israeli Handler of Spy Jonathan Pollard." *The Times of Israel*, November 3, 2022. https://tinyurl.com/58kmnkad.

Toosi, Nahal. "Ivy League Grads Have a Leg up in State Department Promotions, Stats Show." *Politico*, June 14, 2020. https://tinyurl.com/52vb7fab.

Uhlman, Eric Louis et al. "The Motivated Use of Moral Principles." *Judgment and Decision Making* 4, no. 6. October 2009: pp. 476-491. https://journal.sjdm.org/9616/jdm9616.pdf.

"U.S. Capitol Violence." FBI, December 14, 2022. https://www.fbi.gov/wanted/capitol-violence.

"Undercurrents: Black Lives Matter, and Chatham House's Edi Working Group." Chatham House, October 29, 2021. https://tinyurl.com/3wns93x2.

"United States of America: Annual Number of Live Births per 1,000 Population." United Nations Department of Economic and Social Affairs Population Division, December 14, 2022. https://tinyurl.com/muek5bpf.

"University of California." OpenSecrets, December 14, 2022. https://tinyurl.com/yc3adwpe.

Unz, Ron. "The Myth of American Meritocracy." *The American Conservative*, November 28, 2012. https://tinyurl.com/2p8ccxz9.

Uttl, Bob, Victoria Violo, and Lacey Gibson. "Meta-analysis: On Average, Undergraduate Students' Intelligence Is Merely Average." *ScienceOpen Preprints*, 2024. https://doi.org/10.14293/PR2199.000694.v1.

Vaa, Ida Sofia. "Project for the New American Century: How One Think Tank May Influence American Foreign Policy." MA Thesis, The University of Oslo, 2005. https://tinyurl.com/73x37smp.

Vance, J. D. "Fighting Woke Capital." *The American Mind*, June 2, 2021. https://americanmind.org/salvo/fighting-woke-capital/.

Vincent, Isabel. "Security Experts Blast Bank of America for Helping Feds in Capitol Riot Probe." *New York Post*, February 6, 2021. https://tinyurl.com/4667bwc5.

Voytko, Lisette. "Surveillance Video Outside Jeffrey Epstein's Cell Was Deleted in Clerical Error, Jail Says." *Forbes Magazine*, January 9, 2020. https://tinyurl.com/yax2ar6n.

Wai, Jonathan, and Matthew C. Makel. "Why Graduates of Elite Universities Dominate the Time 100 – and What It Means for the Rest of Us." *The Conversation*, December 14, 2022. https://tinyurl.com/5n8f862p.

Ward, Peter. "The Price of Silicon Valley's Obsession with Immortality." *Big Think*, April 21, 2022. https://bigthink.com/health/immortality-race-to-live-forever/.

Watcher II, Washington. "Facebook 'Whistleblower' Frances Haugen Just Wants More Censorship. Real Solution: Mandate Free Speech." *VDARE*, October 7, 2021. https://tinyurl.com/2n2y5m6w.

Watcher II, Washington. "U.S. Ruling Class Reluctant to Accept Ukrainian Refugees–except to Enable Increased Third World Influx." *VDARE*, March 15, 2022. https://tinyurl.com/4u2p9sxs.

Weaver, Sarah. "Elon Musk's Disturbing Dalliance with Transhumanism." *The Federalist*, April 12, 2022. https://tinyurl.com/mtb5c9n4.

Weisgerber, Marcus. "Former Air Force Chief Goldfein Joins Blackstone." *Defense One*, January 14, 2021. https://tinyurl.com/2am56375.

Welton, Lance. "It's Official: Even Hard Science Entering New Dark Age." *VDARE*, October 20, 2018. https://tinyurl.com/3wmcmcfj.

Westhoff, Elise. "How Philanthropy Is Fueling American Division." *National Review*, April 18, 2021. https://tinyurl.com/26acw4ys.

Wexler, Ellen. "Jewish Word: The Hairsplitting Complexity of 'Talmudic.'" *Moment Magazine*, 2021. https://momentmag.com/jewish-word-talmudic/.

"What Are MRNA Vaccines and How Do They Work?" MedlinePlus. National Institutes of Health, December 14, 2022. https://medlineplus.gov/genetics/understanding/therapy/mrnavaccines/.

"Where the Right Went Wrong: How Neoconservatives Subverted the Reagan Revolution and Hijacked the Bush Presidency." *Publishers Weekly*, December 14, 2022. https://www.publishersweekly.com/978-0-312-34115-2.

"Why Tel Aviv Is the Ultimate LGBTQ Travel Destination." Tourist Israel, December 14, 2022. https://tinyurl.com/2p9yr3j3.

Wiker, Benjamin D. "Anthropology Afoul of the Facts." *National Catholic Register*, May 19, 2002. https://tinyurl.com/y6nw6h6u.

Williams, Pete. "FBI Director Wray Says Scale of Chinese Spying in the U.S. 'Blew Me Away.'" *NBC News*, February 1, 2022. https://tinyurl.com/2uvz3f9p.

Williamson, Kevin D. "Codename: Liberal." *National Review*, September 30, 2015. https://tinyurl.com/as994u29.

Winkler, Rolfe. "YouTube: 1 Billion Viewers, No Profit." *The Wall Street Journal*, February 25, 2015. https://tinyurl.com/47767dww.

Wofford, Benjamin. "We're Devastatingly Short on Doctors. Why Doesn't the US Just Make More?" *Washingtonian*, April 13, 2020. https://tinyurl.com/2x7dbywv.

Wuthnow, Joel, Satu Limaye, and Nilanthi Samaranayake. "Brahmaputra: A Conflict-Prone River Takes a Step Backwards." *War on the Rocks*, December 23, 2020. https://tinyurl.com/3y27u3jt.

Xiong, Jack. "The Fake News in 1990 That Propelled the US into the First Gulf War." *Citizen Truth*, May 7, 2018. https://tinyurl.com/yce7txhp.

Yarvin, Curtis. "Big Tech Has No Power at All." *Gray Mirror*, January 12, 2021. https://graymirror.substack.com/p/big-tech-has-no-power-at-all.

Yong, Ed. "Psychology's Replication Crisis Is Running out of Excuses." *The Atlantic*, November 19, 2018. https://tinyurl.com/ykjpws9w.

"You Still Have to Bake the Cake, Bigot." *The American Conservative*, June 30, 2021. https://www.theamericanconservative.com/still-have-to-bake-the-cake-bigot/.

Zollman, Joellyn. "Jewish Immigration to America: Three Waves." *My Jewish Learning*, December 14, 2022. https://tinyurl.com/3vtksew3.

Zuesse, Eric. "Neocons Hate Russia Even More than They Hate Any Other Nation." *Modern Diplomacy*, July 31, 2018. https://tinyurl.com/2kt33wfk.

ENJOYED THIS BOOK?

TO READ MORE, VISIT US AT

ANTELOPEHILLPUBLISHING.COM

www.ingramcontent.com/pod-product-compliance
Lightning Source LLC
Chambersburg PA
CBHW020435130626
46549CB00001B/146